我是医学生

I Am a Medical Student

基础医学汉语 课本 2

Preclinical Medicine Chinese Textbook 2

总 主 编：朱瑞蕾　甄　珍
本册主编：张举英
副 主 编：张杏春　李晓婧
编　　者：张举英　张杏春　李晓婧　朱瑞蕾　甄　珍　张海萍　李婷玉

北京语言大学出版社
BEIJING LANGUAGE AND CULTURE UNIVERSITY PRESS

图书在版编目（CIP）数据

我是医学生. 基础医学汉语. 2. 课本 / 朱瑞蕾，甄珍总主编；张举英分册主编. -- 北京：北京语言大学出版社，2022.11（2025.9 重印）
ISBN 978-7-5619-6181-0

Ⅰ. ①我… Ⅱ. ①朱… ②甄… ③张… Ⅲ. ①医学—汉语—对外汉语教学—教材 Ⅳ. ①H195.4

中国版本图书馆 CIP 数据核字（2022）第 205132 号

我是医学生：基础医学汉语 课本 2
WO SHI YIXUESHENG : JICHU YIXUE HANYU KEBEN 2

排版制作：北京青侣文化创意设计有限公司
责任印制：周 燚

出版发行：北京语言大学出版社
社 址：北京市海淀区学院路 15 号，100083
网 址：www.blcup.com
电子信箱：service@blcup.com
电 话：编辑部 8610-82303395
发行部 8610-82303650/3591/3648
北语书店 8610-82303653
网购咨询 8610-82303908
印 刷：北京市金木堂数码科技有限公司

版 次：2022 年 11 月第 1 版　印 次：2025 年 9 月第 3 次印刷
开 本：787 毫米 × 1092 毫米 1/16　印 张：20.5
字 数：298 千字
定 价：88.00 元

PRINTED IN CHINA

前　言

《我是医学生：基础医学汉语》是一套在“中文＋医学”理念指导下，依据《新汉语水平考试大纲》《国际中文教育中文水平等级标准》《医学汉语水平考试（MCT）大纲》编写的综合性医学专用汉语教材。教材重在提高学习者在日常生活交际和医院日常交际场景中运用汉语的能力，同时也注重提升学习者的文化素养和医生职业素质。

本教材主要适用于来华学习基础医学专业的汉语零起点医学生，同时也适用于：（1）来华学习临床医学专业的医学生；（2）来华学习中医学专业的医学生；（3）来华工作的医学专家以及短期研修的医学生；（4）有汉语学习需求的海外医学生。

一、编写理念

本教材将医学专业汉语学习者的日常汉语学习和HSK应考能力提高相结合，将医学专业知识和社会文化知识相结合，以实现汉语、医学和文化相互融合的编写目标。本教材从零起点开始培养学习者的听、说、读、写技能，帮助学习者逐步掌握HSK一至四级所规定的词汇、语言点和话题任务，熟悉《医学汉语水平考试（MCT）大纲》所规定的医学专业词汇、话题和任务，提高在日常生活交际和医院日常交际场景中运用汉语的能力，同时通过汉语学习了解医生的职业特点，感受“医者仁心”“医德为先”的高尚情操。

二、教材架构

《我是医学生：基础医学汉语》系列教材包括课本4册、配套练习册4册，每册15课。具体安排如下：

第1册侧重汉语日常交际能力的培养，适度增加简单的医学场景交流。其中，正课前的"汉语拼音"和"拼音练习"部分对现代汉语语音知识进行了集中的讲授和练习，后面的1—5课也对其不断进行复现和强化。完成第1册的学习，学习者汉语水平可以达到HSK二级，能够熟悉常用的医学专业词汇，并进行简单的医学场景交流。

第2册将汉语日常交际能力的培养与医学场景中交流能力的提升相结合，所涉及的交际场景更加多样，交流范围更加广阔，所反映的中国社会文化也更加丰富。完成第2册的学习，学习者汉语水平可以达到HSK三级，医学专业词汇进一步增加，并能进行常见的医学场景交流。

第3册和第4册进一步拓展汉语日常交际的广度和深度，日常交际任务更加丰富；所涉医学场景更加侧重医院常见科室的寻医问诊，医患交流场景更加具体、真实，多是通过专科医生了解常见疾病的症状和治疗方案。完成第3册和第4册的学习，学习者汉语水平可以达到甚至超过HSK四级，能够掌握常用的医学专业词汇，了解常见疾病的基本知识，感受医生的职业特点和高尚情操。

三、教材特点

1. 汉语、医学和文化相互融合

《我是医学生：基础医学汉语》的编写目标包括汉语、医学和文化三个方面。汉语目标是核心目标，主要包括汉语知识目标和汉语技能目标，是实现医学目标和文化目标的基础。本教材是医学专用汉语教材，医学目标包括医学词汇目标、医学场景交流目标和医学文化目标，主要通过营造医学场景的方式实现。文化目标包括知识文化目标和交际文化目标，本教材致力于加深学习者对中国社会文化的了解，提高学习者的跨文化交际能力，促进学习者对多元文化的理解。文化目标的实现依赖于语言教学内容中具体文化目标的完成。汉语目标和文化目标属于中文目标，医学目标属于专业目标，三者完美融合于本教材中。

2. 听、说、读、写并重

本教材是综合性医学专用汉语教材，在语言技能培养方面，听、说、读、写并重。教材每篇课文后的“综合练习”部分针对重点词汇、语法、汉字、句型和课文内容进行反复练习，巩固学习者的语言知识；每课后的“语言任务”部分针对口头表达和书面表达能力设计输出型语言任务，重在培养学习者的语言产出能力。配套练习册除进一步巩固汉语重点知识、强化重点能力培养外，还通过丰富的练习题型，训练学习者解决各种语言问题的应用能力，提高 HSK 应考能力。

3. 通用和专用大纲兼顾

通用汉语词汇、语言点和话题任务重点参照《新汉语水平考试大纲》，同时参照《国际中文教育中文水平等级标准》，医用专业词汇、话题和任务重点参照《医学汉语水平考试（MCT）大纲》。本教材覆盖《新汉语水平考试大纲》一至四级全部词汇、语言点和话题任务，同时覆盖《医学汉语水平考试（MCT）大纲》一至三级全部话题和任务，以及大部分词汇。

4. 依据试用反馈不断调整完善

本教材在山东大学临床医学专业（外国留学生）已进行了三轮试用，每次试用后我们都会进行教学效果和学生需求的实证研究和分析，根据教师教学反馈和学生学习反馈进行调整和修改。教材试用结果表明，本教材可以有效满足医学相关专业学生日常交流、临床实习、通过 HSK 四级考试和了解中国社会文化的需要。

除此之外，本教材还在江西中医药大学试用了一个学期，在美国阿拉巴马大学试用了两个学期，都取得了显著的教学效果，并根据试用反馈进行了进一步的调整和修改。

四、编写体例

根据语言学习规律和医学能力培养规律，本教材各册的编写体例略有差异，具体如下：

1. 第 1 册编写体例

◎课本

《课本 1》开篇便针对现代汉语语音基础知识进行了集中的讲授和练习，并在后面的 1—5 课中不断复现和强化。1—15 课每课均由学习目标、热身活动、课文与生词、语言点讲解与操练、综合练习、语言任务等六部分组成。

学习目标：根据课文内容设置语言功能和语言点目标，帮助学习者了解本课的学习重点。鉴于学习者为零起点的外国学生，本部分以英文形式呈现。

热身活动：设置两个问题，引入本课主题，激发学习者对学习内容的兴趣，激活学习者已有的背景知识和相关词汇。问题围绕日常交际话题设计。

课文与生词：每课包含两篇课文，课文（一）和课文（二）均为对话体，以医学生的日常交际话题为主，后期逐渐增加医学场景的交际话题。两篇课文之间注重内容的关联和生词、语法的复现。生词紧扣《新汉语水平考试大纲》和《医学汉语水平考试（MCT）大纲》。

语言点讲解与操练：语言点讲解简洁清晰，例句典型而丰富，同时突出语法格式的归纳、易错点的提醒及近义词的辨析。每个语言点均配有针对性练习。

综合练习：课文（一）和课文（二）后均有紧扣课文内容和知识能力培养的综合练习，前 5 课主要以“听录音，选出你听到的音节”“根据汉字写拼音”“朗读语句”“完成对话”和“汉字书写”为主，后 10 课主要以“根据汉字写拼音”“朗读语句”“替换练习”“选词填空”“根据课文内容回答问题”“根据课文内容填空”和“汉字书写”为主。

语言任务：以现实情景为场景，引导学生完成综合性语言任务，主要包括“阅读理解”和“口头表达”。语言任务以日常交际情景为主，以医学情景为辅。

◎练习册

第 1—5 课所学习的词汇、语言点和课文相对简单，我们将之融入第 6—15

课的练习中。

第6—15课每课包括听力、阅读和书写三个部分。听力部分的练习包括“看图片，听词语，判断对（√）错（×）”“看图片，听句子，判断对（√）错（×）”和“听对话，选择正确答案”，阅读部分的练习包括“看图片，并将图片序号填在相关句子后”“选词填空”和“选出下列词语在句子中的位置”，书写部分的练习包括“读句子，根据拼音写汉字”和“组词成句”。

2. 第2册编写体例

◎课本

《课本2》每课均由学习目标、热身活动、课文与生词、语言点讲解与操练、综合练习、语言任务、补充词汇等七部分组成。

学习目标：根据课文内容设置语言功能、语言点、医学知识和社会文化目标，帮助学习者了解本课的学习重点。同样，鉴于学习者汉语水平较低，本部分以英文形式呈现。

热身活动：设置两个问题，引入本课主题，激发学习者对学习内容的兴趣，激活学习者已有的背景知识和相关词汇。问题主要围绕日常交际话题和医学话题设计。

课文与生词：每课包含两篇课文，课文（一）和课文（二）均为对话体，以医学生的日常交际话题为主，后期逐渐增加医学场景的交际话题。两篇课文之间注重内容的关联和生词、语法的复现。生词紧扣《新汉语水平考试大纲》和《医学汉语水平考试（MCT）大纲》。

语言点讲解与操练：语言点讲解简洁清晰，例句典型而丰富，突出语法格式的归纳、易错点的提醒及近义词的辨析。每个语言点均配有针对性练习。

综合练习：课文（一）和课文（二）后均有紧扣课文内容和知识能力培养的综合练习，题型主要包括“根据拼音写汉字”“辨字组词”“替换练习”“选词填空”“用所给词语完成对话”“根据课文内容回答问题”和“根据课文内容填空”。

语言任务：以现实情景为场景，引导学生完成综合性语言任务，主要包括“阅读理解”“口头表达”和“书面表达”。语言任务以日常交际情景为主，以医学情景为辅。

补充词汇：补充与本课内容密切相关的医学专业词汇，每课补充4—6个词，每个词配有拼音、英文翻译和图片。

◎练习册

《练习册2》每课包括听力、阅读和书写三个部分。听力部分的练习包括“听句子，判断对（√）错（×）”“听对话，选择正确答案”和“听句子，写下你听到的话”，阅读部分的练习包括“选词填空”“选出下列词语在句子中的位置”和“阅读语句，选择正确答案”，书写部分的练习包括“读句子，根据拼音写汉字”和“组词成句”。

3. 第3、4册编写体例

◎课本

《课本3》和《课本4》每课均由学习目标、热身活动、课文与生词、语言点讲解与操练、综合练习、语言任务等六部分组成。

学习目标：根据课文内容设置语言功能、语言点、医学知识和社会文化目标，帮助学习者了解本课的学习重点。随着学习者汉语水平的提高，本部分的呈现形式过渡为中文。

热身活动：设置两个问题，引入本课主题，激发学习者对学习内容的兴趣，激活学习者已有的背景知识和相关词汇。问题主要围绕日常交际话题和医学话题设计。

课文与生词：每课包含三篇课文，课文（一）为医学场景对话，课文（二）为日常交流对话，课文（三）为叙述体，《课本3》以日常交际话题的叙述为主，《课本4》以医学话题的叙述为主。三篇课文之间注重内容的关联和生词、语法的复现。生词紧扣《新汉语水平考试大纲》和《医学汉语水平考试（MCT）大纲》。

语言点讲解与操练：语言点讲解简洁清晰，例句典型而丰富，突出语法格式的归纳、易错点的提醒及近义词的辨析。每个语言点均配有针对性练习。

综合练习：课文（一）、课文（二）和课文（三）后均有紧扣课文内容和知识能力培养的综合练习，题型主要包括“根据拼音写汉字”“辨字组词”“选词填空”“选出下列词语在句子中的位置”“用所给词语完成对话”“根据课文内容回答问题”和“根据课文内容填空”。

语言任务：以现实情景为场景，引导学生完成综合性语言任务，主要包括“阅读理解”“口头表达”和“书面表达”。语言任务以医学情景为主。

◎练习册

《练习册3》和《练习册4》每课包括听力、阅读和书写三个部分。听力部分的练习包括“听句子，判断对错”和“听对话，选择正确答案”，阅读部分的练习包括“选择正确的上下文填空”“选词填空”“排列顺序”和“阅读语段，选择正确答案”，书写部分的练习包括“组词成句”“读句子，根据拼音写汉字”和“看图片，用词造句”。

五、教学建议

本教材建议每课用6—8课时完成。若一周8课时，一学期16周，每学期可完成1册。若选择“主讲＋复练”的教学模式，主讲教师负责教授每课的课文、生词和语言点，并带领学生完成相应课文后的综合练习；复练教师负责生词与语言点的扩展性和交际性练习，并带领学生完成每课的语言任务和练习册上的练习。

六、编写团队

本教材由长期从事一线医学汉语教学工作的教师编写，总主编为朱瑞蕾、甄珍。

《课本1》和《练习册1》由张杏春、甄珍、张举英、李晓婧、朱瑞蕾编写，张杏春负责统稿。

《课本 2》和《练习册 2》由张举英、张杏春、李晓婧、朱瑞蕾、甄珍、张海萍、李婷玉编写，张举英负责统稿。

《课本 3》和《练习册 3》由甄珍、朱瑞蕾、李晓婧、张举英、张杏春编写，甄珍负责统稿。

《课本 4》和《练习册 4》由李晓婧、朱瑞蕾、甄珍、张举英、张杏春编写，李晓婧负责统稿。

七、鸣谢

本教材由张杏春、朱瑞蕾、戴丽华、周汶霏、校潇、张云、蔡燕等任课教师在山东大学进行了三个学期的课堂试用，由张海萍、李婷玉在江西中医药大学进行了一个学期的课堂试用，由马玲在美国阿拉巴马大学进行了两个学期的课堂试用，她们都对教材提出了很多切实的修改意见，在此特别致谢！

在教材编写过程中，山东大学李安老师在词频统计方面提供了强大的技术支持，李静茹、徐紫钰、温璐妃、刘晓洁、齐梓君、张铭心、曾哲宇等同学在语料整理方面提供了周到的帮助，济南市第二人民医院王旭医师、济南市妇幼保健院侯艳梅医师等在医学专业知识和方法方面提供了有力的支持，在此一并感谢。

除此之外，我们还要感谢北京语言大学出版社王俊毅、上官雪娜老师和责任编辑李非飞老师在编辑出版环节对本教材提出的宝贵修改意见。

编写团队

2022 年 4 月

Foreword

With the guidance of "Chinese + medicine" principle, *I Am a Medical Student: Preclinical Medicine Chinese* is a series of integrated medical Chinese textbooks, compiled based on *Chinese Proficiency Test Syllabus*, *Chinese Proficiency Grading Standards for International Chinese Language Education* and *Medical Chinese Test (MCT) Syllabus*. The teaching materials focus on improving the learners' ability to use Chinese for communication in daily life and in the hospital scene, and also focus on improving the learners' cultural literacy and professional quality of doctors.

This set of textbooks is mainly suitable for international preclinical medical students who are the very beginners of Chinese language, and also for: (1) medical students who come to China to study clinical medicine; (2) medical students who come to China to study traditional Chinese medicine; (3) medical experts working in China and medical students for short-term training; (4) international medical students with the need of learning Chinese.

1. Writing Principles

This set of textbooks combines the learning of daily Chinese with the improvement of HSK test-taking ability, and combines medical knowledge with social and cultural knowledge, so as to achieve the goal of integrating Chinese, medicine and culture. This set of textbooks promotes the beginners' listening, speaking, reading and writing skills from scratch, and helps the beginners gradually master the vocabulary, language points and topic tasks stipulated in HSK levels 1 to 4, and acquaint with the medical vocabulary, topics and tasks stipulated in the *Medical Chinese Test (MCT) Syllabus*, improve the ability to use Chinese for communication in daily life and in the hospital scene, understand the professional characteristics of doctors through Chinese, and feel the nobility of "the doctor's benevolence" and "medical morality first" sentiment.

2. Textbook Structure

This set of integrated medical Chinese textbooks includes 4 volumes of textbooks and 4 volumes of workbooks. The textbooks and workbooks are matched together, and each volume has 15 lessons. The specific arrangements are as follows:

Volume 1 focuses on the cultivation of skills of daily communication in Chinese, moderately increases communication in simple medical scenarios. The pre-class parts of "Chinese Pinyin" and "Pinyin exercises" in this textbook focus on teaching and practicing the knowledge of modern Chinese phonetics, which will be repeated and strengthened in the following lessons 1-5. After completing the study of Volume 1, the beginners' Chinese proficiency can reach HSK level 2. They can be familiar with common medical Chinese vocabulary, and communicate in simple medical scenarios.

Volume 2 combines the development of communication skills in daily life with the improvement of communication skills in medical scenarios. The communication scenarios involved are more diverse, the scope of communication is broader, and the Chinese social culture reflected is also richer. After completing the study of Volume 2, the learners' Chinese proficiency can reach HSK level 3. The learners' medical Chinese vocabulary will be further increased, and they can communicate in common medical scenarios.

Volumes 3 and 4 further expand the breadth and depth of daily communication in Chinese, and the daily communication tasks are richer; the medical scenarios involved are more focused on seeing patients in common departments in hospitals, and the doctor-patient communication scenarios are more specific and real, which mostly are about symptoms and treatment options for common diseases through specialists. After completing the study of Volume 3 and Volume 4, the learners' Chinese proficiency can reach or even exceed HSK level 4, they can master common medical Chinese vocabulary, understand the basic knowledge of common diseases, and feel the professional characteristics and noble sentiments of doctors.

3. Characteristics of Textbooks

(1) Integration of Chinese, medicine and culture

The compilation targets of this set of textbooks include three aspects: Chinese, medicine and culture. Chinese is the core target, mainly including targets of Chinese knowledge and Chinese skill, which is the basis for realizing targets of medicine and culture. These textbooks are specialized medical Chinese textbooks. The medical targets mainly include medical vocabulary, medical-scene communication, and medical culture, which are mainly achieved by creating medical scenes. Cultural targets include knowledge culture and communicative culture. These textbooks are committed to deepening learners' understanding of Chinese society and culture, improving learners' cross-cultural communication skills, and promoting learners' understanding of multiculturalism. The realization of cultural targets depends on the completion of specific cultural targets in language teaching. Chinese targets and cultural targets belong to Chinese targets, and medical targets belong to professional targets. These aspects are interactively and perfectly integrated in these textbooks.

(2) Equal emphasis on listening, speaking, reading and writing

This set of textbooks is an integrated medical specialized Chinese textbook. In terms of language skill development, equal emphasis is placed on listening, speaking, reading and writing. The "Comprehensive Exercises" part of the textbooks focuses on repeated exercises on key vocabulary, grammar, Chinese characters, sentence patterns and text contents to consolidate learners' language knowledge; at the same time, the "Language Tasks" part of the textbooks also designs output language tasks to exercise oral and written expressions, focusing on cultivating learning language production ability of the learners. In addition to further consolidating the key knowledge of Chinese and strengthening the cultivation of key abilities, the accompanying workbooks of the textbooks also train learners' application ability to solve various language problems and improve their ability to take the HSK test through a variety of practice questions.

(3) Giving consideration to both general and special syllabuses

For general Chinese vocabulary, language points and topic tasks, this set of textbooks mainly refers to the *Chinese Proficiency Test Syllabus* and *Chinese Proficiency Grading Standards for International Chinese Language Education*. For medical Chinese vocabulary, topics and tasks, this set of textbooks mainly refers to the *Medical Chinese Test (MCT) Syllabus*. This set of textbooks covers all the vocabulary, language points and topic tasks of level 1 to level 4 in *Chinese Proficiency Test Syllabus* and all the topics, tasks and most of vocabulary of level 1 to level 3 in the *Medical Chinese Test (MCT) Syllabus*.

(4) Continuous adjustment and improvement based on trial feedback

This set of textbooks has been tested for three rounds in clinical medicine major (for international students) of Shandong University. After each trial, empirical research and analysis on the teaching effect and students' needs was conducted, and adjustments and revisions were made according to teachers' teaching and students' learning feedbacks. The trail result of these textbooks is sufficient to show that this set of textbooks can effectively meet the needs of medical students for daily communication, clinical practice, passing HSK level 4 test and understanding Chinese social culture.

In addition, this set of textbook has been tried out for one semester at Jiangxi University of Chinese Medicine and two semesters at the University of Alabama in the United States, both of which have achieved remarkable teaching effects, and have led further adjustments and revisions based on the trial feedbacks.

4. Compilation Layouts

According to the law of language learning and medical ability training, the compilation layouts of each volume of this set of textbooks are slightly different. The specific compilation layouts are as follows:

(1) The compilation layout of Volume 1

◎ Textbook

The first chapter of Volume 1 arranges three concentrated lectures, focusing on the basic knowledge of modern Chinese phonetics and recurring and strengthening in the following lessons 1 to 5. Each lesson from 1 to 15 consists of six parts: learning objectives, warming-up, texts and new words, language points explanation and practice, comprehensive exercises, and language tasks.

Learning objectives: Targets for language functions and language points are set according to the content of the text to help learners understand the key points of each lesson. Since the learners are beginners, this part is presented in English.

Warming-up: Two questions are set to introduce the theme of the lesson, stimulate learners' interest in the content, and activate learners' existing background knowledge and related vocabulary. The two questions focus on topics of daily communication.

Texts and new words: Each lesson includes two texts. Text 1 and Text 2 are both conversational, focusing on the daily communication topics of medical students, and gradually increasing the communication topics in medical scenes. The relationship between the two texts and the repetition of new words and grammar are emphasized. The new words stick to *Chinese Proficiency Test Syllabus* and *Medical Chinese Test (MCT) Syllabus*.

Language points explanation and practice: The language points explanation is concise and clear, and the example sentences are typical and rich, highlighting grammatical formats induction, error-prone reminders, and synonym identification. Each language point comes with targeted exercises.

Comprehensive exercises: After Text 1 and Text 2, there are comprehensive exercises sticking to the content of the texts and the cultivation of knowledge and ability. The first 5 lessons mainly focus on "listen to the recording and pick out the syllables you hear", "write Pinyin according to Chinese characters", "read aloud", "complete dialogues", and "write Chinese characters". And the last 10 lessons are mainly about "write Pinyin according to Chinese characters", "read aloud", "substitution drills", "use the following words to fill in the blanks", "answer the following questions according to the text", "fill in the blanks according to the text", and "write Chinese characters".

Language tasks: The compilers take realistic situations as scenarios, and guide students to complete comprehensive language tasks, mainly including "reading comprehension" and "oral expression". The language tasks are mainly based on daily communication situations, supplemented by medical situations.

◎ Workbook

The vocabulary, language points and texts learned in Lessons 1 to 5 are relatively simple, and we incorporate them into the practice in Lessons 6 to 15.

Lessons 6 to 15 consist of three parts: listening, reading and writing. The listening exercises include "look at the pictures, listen to the words and judge right (√) or wrong (×)", "look at the pictures, listen to the sentences and judge right (√)

or wrong (×)", and "listen to the dialogues and choose the correct answers". The reading exercises include "look at the pictures and fill in the picture numbers after the relevant sentences", "use the following words to fill in the blanks", and "choose the correct position of the following words in the sentences". The writing exercises include "read the following sentences and write Chinese characters according to Pinyin" and "group the following words into sentences".

(2) The compilation layout of Volume 2

◎ Textbook

Each lesson consists of seven parts: learning objectives, warming-up, texts and new words, language points explanation and practice, comprehensive exercises, language tasks, and supplementary words.

Learning objectives: Targets for language functions, language points, medical knowledge, and social culture are set according to the content of the text to help learners understand the key points of each lesson. Since the learners' Chinese level is limited, this part is also presented in English.

Warming-up: Two questions are set to introduce the theme of the lesson, stimulate learners' interest in the content, and activate learners' existing background knowledge and related vocabulary. The two questions focus on topics of daily communication and medicine.

Texts and new words: Each lesson includes two texts. Text 1 and Text 2 are both conversational, focusing on the daily communication topics of medical students, and gradually increasing the communication topics in medical scenes. The relationship between the two texts and the repetition of new words and grammar are emphasized. The new words stick to *Chinese Proficiency Test Syllabus* and *Medical Chinese Test (MCT) Syllabus*.

Language points explanation and practice: The language points explanation is concise and clear, and the example sentences are typical and rich, highlighting grammatical formats induction, error-prone reminders, and synonym identification. Each language point comes with targeted exercises.

Comprehensive exercises: After Text 1 and Text 2, there are comprehensive exercises sticking to the content of the texts and the cultivation of knowledge and ability. The types of questions mainly include "write Chinese characters according to Pinyin", "discriminate between Chinese characters and make words", "substitution drills", "use the following words to fill in the blanks", "complete the dialogues with given words", "answer the following questions according to the text", and "fill in the blanks according to the text".

Language tasks: The compilers take realistic situations as scenarios, and guide students to complete comprehensive language tasks, mainly including "reading comprehension", "oral expression" and "written expression". The language tasks are mainly based on daily communication situations, supplemented by medical situations.

Supplementary words: It mainly includes medical Chinese words closely related to each lesson. Each lesson is supplemented with 4-6 words with Pinyin, English translations and pictures.

◎ Workbook

Each lesson consists of three parts: listening, reading and writing. The listening exercises include "listen to sentences and judge right (√) or wrong (×)", "listen to dialogues and choose the correct answers", and "listen to sentences and write down what you heard". The reading exercises include "use the following words to fill in the blanks", "choose the correct position of the following words in the sentences", and "read the following sentences and choose the correct answers". The writing exercises include "read the following sentences and write Chinese characters according to Pinyin" and "group the following words into sentences".

(3) The compilation layout of Volumes 3 and 4

◎ Textbooks

Each lesson consists of six parts: learning objectives, warming-up, texts and new words, language points explanation and practice, comprehensive exercises, and language tasks.

Learning objectives: Targets for language functions, language points, medical knowledge, and social culture are set according to the content of the text to help learners understand the key points of each lesson. With the improvement of the learners' Chinese level, this part is presented in Chinese.

Warming-up: Two questions are set to introduce the theme of the lesson, stimulate learners' interest in the content, and activate learners' existing background knowledge and related vocabulary. The two questions focus on topics of daily communication and medicine.

Texts and new words: Each lesson includes three texts. Text 1 is a dialogue in medical scenarios, Text 2 is a daily communication dialogue, and Text 3 is a narration. Volume 3 is mainly about the narration of daily communication topics, and Volume 4 is mainly about the narration of medical topics. The relationship between the three texts and the repetition of new words and grammar are emphasized. The new words stick to *Chinese Proficiency Test Syllabus* and *Medical Chinese Test (MCT) Syllabus*.

Language points explanation and practice: The language points explanation is concise and clear, and the example sentences are typical and rich, highlights grammatical formats induction, error-prone reminders, and synonym identification. Each language point comes with targeted exercises.

Comprehensive exercises: After Text 1, Text 2 and Text 3, there are comprehensive exercises sticking to the content of the texts and the cultivation of knowledge and ability. The types of questions mainly include "write Chinese characters according to Pinyin", "discriminate between Chinese characters and make words", "use the following words to fill in the blanks", "choose the correct position of the following words in the sentences", "complete the dialogues with given words", "answer the following questions according to the text", and "fill in the blanks according to the text".

Language tasks: Take realistic situations as scenarios, guide students to complete comprehensive language tasks, mainly including "reading comprehension", "oral expression" and "written expression". The language tasks are mainly based on medical situations.

◎ Workbook

Each lesson consists of three parts: listening, reading and writing. The listening exercises include "listen to sentences and judge right or wrong", and "listen to dialogues and choose the correct answers". The reading exercises include "choose the correct context to fill in the blanks", "use the following words to fill in the blanks", "sort sentences", and "read the following paragraphs and choose the correct answers". The writing exercises include "group the following words into sentences", "read the following sentences and write Chinese characters according to Pinyin", and "look at pictures and make sentences with given words".

5. Teaching Suggestions

We suggest that teachers use 6-8 hours to complete each lesson of this set of textbooks. If there are 8 lessons per week, 16 weeks per semester, one volume could be completed per semester. If you choose the teaching mode of "main lecture + repractice", the main lecture teacher is responsible for teaching the texts, new words and language points, and guiding students to complete comprehensive exercises after the corresponding text; the re-practice teacher is responsible for teaching extension knowledge of new words and language points, and leading students to complete the language tasks and exercises in the workbook for each lesson.

6. Compilation Team

This set of textbooks are written by teachers who have long been engaged in the teaching front-line of medical Chinese. The chief compilers are Zhu Ruilei and Zhen Zhen.

The first volumes of the textbooks and workbooks are compiled by Zhang Xingchun, Zhen Zhen, Zhang Juying, Li Xiaojing, Zhu Ruilei. Zhang Xingchun is responsible for the final compilation and edit.

The second volumes of the textbooks and workbooks are compiled by Zhang Juying, Zhang Xingchun, Li Xiaojing, Zhu Ruilei, Zhen Zhen, Zhang Haiping, and Li Tingyu. Zhang Juying is responsible for the final compilation and edit.

The third volumes of the textbooks and workbooks are compiled by Zhen Zhen, Zhu Ruilei, Li Xiaojing, Zhang Juying, and Zhang Xingchun. Zhen Zhen is responsible for the final compilation and edit.

The fourth volumes of the textbooks and workbooks are compiled by Li Xiaojing, Zhu Ruilei, Zhen Zhen, Zhang Juying and Zhang Xingchun. Li Xiaojing is responsible for the final compilation and edit.

7. Acknowledgments

This set of textbooks was tested in Shandong University for three semesters by the teacher Zhang Xingchun, Zhu Ruilei, Dai Lihua, Zhou Wenfei, Xiao Xiao, Zhang Yun and Cai Yan. Zhang Haiping and Li Tingyu tested in Jiangxi University of Chinese Medicine for one semester. Ma Ling conducted a two-semester classroom trial at the University of Alabama. All of them have put forward many practical suggestions for revision of the textbook, and I would like to express my special thanks here.

In the process of compiling these textbooks, Li An, from Shandong University, provided strong technical support on statistics of word frequency, and students, such as Li Jingru, Xu Ziyu, Wen Lufei, Liu Xiaojie, Qi Zijun, Zhang Mingxin, and Zeng Zheyu, provided thoughtful help in corpus organization. Physician Wang Xu, from Jinan Second People's Hospital, and Physician Hou Yanmei, from Jinan Maternal and Child Health Hospital, provided their strong support in terms of medical expertise and methods, and we would like to thank them all, too.

In addition, we would also like to thank senior editors Wang Junyi and Shangguan Xuena, the editors-in-chief, and Li Feifei, the editor in charge, from Beijing Language and Culture University Press, for their valuable comments on the revision of this textbook during the editing and publishing process.

Compilation team

April 2022

主要人物简介

Introductions to Major Characters

王　晨 / Wang Chen

中国人，男，19 岁，东山大学基础医学院一年级学生。

Chinese, Male, 19 years old, Freshman of School of Basic Medical Science, Dongshan University.

李　真 / Li Zhen

中国人，女，18 岁，东山大学文学院一年级学生。

Chinese, Female, 18 years old, Freshman of School of Literature, Dongshan University.

美　丽 / Meili

南非人，女，19 岁，东山大学基础医学院一年级留学生。

South African, Female, 19 years old, International Freshman of School of Basic Medical Science, Dongshan University.

金　龙 / Jin Long

泰国人，男，21 岁，东山大学基础医学院一年级留学生。

Thai, Male, 21 years old, International Freshman of School of Basic Medical Science, Dongshan University.

马大为 / Ma Dawei

尼泊尔人，男，20 岁，东山大学基础医学院一年级留学生，金龙的同屋。

Nepalese, Male, 20 years old, International Freshman of School of Basic Medical Science, Dongshan University, Jin Long's roommate.

月　亮 / Yueliang

巴林人，女，20岁，东山大学基础医学院一年级留学生，美丽的同屋。

Bahraini, Female, 20 years old, International Freshman of School of Basic Medical Science, Dongshan University, Meili's roommate.

吉　米 / Jimmy

俄罗斯人，男，21岁，东山大学口腔医学院一年级留学生，马大为的朋友。

Russian, Male, 21 years old, International Freshman of School of Stomatology, Dongshan University, Ma Dawei's friend.

王　东 / Wang Dong

中国人，男，31岁，东山医院外科医生，王晨的哥哥。

Chinese, Male, 31 years old, Surgeon of Dongshan Hospital, Wang Chen's elder brother.

艺　文 / Yi Wen

中国人，女，32岁，东山医院眼科医生，王东的妻子。

Chinese, Female, 32 years old, Ophthalmologist of Dongshan Hospital, Wang Dong's wife.

张佳乐 / Zhang Jiale

中国人，女，28岁，东山医院护士，王东、艺文的朋友。

Chinese, Female, 28 years old, Nurse of Dongshan Hospital, Wang Dong and Yi Wen's friend.

刘一鸣 / Liu Yiming

中国人，男，30岁，律师，张佳乐的男朋友。

Chinese, Male, 30 years old, Lawyer, Zhang Jiale's boyfriend.

语法术语及缩略形式参照表

Grammar Terms and Their Abbreviations

Grammar Terms in Chinese	Grammar Terms in Pinyin	Grammar Terms in English	Abbreviations
名词	míngcí	noun	*n.*
代词	dàicí	pronoun	*pron.*
数词	shùcí	numeral	*num.*
量词	liàngcí	measure word	*m.*
数量词	shùliàngcí	numeral measure word	*num.-m.*
动词	dòngcí	verb	*v.*
能愿动词	néngyuàn dòngcí	modal verb	*mod. v.*
形容词	xíngróngcí	adjective	*adj.*
副词	fùcí	adverb	*adv.*
介词	jiècí	preposition	*prep.*
连词	liáncí	conjunction	*conj.*
助词	zhùcí	particle	*part.*
拟声词	nǐshēngcí	onomatopoeia	*onom.*
叹词	tàncí	interjection	*int.*
前缀	qiánzhuì	prefix	*pref.*
后缀	hòuzhuì	suffix	*suf.*
成语	chéngyǔ	idiom	*idm.*
主语	zhǔyǔ	subject	*S*
谓语	wèiyǔ	predicate	*P*
宾语	bīnyǔ	object	*O*
补语	bǔyǔ	complement	*C*
动宾结构	dòngbīn jiégòu	verb-object	*VO*
动补结构	dòngbǔ jiégòu	verb-complement	*VC*
动词性短语	dòngcíxìng duǎnyǔ	verbal phrase	*VP*
形容词性短语	xíngróngcíxìng duǎnyǔ	adjectival phrase	*AP*

目　录

Contents

第一课 Lesson 1

Nǐ liáng xuèyā le ma?

你量 血压了吗？

Have you had your blood pressure taken?

学习目标 Learning Objectives

1. Language functions: Students are able to master common expressions at the outpatient and routine examinations; students can briefly describe the condition; students are able to make arrangements.
2. Language points: Modal particle “了” (2); Fixed structure “虽然……但是……”; Pivotal sentence (1) “A + 叫 + B + verb/verbal phrase”; Preposition “从” (1); Adverb “一直” (2); Preposition “往”; Adverb “已经”; Fixed structure “除了……以外” (1).
3. Medical knowledge: Students are expected to understand the basic knowledge of blood pressure measurement.
4. Social culture: Students are expected to understand the living habits of young people in China.

热身活动 Warming-up

1. 在你们国家，已经工作的年轻人喜欢住在家里还是住在外边？为什么？

In your country, do young people prefer to live at home or alone after they begin to work? Why?

2. 你了解高血压吗？高血压有哪些症状？

Do you know about high blood pressure? What are the symptoms of high blood pressure?

课文（一）
Text（Ⅰ）

Wáng Chén hé Mǎ Dàwéi zài pá shān.
（王 晨 和 马 大为 在 爬 山。）

Wáng Chén: Wǒ gēge zuìjìn bānjiā le.
王晨：我哥哥最近搬家了。

Mǎ Dàwéi: Bānjiā le? Wèi shénme?
马大为：搬家了？为什么？

Wáng Chén: Zhù zài jiā li suīrán hěn shūfu, dànshì shàngbān yǒudiǎnr yuǎn.
王晨：住在家里虽然很舒服，但是上班 有点儿 远。

Tā de xīn fángzi lí yīyuàn hěn jìn.
他的新房子离医院 很近。

Mǎ Dàwéi: Tài hǎo le!
马大为：太好了！

Wáng Chén: Tā jiào wǒmen zhōumò qù tā de xīn jiā chīfàn.
王晨：他叫 我们 周末 去他的新家吃饭。

Mǎ Dàwéi: Hǎo. Chīle fàn, wǒ qǐng nǐmen qù chànggē ba.
马大为：好。吃了饭，我请 你们去 唱歌 吧。

Wáng Chén: Qù nǎr chànggē?
王晨：去哪儿唱歌？

Mǎ Dàwéi: Cóng xuéxiào ménkǒu yìzhí wǎng xī zǒu, dàgài 700 mǐ, yǒu yì jiā hěn búcuò de KTV.
马大为：从 学校 门口 一直 往 西走，大概700米，有一家很不错的KTV。

Wáng Chén: Nǐ huì chàng zhōngguógē ma?
王晨：你会 唱 中国歌 吗？

Mǎ Dàwéi: Dāngrán! Wǒ huì chàng hěn duō zhōngguógē.
马大为：当然！我会 唱 很 多 中国歌。

(Wang Chen and Ma Dawei are climbing the mountain.)

Wang Chen: My brother moved house recently.

Ma Dawei: Moved? Why?

Wang Chen: Comfortable as living at home is, it is far for him to go to work. His new house is close to the hospital.

Ma Dawei: Good for him!

Wang Chen: He invited us to have meal at his new house this weekend.

Ma Dawei: OK. After the meal, let me treat you to singing.

Wang Chen: Where shall we sing?

Ma Dawei: There is a pretty good KTV about 700 meters towards the west of the school gate.

Wang Chen: Can you sing Chinese songs?

Ma Dawei: Of course. I can sing many Chinese songs.

生词 New words

1. 最近	zuìjìn	*n.*	recently
2. 搬家	bānjiā	*v.*	to move house
搬	bān	*v.*	to move
3. 虽然……但是……	suīrán…dànshì…		although…
虽然	suīrán	*conj.*	although
但是	dànshì	*conj.*	but
4. 舒服	shūfu	*adj.*	comfortable
5. 上班	shàngbān	*v.*	to go to work
6. 房子	fángzi	*n.*	house
7. 叫	jiào	*v.*	to ask, to order
8. 周末	zhōumò	*n.*	weekend

9. 请	qǐng	*v.*	to invite
10. 唱歌	chànggē	*v.*	to sing (a song)
唱	chàng	*v.*	to sing
歌	gē	*n.*	song
11. 从	cóng	*prep.*	from
12. 门口	ménkǒu	*n.*	gate
13. 一直	yìzhí	*adv.*	straight, straight forward
14. 往	wǎng	*prep.*	towards
15. 西	xī	*n.*	west
16. 走	zǒu	*v.*	to walk, to go
17. 大概	dàgài	*adv.*	probably
18. 米	mǐ	*m.*	meter
19. 家	jiā	*m.*	used for households or businesses
20. KTV	KTV	*n.*	Karaoke TV

语言点 Language Points

一、语气助词“了”（2） Modal particle “了” (2)

语气助词“了”一般用在句尾，表示某种情况已经发生，有成句的作用。例如：

The modal particle “了” is usually used at the end of a sentence to indicate that a certain situation has occurred and has the function of forming a sentence. For example:

1. 我哥哥最近搬家了。
2. 哥哥去医院了。

3. 病人做手术了吗？

※ 练习：请用语气助词“了”和所给词语完成对话 Please use the modal particle “了” and the given words to complete dialogues

1. A：我们一起去吃饭吧。

   B：你们去吧，我 ______________________________。（吃饭）

2. A：你想不想去爬山？

   B：我昨天 ______________________________。（爬山）

3. A：昨天上午你们做什么了？

   B：我们 ______________________________。（上课）

4. A：我们明天去李真家玩儿吧。

   B：星期六 ______________________________。（去李真家）

二、固定结构“虽然……但是……” Fixed structure “虽然……但是……”

“虽然……但是……”用于连接两个意思相反的分句。“虽然”可以用在主语前面或后面，“但是”只能用在主语前面。例如：

“虽然……但是……” is used to connect two clauses of opposite meanings. “虽然” can be used before or after the subject, while “但是” can only be used before the subject. For example:

1. 住在家里虽然很舒服，但是上班有点儿远。
2. 我虽然很爱运动，但是常常没有时间。
3. 虽然哥哥做饭很好吃，但是他不常做。

※ 练习：请用固定结构“虽然……但是……”完成句子 Please complete the sentences with the fixed structure “虽然……但是……”

1. 虽然这家饭店的菜很好吃，______________________________。

2. ________________________________，但是新房子离医院很近。

3. 虽然我没有车，________________________________。

4. ________________________________，但是我有课。

三、兼语句（1）：A + 叫 + B + 动词 / 动词性短语　Pivotal sentence (1): A + 叫 + B + verb/verbal phrase

“叫”表示容许或听任。在“A + 叫 + B + 动词 / 动词性短语”结构中，A 是句子的主语，“叫 + B + 动词 / 动词性短语”是句子的谓语，B 是“叫”的宾语，同时又是后面动词 / 动词性短语的主语。否定形式常在“叫”前加“不”或“没”。例如：

“叫” means to allow. In the structure of “A + 叫 + B + verb/verbal phrase”, A is the subject of the sentence, “叫 + B + verb/verbal phrase” is the predicate of the sentence, and B is the object of “叫” and the subject of the following verb/verbal phrase. The negative form is often to put “不” or “没” before “叫”. For example:

1. 他叫我们周末去他的新家吃饭。
2. 马大为叫我去健身房运动。
3. 哥哥不叫我开车去学校。

※ 练习：选出“叫”在句子中的位置　Choose the position of “叫” in sentences

1. A 妈妈 B 哥哥 C 给我 D 做饭。　（　）
2. 王晨 A 马大为 B 骑共享单车 C 去 D 爬山。　（　）
3. 李真 A 美丽 B 星期六 C 去 D 她家玩儿。　（　）
4. 王晨 A 金龙 B 晚上 C 去看电影 D。　（　）

四、介词“从”（1）　Preposition “从” (1)

介词“从”可表示距离、空间的起点，常用在“从……到……”结构中。例如：

The preposition “从” can indicate the start point of the distance or space, and is often used in the form of “从……到……”. For example:

1. 从学校门口一直往西走，大概 700 米，有一家很不错的 KTV。

2. 从宿舍到教室，大概有800米。

3. 从我家到学校，大概要15分钟。

※ 练习：请用介词“从”完成句子或对话 Please complete the sentences or dialogues with the preposition “从”

1. 哥哥的新房子离医院很近，______________________。

2. ______________________，坐公共汽车只要两站。

3. A：李真，你家离学校远吗？

   B：______________________。

4. A：美丽，住在学校宿舍方便吗？

   B：______________________。

五、副词“一直”（2） Adverb “一直” (2)

副词“一直”可以表示动作的方向不变。例如：

The adverb “一直” can be used to indicate that the direction of the action remains unchanged. For example:

1. 从学校门口一直往西走，大概700米，有一家很不错的KTV。

2. 你一直往前走，医院就在前边。

3. A：请问，图书馆在什么地方？

   B：你们一直往东走，图书馆就在宿舍的东边。

※ 练习：请用副词“一直”完成句子或对话 Please complete the sentences or dialogues with the adverb “一直”

1. 图书馆不远，______________________。

2. A：请问，卫生间在哪儿？

   B：______________________。

3. A：我在学校门口，你说的那家饭店在哪儿？

B：______________________________。

4. ______________________________，我家就在花园旁边。

六、介词“往”　Preposition “往”

介词“往”后面常加方位名词或者处所名词，表示动作或行为的方向。例如：

The preposition “往” is often followed by a locative noun or a place noun to indicate the direction of the action or behavior. For example:

1. 从学校门口一直往西走，大概 700 米，有一家很不错的 KTV。
2. 你一直往前走，医院就在不远的地方。
3. A：同学，解剖楼往哪儿走？

   B：你知道图书馆在哪儿吗？

   A：知道。

   B：你往图书馆走，解剖楼就在图书馆旁边。

※ 练习：请用介词“往”完成句子　Please complete the sentences with the preposition “往”

1. 图书馆不在东边，______________________________。
2. 李真家离学校不太远，学校门口______________________________。
3. 我在饭店门口，你______________________________。
4. 宿舍在图书馆的前边，你______________________________。

综合练习 Comprehensive Exercises

一、根据拼音写汉字 Write Chinese characters according to Pinyin

1. suīrán________ 3. shūfu________ 5. chànggē________

2. dànshì________ 4. zhōumò________ 6. dàgài________

二、辨字组词 Discriminate between Chinese characters and make words

1. 房________ 方________
2. 西________ 四________
3. 舒________ 舍________
4. 米________ 来________

三、替换练习 Substitution drills

1. 我哥哥最近<u>搬家了</u>。

上班了
做手术了
买电脑了

2. 住在家里虽然<u>很舒服</u>，但是<u>上班有点儿远</u>。

很好	离学校太远了
上班有点儿远	可以每天看到家人（family member）
有点儿不方便	可以每天吃到妈妈做的饭

3. 他叫我们周末<u>去他的新家吃饭</u>。

去 KTV 唱歌
去学校踢足球
一起去看电影

四、选词填空 Use the following words to fill in the blanks

往　叫　大概　虽然　最近

1. 我________不认识他，但是我认识他的爸爸。
2. 哥哥的新房子离医院很近，________1000 米。
3. 我________要搬家，搬到医院旁边住。
4. 医生________病人多休息，少抽烟。
5. 王医生________病房（bìngfáng，ward）那边去了。

五、用所给词语完成对话 Complete the dialogues with given words

1. 美丽：李真，你家离学校远吗？

   李真：不远，____________________。（一直）
2. 同学：____________________。（叫）

   美丽：好的，我现在就去他宿舍。
3. 王晨：大为，我们明天什么时候去健身房？

   大为：____________________。（大概）
4. 金龙：大为，你明天想和我一起去图书馆吗？

   大为：我很想去，____________________。（但是）
5. 病人：请问，王医生在吗？

   护士：他不在，____________________。（了）

六、根据课文内容回答问题 Answer the following questions according to the text

1. 谁最近搬家了？
2. 他为什么搬家？

3. 王晨和马大为周末要去哪儿吃饭？
4. 马大为请王晨他们去哪儿唱歌？

七、根据课文内容填空 Fill in the blanks according to the text

我哥哥_______了。住在家里_______很舒服，_______上班有点儿远。他的新房子_______医院很近。他_______我们_______去他的新家吃饭。从学校门口一直_______西走，_______700 米，有一_______很不错的 KTV。吃了饭，马大为想_______去那儿唱歌。马大为_______唱很多中国_______。

课文（二）
Text（II）

Nèikē zhěnshì, yīshēng zài wènzhěn.
（内科 诊室， 医生 在 问诊。）

yīshēng: Nǐ nǎr bù shūfu?
医生：你哪儿不舒服？

bìngrén: Wǒ zuìjìn chángcháng tóuyūn.
病人：我 最近 常常 头晕。

yīshēng: Nǐ liáng xuèyā le ma?
医生：你 量 血压了吗？

bìngrén: Liáng le, gāoyā 160, dīyā 110.
病人：量 了，高压 160，低压 110。

yīshēng: Duō cháng shíjiān le?
医生：多 长 时间了？

bìngrén: Yǐjīng yí gè xīngqī le.
病人：已经一个星期了。

yīshēng: Chúle tóuyūn yǐwài, nǐ hái yǒu nǎr bù shūfu?
医生：除了头晕 以外，你还有哪儿不舒服？

bìngrén: Méiyǒu le.
病人：没有 了。

yīshēng: Nǐ xiān qù zuò gè xīndiàntú ba.
医生：你先 去做 个心电图吧。

bìngrén: Hǎo de. Xièxie yīshēng!
病人：好 的。谢谢 医生！

(The doctor is inquiring in the medical consulting room.)

Doctor: What's wrong with you?

Patient: I often feel dizzy recently.

Doctor: Have you had your blood pressure taken?

Patient: Yes. The systolic blood pressure is 160 and the diastolic blood pressure is 110.

Doctor: How long have you been like this?

Patient: For one week.

Doctor: Except for dizziness, what else do you feel?

Patient: Nothing else.

Doctor: Go to have an electorcardiogram examination first.

Patient: OK. Thank you, doctor.

生词 New words

1. 常常	chángcháng	*adv.*	often, usually
2. 头晕	tóuyūn	*v.*	to be dizzy
头	tóu	*n.*	head
晕	yūn	*adj.*	dizzy, faint
3. 量	liáng	*v.*	to measure
4. 血压	xuèyā	*n.*	blood pressure
5. 高压	gāoyā	*n.*	systolic blood pressure
高	gāo	*adj.*	high
6. 低压	dīyā	*n.*	diastolic blood pressure
低	dī	*adj.*	low
7. 长	cháng	*adj.*	long
8. 已经	yǐjīng	*adv.*	already
9. 除了……以外	chúle…yǐwài		except, besides
除了	chúle	*prep.*	except, besides

以外	yǐwài	*n.*	except, beyond
10. 先	xiān	*adv.*	first, firstly
11. 做心电图	zuò xīndiàntú	*VO*	to take an ECG
心电图	xīndiàntú	*n.*	electrocardiogram

语言点 Language Points

一、副词“已经” Adverb “已经”

副词“已经”表示动作行为完成了或者性质状态达到了某种程度，句尾常有语气助词“了”与之呼应。例如：

The adverb “已经” indicates that the action or behavior has been completed or the nature has reached a certain level, and the modal particle “了” often echoes it at the end of the sentence. For example:

1. 他头晕已经一个星期了。
2. 病人已经量血压了。
3. 山上的树叶已经红了。

※ 练习：请用副词“已经”和所给词语完成句子或对话 Please use the adverb “已经” and the given words to complete the sentences or dialogues

1. 他不在家，________________________。（去学校）
2. 我不饿（è，hungry），________________________。（吃早饭）
3. A：马大为不在宿舍吗？

   B：________________________。（上课）

4. A：你写作业了吗？

B：________________________________。（写）

二、固定结构“除了……以外”（1） Fixed structure “除了……以外” (1)

固定结构“除了……以外”可以表示排除已知，还有别的。此时，该结构常用在“除了……（以外），……还/也……”句式中，“以外”可以省略。例如：

The fixed structure “除了……以外” means that there are other possibilities, besides the known ones. In this case, this structure is often used in the format of “除了……（以外），……还/也……”, and “以外” can be omitted. For example:

1. 除了头晕以外，你还有哪儿不舒服？
2. 除了踢足球以外，我也很喜欢爬山。
3. 除了美丽，月亮也是我的好朋友。

※ 练习：请用固定结构“除了……以外”完成对话 Please complete the dialogues with the fixed structure “除了……以外”

1. A：今天谁去爬山？金龙去吗？

   B：________________________________。

2. A：今天你有汉语课吗？

   B：________________________________。

3. A：星期六你做什么了？

   B：________________________________。

4. A：你喜欢什么运动？

   B：________________________________。

综合练习 Comprehensive Exercises

一、根据拼音写汉字 Write Chinese characters according to Pinyin

1. cháng__________ 3. xiān__________ 5. chúle__________
2. yǐwài__________ 4. yǐjīng__________ 6. liáng__________

二、辨字组词 Discriminate between Chinese characters and make words

1. 常________ 学________
2. 头________ 兴________
3. 量________ 里________
4. 先________ 生________

三、替换练习 Substitution drills

1. 我最近常常<u>头晕</u>。

不舒服
不来上班
睡得很晚

2. 除了<u>头晕</u>以外，你还<u>有哪儿不舒服</u>？

会说英语	会说什么
学习医学（medical science）	学习什么
喜欢运动	喜欢什么

3. 你先<u>去做个心电图</u>吧。

去买一瓶水
去写作业
喝点儿茶

四、选词填空 Use the following words to fill in the blanks

常常	已经	除了	先	血压

1. 现在________八点半了，你快起床吧。
2. 这一个月我们________去学校旁边的饭店吃饭。
3. ________头晕，我还肚子疼。
4. 我现在有点儿忙，你________去教室上课吧。
5. 他最近________有点儿高，高压160，低压110。

五、用所给词语完成对话 Complete the dialogues with given words

1. 爸爸：快点儿吃饭吧。

   妈妈：________________________，我去打个电话。（先）

2. 医生：你哪儿不舒服？

   病人：________________________。（常常）

3. 王晨：我下（the next）个周末要去北京。

   朋友：________________________？（多长）

4. 王晨：你是不是常运动？

   大为：________________________。（除了……以外）

5. 医生：量血压了吗？

   病人：________________________。（已经）

六、根据课文内容回答问题 Answer the following questions according to the text

1. 病人哪儿不舒服？
2. 他头晕多长时间了？

3. 除了头晕以外，他还有哪儿不舒服？
4. 医生叫他先做什么？

七、根据课文内容填空 Fill in the blanks according to the text

有个病人最近________，________一个星期了。他________血压，高压 160，低压 110。__________头晕以外，他没有别的不舒服。医生叫他去做个心电图。

语言任务 Language Tasks

一、阅读理解 Reading comprehension

最近我搬到学校宿舍了。住在家里虽然很舒服，但是离学校太远了。我每天要六点前起床，还要坐四十分钟的公共汽车到学校，太不方便了。宿舍虽然有点儿小，但是住在这儿非常方便。我常常七点四十起床，五分钟就能到教室。

读后判断 True or false

1. 我最近不在家住了。 ( )
2. 住在家里很舒服，但是上学不太方便。 ( )
3. 住在学校宿舍很方便。 ( )
4. 从宿舍到教室五分钟就能到。 ( )
5. 搬家前我常常七点四十起床。 ( )

二、口头表达 Oral expression

任务名称：头晕去医院看病。

Task: Go to see the doctor for dizziness.

任务要求：1. 两个学生一组，一个是病人，一个是医生。

2. 医生询问病人的身体情况，病人描述头晕和血压情况。

Requirements: 1. Two students work in a group. One acts as the patient, the other as the doctor.

2. The doctor inquires about the patient's physical condition, and the patient describes about his/her dizziness and blood pressure.

Reference words: 常常　量　血压　高压　低压　已经　除了……以外　先

三、书面表达 Written expression

任务名称：住在哪里好？

Task: Where is better to live?

任务要求：分别列出住在家里和住在学校宿舍的好处，并做出适合自己的选择。

Requirement: List the advantages of living at home and living in the school dormitory, and make a choice that suits you.

住在家里的好处 Benefits of living at home	1.
	2.
	3.
住在学校宿舍的好处 Benefits of living in the school dormitory	1.
	2.
	3.
我的选择 My choice	

Reference words: 虽然……但是…… 最近 除了……以外 常常
大概 已经 舒服 方便 远 近

补充词汇 Supplementary Words

xuèjiǎn
血检
blood test

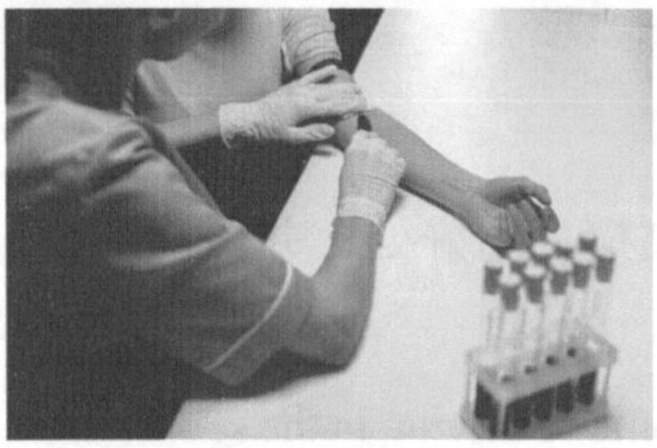

niàojiǎn
尿检
urinalysis

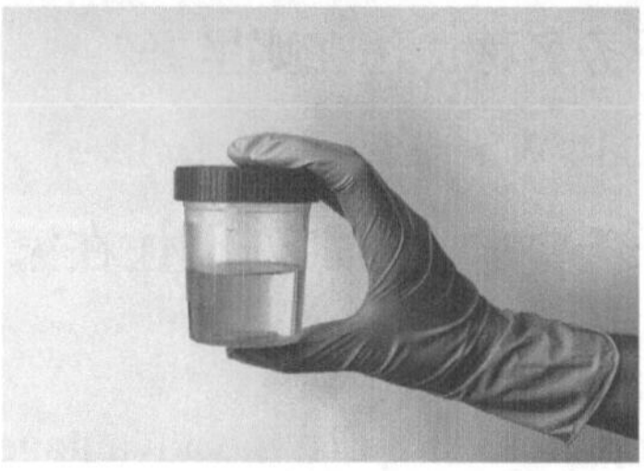

cǎichāo
彩超
color doppler ultrasound

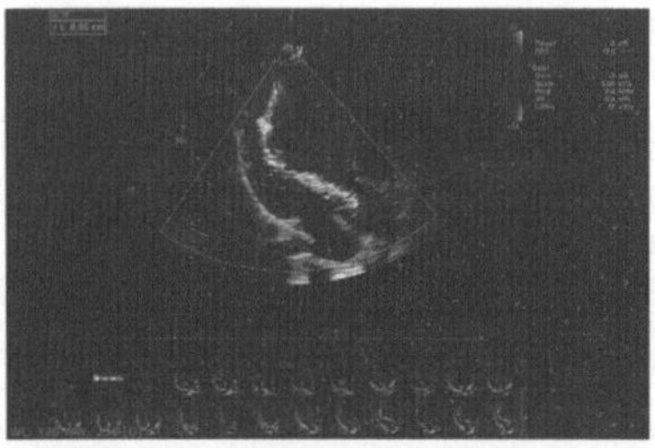

hécígòngzhèn
核磁共振
nuclear magnetic resonance

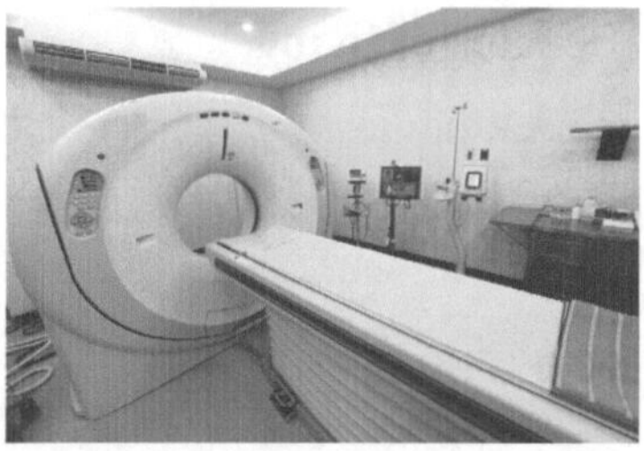

第二课
Lesson 2

Shēnglǐxué wǒmen yǐjīng xuéwán le
生理学 我们已经 学完 了
The physiology course has been finished

学习目标 Learning Objectives

1. Language functions: Students can briefly introduce the subjects and examinations; students can comfort others in Chinese.
2. Language points: Temporal noun “刚才”; Adverb “没(有)”; Resultative complement (1); Personal pronoun “咱们”; Adverb “还” (2); Fixed structure “又……又……”; Adverb “特别”; Imperative sentence (2) “不要……了”.
3. Medical knowledge: Students are expected to understand the main courses of medical specialty.
4. Social culture: Students are expected to learn about the examinations of Chinese universities.

热身活动 Warming-up

1. 你学过哪些医学科目?
Which medical subjects have you studied?

2. 你觉得最难学的科目是什么?
Which subject do you think is the most difficult to learn?

课文（一）
Text（Ⅰ）

Mǎ Dàwéi zài gěi tā de péngyou Jímǐ dǎ diànhuà.
（马 大为 在 给 他的 朋友 吉米 打 电话。）

Mǎ Dàwéi: Jímǐ, wǒ gāngcái gěi nǐ fā wēixìn le, nǐ méiyǒu huí.
马大为：吉米，我 刚才 给你发微信了，你没有 回。

Jímǐ: Bù hǎoyìsi, wǒ yìzhí zài sùshè xuéxí, méi kànjiàn. Yǒu shìr ma?
吉米：不好意思，我 一直 在 宿舍 学习，没 看见。有 事儿吗？

Mǎ Dàwéi: Zánmen xiàwǔ qù dǎ lánqiú, zěnmeyàng?
马大为：咱们 下午去打篮球，怎么样？

Jímǐ: Jīntiān bùxíng, wǒmen shēnglǐxué yǒu hěn duō zuòyè, wǒ hái méi xiěwán. Nǐmen méiyǒu ma?
吉米：今天 不行，我们 生理学 有 很 多 作业，我 还 没 写完。你们 没有 吗？

Mǎ Dàwéi: Méiyǒu, yīnwèi wǒmen yǐjīng xuéwán le.
马大为：没有，因为 我们 已经 学完 了。

Jímǐ: Xuéwán le? Zhème kuài?
吉米：学完 了？这么 快？

Mǎ Dàwéi: Suīrán xuéwán le, dànshì wǒ hái méi xuéhuì.
马大为：虽然 学完 了，但是 我 还 没 学会。

(Ma Dawei is calling up his friend Jimmy.)

Ma Dawei: Jimmy, I just sent you Wechat messages, but you didn't reply.

Jimmy: Sorry, I have been learning in dorm and don't see that. What's the matter?

Ma Dawei: How about playing basketball this afternoon?

Jimmy: Not today. We have a lot of physiology homework and I haven't finished it yet. Don't you have that?

Ma Dawei: No. We have finished the study of physiology.

Jimmy: Finished? So fast?

Ma Dawei: Although we have finished this course, I haven't understood it yet.

生词 New words

1. 刚才	gāngcái	*n.*	just now
2. 发微信	fā wēixìn	*VO*	to send a message on WeChat
发	fā	*v.*	to send
微信	wēixìn	*n.*	WeChat
3. 回	huí	*v.*	to reply, to answer
4. 看见	kànjiàn	*v.*	to see
5. 事儿	shìr	*n.*	matter
6. 咱们	zánmen	*pron.*	we, us
7. 打篮球	dǎ lánqiú	*VO*	to play basketball
打	dǎ	*v.*	to play
篮球	lánqiú	*n.*	basketball
8. 生理学	shēnglǐxué	*n.*	physiology
9. 完	wán	*v.*	to finish, to be over
10. 因为	yīnwèi	*conj.*	because
11. 学	xué	*v.*	to learn
12. 这么	zhème	*pron.*	so, such

专名 Proper nouns

吉米	Jímǐ	name of a Russian student

语言点 Language Points

一、时间名词“刚才” Temporal noun “刚才”

时间名词“刚才”表示不久以前的时间。在句中，它既可以位于主语后，也可以位于句首。例如：

The temporal noun “刚才” refers to the time not long ago. In a sentence, it can be put either after the subject or at the beginning of the sentence. For example:

1. 我刚才给你发微信了。
2. 病人刚才量血压了。
3. 刚才我们去踢足球了。

※ 练习：请用时间名词“刚才”完成对话 Please complete dialogues with the temporal noun “刚才”

1. A：你刚才去哪儿了？

   B：______________________________。

2. A：你想去图书馆吗？

   B：______________________________。

3. A：马大为去哪儿了？

   B：______________________________。

4. A：你给他发微信了吗？

   B：______________________________。

二、副词“没（有）” Adverb “没（有）”

否定副词“没（有）”否定某一动作或状态已经发生，后面可以接动词或形容词性成分。表示疑问时，其结构是“动词 / 形容词性成分 + 了 + 没（有）/ 吗？”。“没（有）”还可以单独回答问题。例如：

The negative adverb "没（有）" negates that an action or a state has occurred. It can be followed by a verb or an adjective. When it is used to ask a question, the structure is "verbal/adjectival component + 了 + 没（有）/吗？". "没（有）" can be used to answer the question separately. For example:

1. 我刚才给你发微信了，你没有回。

2. 虽然昨天爬山了，但是今天我没有很累。

3. 你去健身房了没有？

4. A：你看电影了吗？

B：没有。

没 VS 不

1. "不"一般用来否定主观意愿，可以指过去、现在和将来；"没"一般用来否定客观情况，不能指将来。例如：

"不" is usually used to deny subjective willings, and can refer to the past, the present and the future; "没" generally negates objective conditions and cannot refer to the future. For example:

（1）我昨天没去爬山。

（2）我明天不去爬山。

2. 否定"有"只能用"没"。例如：

Only "没" can be used to negate "有". For example:

（3）她没有哥哥。

3. 否定能愿动词一般用"不"。例如：

"不" is usually used to negate the negative modal verb. For example:

（4）这里不可以用手机支付。

※ 练习：请选择"不"或"没"填空　Please select "不" or "没" to fill in blanks

1. 昨天晚上我 _____ 吃饭。

2. 我今天 _____ 想去健身房。

3. 金龙 ______ 有妹妹。

4. A：医学院有三千个留学生？

B：这 ______ 可能。

三、结果补语（1） Resultative complement (1)

结果补语常用在动词后面，补充说明动词所引起的结果。常用的结果补语有“见、完、会、好、到”等。例如：

The resultative complement is often used after the verb to introduce the result caused by the verb. The frequently used resultative complements are “见, 完, 会, 好, 到” etc. For example:

1. 我没看见 / 看到你发的微信。
2. 生理学我们已经学完了，但我还没学会。
3. 饭做好了吗？
4. 今天的汉语课上，你学到了什么？

※ 练习：请用合适的结果补语填空 Please fill in blanks with the appropriate resultative complements

见 完 会 好 到

1. 马大为在哪儿？你看 ______ 他了吗？
2. 你写 ______ 作业了吗？
3. 我们已经点 ______ 菜了。
4. 你最近见 ______ 王老师了吗？

四、人称代词“咱们” Personal pronoun “咱们”

人称代词“咱们”表示说话人和听话人双方，一般用在口语中。例如：

The personal pronoun “咱们” refers to both the speaker and the hearer, and is usually used in spoken Chinese. For example:

1. 咱们下午去打篮球，怎么样？

2. 山上的叶子都红了，很漂亮，咱们去看看吧。

3. 咱们一起去上课吧。

咱们 VS 我们

“咱们”和“我们”都是第一人称代词。

“咱们” and “我们” are both first personal pronouns.

1. “咱们”多用在口语中，“我们”口语和书面语中都可以用。

“咱们” are mostly used in spoken language, and “我们” can be used both in spoken and written Chinese.

2. 指代说话人和听话人双方时，用“咱们”“我们”都可以；如果只指说话人一方，用“我们”，不能用“咱们”。例如：

When referring to both the himself/herself and the hearer, he/she can use both “咱们” and “我们”; when referring to the speaker himself/herself only, he/she should use “我们”, not “咱们”. For example:

（1）金龙，我们 / 咱们明天去爬山吧。

（2）金龙，明天我们（* 咱们）想去爬山，你去吗？

（3）我们（* 咱们）学完生理学了，你们呢？

※ 练习：请选择“咱们”或“我们”填空　Please select “咱们” or “我们” to fill in blanks

1. 上午有课，________ 走吧。

2. 星期六你来 ________ 家玩儿吧。

3.________ 去饭店吃饭吧。

4.________ 已经点好菜了，你快来吧。

五、副词“还”（2） Adverb “还” (2)

副词“还”可以表示动作或状态持续不变。例如：

The adverb “还” can indicate that the action or state remains unchanged. For example:

1. 我们生理学有很多作业，我还没写完。
2. 虽然学完了，但是我还没学会。
3. A：外边还在下雨吗？

   B：还在下。

※ 练习：请用副词“还”和所给词语完成句子 Please use the adverb “还” and the given words to complete sentences

1. 已经上课了，马大为 ______________________________。（睡觉）
2. 已经头晕一个星期了，他 ____________________________。（去医院）
3. 你到了吗？我 ______________________________。（公共汽车）
4. ______________________________，我们开车去吧。（下雨）

综合练习 Comprehensive Exercises

一、根据拼音写汉字 Write Chinese characters according to Pinyin

1. gāngcái________	3. shìr________	5. zánmen________
2. kànjiàn________	4. zhème________	6. fā________

二、辨字组词 Discriminate between Chinese characters and make words

1. 因________ 国________	2. 完________ 元________	3. 回________ 四________	4. 篮________ 蓝________

三、替换练习 Substitution drills

1. 我刚才<u>给你发微信</u>了。

去卫生间
去买东西
去图书馆

2. 我没看见<u>你发的微信</u>。

你写的电话号码
你买的手机
你订的外卖

3. 我还没<u>写</u>完<u>生理学作业</u>。

吃	早饭
打	电话
看	电影

四、选词填空 Use the following words to fill in the blanks

会　完　发　看见　刚才

1. 你有事儿就给我_______微信。
2. 王医生做_______手术了吗？
3. 我们学的生词（shēngcí，new words）你都学_______了吗？
4. 我上午没_______你，你没去上课？
5. 那个病人_______去哪儿了？

五、用所给词语完成对话 Complete the dialogues with given words

1. 李真：妈妈，你去哪儿了？

   妈妈：________________。（刚才）

2. 美丽：咱们去看电影吧，王老师说最近有个很好看的电影。

   朋友：____。（V 完）

3. 老师：今天上课学的生词简单不简单？

   金龙：很简单，__________________________。（V 会）

4. 女儿：爸爸，你明天为什么不和我们一起去爬山？

   爸爸：____________________________________。（因为）

5. 医生：你明天的手术大概要三个半小时。

   病人：____________________________？（这么）

六、根据课文内容回答问题 Answer the following questions according to the text

1. 吉米为什么没回马大为的微信？
2. 吉米为什么不去打篮球？
3. 马大为怎么没有生理学作业？
4. 马大为生理学学得怎么样？

七、根据课文内容填空 Fill in the blanks according to the text

马大为______给吉米______微信，但是吉米______。因为吉米一直在宿舍______，没______马大为发的微信。马大为想请吉米下午一起去______，可是吉米有很多______作业，他______，不能去。马大为没有生理学作业，因为他已经______生理学。马大为虽然______生理学，但是他还没______。

课文（二）
Text（II）

Měilì zài zìxíshì yùjiàn Jīn Lóng.
（美丽在自习室遇见金龙。）

Měilì: Jīn Lóng, nǐ de liǎnsè bú tài hǎo, shēngbìng le ma?
美丽：金龙，你的脸色不太好，生病了吗？

Jīn Lóng: Zuìjìn wǒ měi tiān dōu áoyè fùxí, yòu lèi yòu kùn.
金龙：最近我每天都熬夜复习，又累又困。

Měilì: Nǐmen kǎowán le ma?
美丽：你们考完了吗？

Jīn Lóng: Méiyǒu, shēnglǐxué hòutiān kǎo.
金龙：没有，生理学后天考。

Měilì: Nǐ fùxí hǎo le ma?
美丽：你复习好了吗？

Jīn Lóng: Dāngrán méiyǒu. Zhè mén kǎoshì hěn nán, tèbié shì tiánkòng hé pànduàn.
金龙：当然没有。这门考试很难，特别是填空和判断。

Měilì: Nǐ yào hǎohāor xiūxi, búyào tài lèi le.
美丽：你要好好儿休息，不要太累了。

Jīn Lóng: Fàngxīn ba, méi wèntí!
金龙：放心吧，没问题！

(Meili meets Jin Long in the study room.)

Meili: Jin Long, you doesn't look good. Are you ill?

Jin Long: Recently I stay up all night for reviewing everyday. I feel tired and sleepy.

Meili: Have you finished the exam?

Jin Long: No. The physiology will be tested on the day after tomorrow.

Meili: Have you prepared well?

Jin Long: Of course not. This examination is very difficult, especially the blank filling part and the true or false part.

Meili: You should have a good rest. Don't get too tired.

Jin Long: Don't worry. No problem!

生词 New words

1. 脸色	liǎnsè	*n.*	complexion
2. 生病	shēngbìng	*v.*	to get sick
病	bìng	*n./v.*	illness; to fall ill
3. 熬夜	áoyè	*v.*	to stay up
4. 复习	fùxí	*v.*	to review
5. 又……又……	yòu…yòu…		both…and…
6. 困	kùn	*adj.*	sleepy
7. 考	kǎo	*v.*	to test, to examine
8. 后天	hòutiān	*n.*	the day after tomorrow
9. 门	mén	*m.*	branch of study
10. 考试	kǎoshì	*v.*	to test, to exam
11. 难	nán	*adj.*	difficult
12. 特别	tèbié	*adv./adj.*	especially; special
13. 填空	tiánkòng	*v.*	to fill in the blank
填	tián	*v.*	to fill
14. 判断	pànduàn	*v.*	to judge
15. 好好儿	hǎohāor	*adv.*	well

16. 不要	búyào	*adv.*	do not
17. 放心	fàngxīn	*v.*	to be at ease, don't worry
18. 问题	wèntí	*n.*	question, problem, matter

语言点 Language Points

一、固定结构"又……又……"　Fixed structure"又……又……"

固定结构"又……又……"可以用来连接形容词、动词或动词性短语，表示主语同时具有两种性质状态或者同时存在两种情况。例如：

The fixed structure "又……又……" can be used to connect adjectives, verbs or verbal phrases, indicating that the subject has two states or two situations at the same time. For example:

1. 最近我每天都熬夜复习，又累又困。
2. 哥哥的新房子又漂亮又舒服。
3. 这个小区又近又方便。
4. 星期五考生理学，这几天我又早起又熬夜，还没复习好。
5. 在 KTV 里，马大为又唱又跳（tiào，dance），非常高兴。

※ 练习：请用固定结构"又……又……"和所给词语完成对话　Please use the fixed structure "又……又……" and the given words to complete dialogues

1. A：你的宿舍怎么样？

   B：______________________________。（漂亮　舒服）

2. A：你住的小区好不好？

B：______________________________。（漂亮　干净）

3. A：你怎么了？不舒服吗？

B：______________________________。（头晕　肚子疼）

4. A：你们上午做什么了？

B：______________________，太累了。（爬山　踢足球）

二、副词"特别"　Adverb "特别"

副词"特别"表示尤其，常用在后面小句的开头，其后常与"是"连在一起说。例如：

The adverb "特别" means especially. It is often used at the beginning of the following clause, followed by "是". For example:

1. 这门考试很难，特别是填空和判断。
2. 马大为很喜欢运动，特别是爬山。
3. 哥哥每天工作都很忙，特别是星期一。

※ 练习：请用副词"特别"完成句子　Please complete sentences with the adverb "特别"

1. 北京夏天很热，______________________________。
2. 我很喜欢吃中国菜，__________________________。
3. 你穿裙子很好看，____________________________。
4. 你最近脸色不太好，__________________________。

三、祈使句（2）："不要……了"　Imperative sentence (2): "不要……了"

"不要……了"是祈使句的一种，表示劝阻、禁止。例如：

"不要……了" is a kind of imperative sentence, indicating dissuasion or prohibition. For example:

1. 你要好好儿休息，不要太累了。
2. 不要看电影了，早点儿睡吧。
3. 不要睡了，马上上课了！

※ 练习：请用祈使句“不要……了”完成句子　Please complete sentences with the imperative structure “不要……了”

1. ____________________，咱们休息一下吧。
2. ____________________，我们订外卖吧。
3. ____________________，你写完作业了吗？
4. 已经十二点了，____________________。

综合练习 Comprehensive Exercises

一、根据拼音写汉字 Write Chinese characters according to Pinyin

1. shēngbìng__________　3. hòutiān__________　5. kǎoshì__________
2. fùxí__________　4. tèbié__________　6. fàngxīn__________

二、辨字组词 Discriminate between Chinese characters and make words

1. 难________ 谁________
2. 放________ 方________
3. 困________ 因________
4. 病________ 疼________

三、替换练习 Substitution drills

1. 我最近每天都 又累又困。

他姐姐	又高又漂亮
他买的苹果	又红又大
那家饭店的菜	又贵又不好吃

2. 你 复习 好了吗？

妈妈	休息
饭	做
房间	订

3. 你要好好儿 休息 。

吃饭

复习

工作

四、选词填空 Use the following words to fill in the blanks

特别　好好儿　门　好　放心

1. 你为什么不喜欢这_______课？
2. 你的生理学复习_______了吗？
3. 你生病了，要_______休息，不要工作了。

4. 汉语很难学，________是汉字（Hànzì，Chinese character）。

5. 爸爸和妈妈都不________我一个人去中国留学。

五、用所给词语完成对话 Complete the dialogues with given words

1. 妈妈：你不能一个人去，我和你一起去吧。

   王晨：________________________________。（放心）

2. 美丽：这件衣服怎么样？

   朋友：________________________________。（又……又……）

3. 朋友：医学（medical science）难学吗？

   金龙：非常难，__________________。（特别）

4. 李真：爸爸，我今天很累。

   爸爸：不要写作业了，今天________________。（好好儿）

5. 医生：明天是周末，你不用来上班，对吧？

   护士：________________________________。（虽然……但是……）

六、根据课文内容回答问题 Answer the following questions according to the text

1. 金龙为什么脸色不好？
2. 金龙考完了吗？
3. 金龙什么时候考生理学？
4. 金龙为什么说还没复习好？

七、根据课文内容填空 Fill in the blanks according to the text

金龙的脸色________，因为最近他每天都熬夜复习，________。他________考生理学，但是现在还没________呢。这________考试很难，________填空和判断。美丽叫他________休息，不要太累了。

语言任务 Language Tasks

一、阅读理解 Reading comprehension

我们班（class）有一些同学，常常不好好儿上课，想出去玩儿。考试前几天，他们每天都熬夜复习，又累又困，脸色也不好。长时间不睡觉，有的考试前就生病了，不能参加（cānjiā，take part in）考试，真是太糟糕（zāogāo，bad）了。

读后判断 True or false

1. 我们班的同学都喜欢学习。（ ）
2. 有的同学考试前熬夜复习。（ ）
3. 常熬夜对身体（shēntǐ，health）不好。（ ）
4. 熬夜的同学都生病了。（ ）
5. 很多同学考完试生病了。（ ）

二、口头表达 Oral expression

任务名称：我不想去踢球。

Task: I don't want to play soccer.

任务要求：1. 两个学生一组，一个有考试，要复习；另一个没有考试，想去踢球。
2. 后者询问不能去的原因，劝慰前者注意身体，不要熬夜。

Requirements: 1. Two students work in a group. One pretends to have an exam and needs to review; the other one pretends to not have an exam and wants to play soccer.
2. The latter one asks why the former one can't go to play soccer, and comforts him/her, reminding him/her to take care of him/her and not to stay up late.

Reference words: 发　微信　回　一直　踢足球　复习　考试　这么
完　会　熬夜　脸色　好好儿　不要

三、书面表达 Written expression

任务名称：不要熬夜。

Task: Don't stay up late.

任务要求：写出熬夜的坏处。

Requirement: List the disadvantages of staying up late.

熬夜的坏处 The disadvantages of staying up late	1.
	2.
结论 Conclusion	

Reference words: 每天　熬夜　又……又……　累　脸色　困　复习　好
特别　门　好好儿　考试

补充词汇 Supplementary Words

bìnglǐxué
病理学
pathology

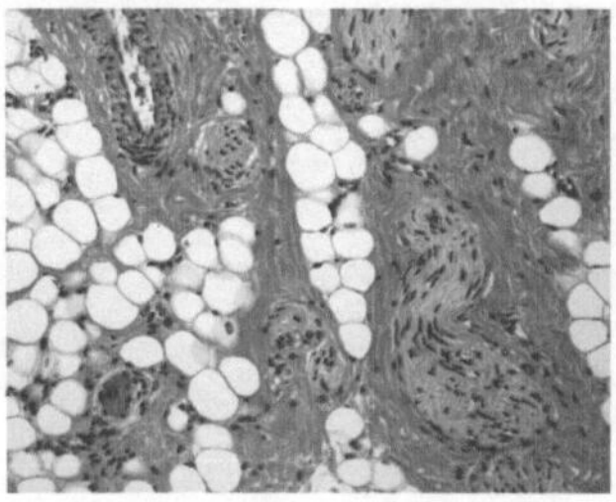

shēngwù huàxué
生物化学
biochemistry

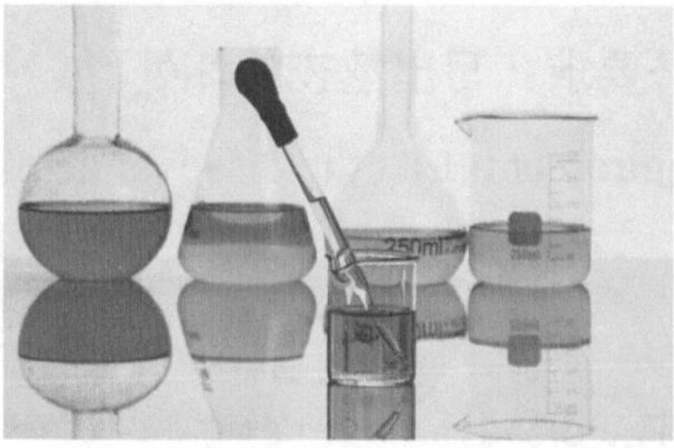

jiěpōuxué
解剖学
anatomy

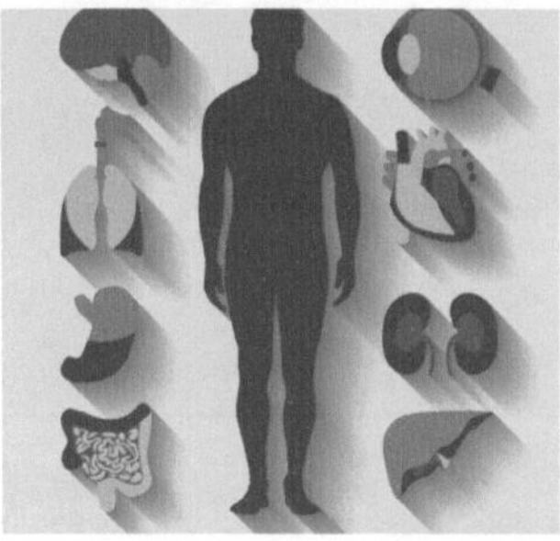

yàolǐxué
药理学
pharmacology

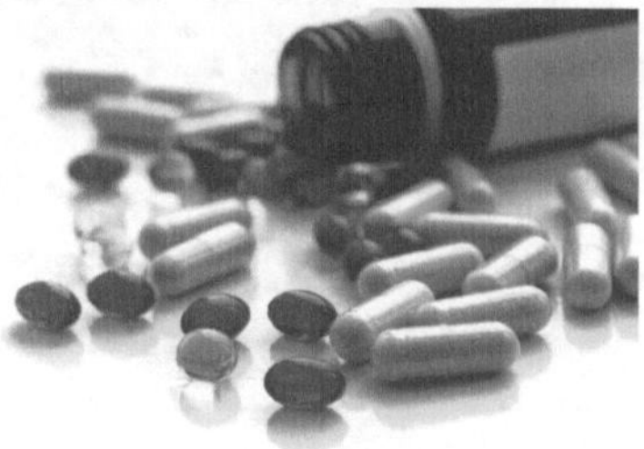

第三课
Lesson 3

Wǒ guòlai kànkan tā
我过来看看他
I come to see him

学习目标 Learning Objectives

1. Language functions: Students can describe or inquire about someone's condition and hospitalization; students are able to express permission.
2. Language points: Simple directional complement (1) "来/去"; Adverb "挺"; Adverb "刚"; Modal particle "吧" (3); Fixed structure "如果……就……"; Preposition "从" (2).
3. Medical knowledge: Students are expected to understand nursing.
4. Social culture: Students are expected to understand the basic situation of the accommodation of Chinese college students.

热身活动 Warming-up

1. 你自己或者家人有过住院的经历吗？是谁在医院照顾病人呢？
Have you or your family member(s) ever been hospitalized? Who cared for the patient(s) in the hospital?

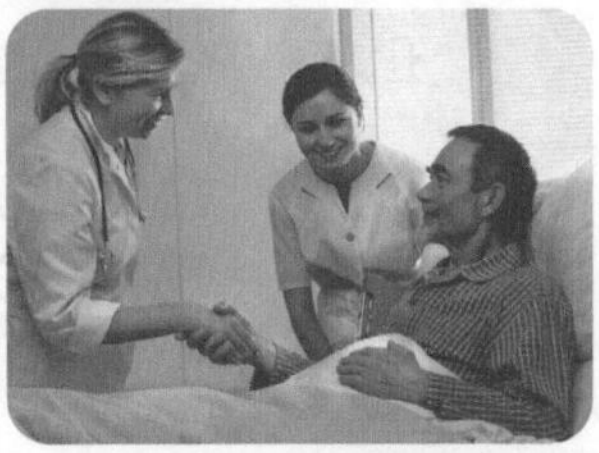

2. 学习的时候遇到不会的问题，你一般会怎么做？
What do you usually do when you encounter problems that you don't know in your study?

课文（一）
Text（I）

Wáng Dōng zài bìngfáng ménkǒu yùdào Mǎ Dàwéi.
（王　东 在 病房　门口 遇到 马 大为。）

Wáng Dōng: Dàwéi, nǐ zěnme lái le?
王东：大为，你怎么来了？

Mǎ Dàwéi: Wǒ péngyou tī zúqiú shuāishāng le, zài zhèr zhùyuàn, wǒ guòlai kànkan tā.
马大为：我 朋友 踢足球 摔伤 了，在这儿住院，我过来看看 他。

Wáng Dōng: Yánzhòng ma?
王东：严重 吗？

Mǎ Dàwéi: Tǐng yánzhòng de, gāng zuòwán shǒushù.
马大为：挺 严重 的，刚 做完 手术。

Wáng Dōng: Tài zāogāo le. Xiànzài shéi zhàogù tā?
王东：太 糟糕 了。现在 谁 照顾 他？

Mǎ Dàwéi: Péngyoumen zhàogù tā, yǒude báitiān guòlai, yǒude wǎnshang guòlai.
马大为：朋友们 照顾 他，有的 白天 过来，有的 晚上 过来。

Wáng Dōng: Nǐmen zhèxiē péngyou zhēn búcuò.
王东：你们 这些 朋友 真 不错。

Mǎ Dàwéi: Tā de jiārén bú zài Zhōngguó, wǒmen yào hǎohāor zhàogù tā.
马大为：他的家人不在 中国，我们 要 好好儿照顾他。

(Wang Dong meets Ma Dawei at the door of the ward.)

Wang Dong: Dawei, why do you come?

Ma Dawei: My friend fell down and got hurt when playing soccer. He is in hospital and I come to see him.

Wang Dong: Did he hurt seriously?

Ma Dawei: Yes, very much. He just had a surgery.

Wang Dong: That's too bad. Who is taking care of him?

Ma Dawei: His friends are taking care of him. Some come by day, and some by night.

Wang Dong: His friends like you are so nice.

Ma Dawei: His family is not in China. We shall take good care of him.

生词 New words

1. 摔	shuāi	*v.*	to fall
2. 伤	shāng	*v.*	to hurt
3. 住院	zhùyuàn	*v.*	to be hospitalized
4. 过来	guòlai	*v.*	to come over
过	guò	*v.*	to cross
5. 严重	yánzhòng	*adj.*	serious
6. 挺	tǐng	*adv.*	quite
7. 刚	gāng	*adv.*	just
8. 糟糕	zāogāo	*adj.*	bad
9. 照顾	zhàogù	*v.*	to take care of
10. 有的……有的……	yǒude…yǒude…		some...some...
有的	yǒude	*pron.*	some
11. 白天	báitiān	*n.*	daytime
12. 家人	jiārén	*n.*	family member

语言点 Language Points

一、简单趋向补语(1): 来/去　Simple directional complement (1): 来/去

“来/去”用在动词后边，可补充说明动作行为的方向。其中，“来”表示动作行为向着说话人所在的方向，“去”表示动作行为向着与说话人相反的方向。例如：

“来/去” are used after the verb to indicate the direction of the action. “来” means that the action moves toward the speaker, and “去” means that the action moves against the speaker. For example:

1. 我朋友在这儿住院，我过来看看他。
2. 老师，马大为说他在宿舍肚子疼，您可以过去看看他吗？
3. 前面走来一个人，穿一件白大褂。

※ 练习：请选择“来”或“去”填空　Please select “来” or “去” to fill in blanks

1. 妈妈：你什么时候回（huí，return）家？

   李真：妈妈，我六点前就回 ________。

2. A：你为什么来医院？

   B：我朋友生病了，我过 ________ 看他。

3. A：我们点好菜了，你快过 ________ 吧。

   B：好，我现在过 ________。

4. 山上很漂亮，咱们快上（go up）________ 看看吧。

二、副词“挺”　Adverb “挺”

副词“挺”表示程度相当高，但是比“很”的程度略低；一般用在口语中，常

用在“挺+形容词/动词+的”结构中。例如：

The adverb “挺” indicates quite high degree, but slightly lower than “很”; it is usually used in spoken Chinese in the structure of “挺 + adjective/verb + 的”. For example:

1. 我们宿舍挺大的。
2. 这个小区挺好的。
3. 手机支付挺方便的。
4. 这门考试挺难的。
5. 我挺想爸爸妈妈的。
6. 马大为挺喜欢运动的。

※ 练习：请用副词“挺”完成对话　Please complete dialogues with the adverb “挺”

1. A：生理学考试怎么样？

   B：________________________________。

2. A：哥哥做饭怎么样？

   B：________________________________。

3. A：哥哥的新房子怎么样？

   B：________________________________。

4. A：图书馆远不远？

   B：________________________________。

三、副词“刚”　Adverb “刚”

副词“刚”表示动作行为或情况发生在不久之前。例如：

The adverb “刚” means that the action or situation occurred not long ago. For example:

1. 朋友刚做完手术。

2. 我刚写完作业。

3. 我们刚认识。

刚 VS 刚才

“刚”和“刚才”都表示动作行为或情况发生在不久之前，都可以做状语。

“刚” and “刚才” both indicate that the action or situation occurs not long ago, and both can be used as adverbial.

1. “刚”是副词，只能用在动词前；“刚才”是名词，可以用在主语前面，也可以用在动词、形容词前面。例如：

“刚” is an adverb and can only be used before a verb; “刚才” is a noun, which can be used before the subject or verbs and adjectives. For example:

（1）我刚踢完球。（* 刚我踢完球。）

（2）我刚才去踢足球了。（刚才我去踢球了。）

2. “刚”前面可以有表示时间的词语，“刚才”不行。例如：

“刚” can have words indicating time before it, but “刚才” cannot. For example:

（3）我今天早上刚看了这个电影。（* 我今天早上刚才看了这个电影。）

3. “刚才”后面可以加否定词，“刚”不行。例如：

“刚才” can be followed by negative words, but “刚” cannot. For example:

（4）你刚才为什么不去看电影？（* 你刚为什么不去看电影。）

※ 练习：请选择“刚”或“刚才”填空　Please select “刚” or “刚才” to fill in blanks

1. 我 ________ 认识马大为。

2. ________ 我看见马大为了。

3. ________ 你去哪儿了？不在宿舍吗？

4. 我们昨天 ________ 去爬了山。

综合练习 Comprehensive Exercises

一、根据拼音写汉字 Write Chinese characters according to Pinyin

1. zāogāo__________　　3. tǐng__________　　5. yǒude__________

2. yánzhòng__________　　4. zhàogù__________　　6. shuāi__________

二、辨字组词 Discriminate between Chinese characters and make words

1. { 重________ / 里________ }　　2. { 白________ / 百________ }　　3. { 摔________ / 球________ }　　4. { 挺________ / 庭________ }

三、替换练习 Substitution drills

1. 我朋友踢足球摔伤了，我过来看看他。

过去

进（jìn，enter）去

上来

2. 我朋友伤得挺严重的。

我最近	忙
哥哥上班	累
你的汉语说得	好

3. 他刚 做完手术 。

吃完饭
考完试
打完电话

四、选词填空 Use the following words to fill in the blanks

挺　刚　过来　有的　糟糕

1. 我______给他打完电话，他就来了。
2. 王医生______看你了。
3. 他摔得______严重的，要马上去医院。
4. 上课了，同学们______写汉字（Hànzì，Chinese character），______读课文（kèwén，text）。
5. 今天我和金龙都不高兴，因为我们昨天考试考得都很______。

五、用所给词语完成对话 Complete the dialogues with given words

1. 美丽：妈妈，你今天过得怎么样？
   妈妈：____________________。（挺）
2. 美丽：你今天回（huí，return）来得这么早啊。
   朋友：____________________。（刚）
3. 病人：护士，我现在特别不舒服。
   护士：____________________。（过来）
4. 李真：你们医院的医生都是中国人吗？
   爸爸：____________________。（有的）

5. 病人：我可以进（jìn，enter）去吗？

护士：______________________。（进来）

六、根据课文内容回答问题 Answer the following questions according to the text

1. 马大为为什么来医院？
2. 他的朋友伤得怎么样？
3. 现在谁照顾他的朋友？
4. 朋友们为什么来医院照顾他？

七、根据课文内容填空 Fill in the blanks according to the text

马大为的朋友踢足球________了，伤得________，________手术，现在在医院________。他的朋友们都来医院________他，________白天________，________晚上________。因为他的家人________，朋友们都想好好儿________他。

课文（二）
Text（II）

Jīn Lóng qù bàngōngshì wèn lǎoshī wèntí.
（金龙 去 办公室 问 老师 问题。）

Jīn Lóng: Lǎoshī, dǎrǎo yíxià, wǒ kěyǐ jìnqu ma?
金龙：老师，打扰一下，我可以进去吗？

lǎoshī: Jìnlai ba.
老师：进来吧。

Jīn Lóng: Wǒ yǒu jǐ gè wèntí xiǎng wèn nín, kěyǐ ma?
金龙：我有几个问题 想 问 您，可以吗？

lǎoshī: Dāngrán kěyǐ.
老师：当然 可以。

Lǎoshī gěi Jīn Lóng jiǎngjiě.
（老师 给 金 龙 讲解。）

Jīn Lóng: Xiànzài wǒ dōu míngbai le, xièxie nín!
金龙：现在 我都 明白 了，谢谢您！

lǎoshī: Bú kèqi. Rúguǒ nǐ yǒu bú huì de wèntí, jiù guòlai wèn wǒ.
老师：不客气。如果你有不会的问题，就过来问 我。

Jīn Lóng: Hǎo de. Qǐngwèn nín shénme shíhou zài bàngōngshì?
金龙：好 的。请问 您 什么 时候 在 办公室？

lǎoshī: Wǔfàn yǐhòu, cóng yī diǎn dào wǔ diǎn, wǒ dōu zài bàngōngshì.
老师：午饭以后，从一点 到 五 点，我都 在 办公室。

(Jin Long goes to the office to ask the teacher questions.)

Jin Long: Excuse me, sir, may I come in?

Teacher: Yes, please.

Jin Long: I want to ask you some questions, may I?

Teacher: Of course.

(The teacher answers Jin Long's questions.)

Jin Long: I understand all these questions now. Thank you!

Teacher: You are welcome. If you have any questions, you may come and ask me.

Jin Long: OK. May I ask when you are in the office?

Teacher: I am in the office after lunch, from one o'clock to five o'clock.

生词 New words

1. 打扰	dǎrǎo	*v.*	to interrupt, to bother
2. 进去	jìnqu	*v.*	to enter, to get in
进	jìn	*v.*	to enter
3. 进来	jìnlai	*v.*	to come in
4. 明白	míngbai	*v./adj.*	to understand; clear, obvious
5. 如果……就……	rúguǒ…jiù…		if...
如果	rúguǒ	*conj.*	if
就	jiù	*adv.*	will
6. 午饭	wǔfàn	*n.*	lunch

语言点 Language Points

一、语气助词“吧”（3） Modal particle “吧” (3)

“吧”用在后续句句尾，表示同意或者允许。例如：

“吧” is used at the end of the following-sentence to indicate approval or permission. For example:

1. A：老师，我可以进去吗？

   B：进来吧。

2. A：我可以去一下卫生间吗？

   B：你去吧。

3. A：妈妈，我现在可以看电视吗？

   B：看吧。

※ 练习：请用语气助词“吧”完成对话 Please complete dialogues with the modal particle “吧”

1. A：星期六我们去李真家玩儿，好吗？

   B：________________________________。

2. A：老师，十二点了，我们可以下课了吗？

   B：________________________________。

3. A：爸爸，我今天想吃外卖，可以吗？

   B：________________________________。

4. A：下午我们去健身房，好吗？

   B：________________________________。

二、固定结构“如果……就……” Fixed structure “如果……就……”

“如果……就……”连接两个分句，其中前一分句是假设的条件，后一分句是在假设条件下产生的结果。前后两个分句的主语可能一样，也可能不一样。例如：

“如果……就……” connects two clauses. The first clause is a hypothetical condition, and the last clause is the result of the hypothetical condition. The subject of the two clauses could be the same or different. For example:

1. 如果你有不会的问题，就过来问我。
2. 如果你星期六没有课，就来我家玩儿吧。
3. 如果明天不下雨，咱们就去爬山吧。

※ 练习：请用固定结构“如果……就……”完成句子 Please complete sentences with the fixed structure “如果……就……”

1. 如果明天早上没有课，______________________________。
2. ______________________________，就订外卖吧。
3. 如果你写完作业了，______________________________。
4. ______________________________，就去医院看看医生吧。

三、介词“从”（2） Preposition “从” (2)

介词“从”可表示时间的起点，常用在“从……到……”结构中。例如：

The preposition “从” can indicate the start of a time, and is often used in the structure of “从……到……”. For example:

1. 午饭以后，从一点到五点，我都在办公室。
2. 从星期一到星期五，我们每天都有课。
3. 从早上到现在，她一直在宿舍看电影。

※ 练习：请用固定结构“从……到……”完成对话 Please complete dialogs with the fixed structure “从……到……”

1. A：你们星期几有课？

B：________________________________。

2. A：你今天几点有课？

B：________________________________。

3. A：你什么时候有考试？

B：________________________________。

4. A：你脸色不太好，昨天都做什么了？

B：________________________________。

综合练习 Comprehensive Exercises

一、根据拼音写汉字 Write Chinese characters according to Pinyin

1. dǎrǎo________ 3. míngbai________ 5. wǔfàn________

2. jìnqu________ 4. rúguǒ________ 6. jìnlai________

二、辨字组词 Discriminate between Chinese characters and make words

1. {果________ 里________} 2. {进________ 近________} 3. {如________ 和________} 4. {午________ 牛________}

三、替换练习 Substitution drills

1. 我可以<u>进去</u>吗？

过来
进来
过去

2. 如果你<u>有不会的问题</u>，就<u>过来问我</u>。

不舒服	去医院看看
有时间	过去看看他
没有课	去图书馆看看书

3. 从<u>一点</u>到<u>五点</u>，我都在办公室。

星期一	星期五
午饭以后	现在
早上	下午两点

四、选词填空 Use the following words to fill in the blanks

如果　从　进去　打扰　明白

1. 很晚了，不要______病人休息。

2. 中国人的上班时间常常是______早上九点到下午五点。

3. 医生在办公室，你______找（zhǎo，look for）他吧。

4. ________晚上没有人照顾他，我就过去照顾。

5. 这个问题我不太________，我去问问老师。

五、用所给词语完成对话 Complete the dialogues with given words

1. 妈妈：晚上你在家吃饭吗？

   王晨：________________________。（如果……就……）

2. 美丽：你哪天有课？

   朋友：________________________。（从……到……）

3. 金龙：老师，我有几个问题想问您，____________________？（可以）

   老师：当然可以。

4. 大为：________________________，请问解剖楼怎么走？

   同学：从教学楼一直往东走，就能看见。（打扰）

5. 护士：这个病人做完手术了吗？

   家属：__________________________。（刚）

六、根据课文内容回答问题 Answer the following questions according to the text

1. 老师让金龙做什么？
2. 金龙为什么去老师办公室？
3. 如果有不会的问题，金龙可以怎么做？
4. 老师什么时候在办公室？

七、根据课文内容填空 Fill in the blanks according to the text

金龙有几个问题________，他来办公室________。老师说完，他都________了。老师说________有不会的________，________问他。老师午饭________，________一点________五点都在办公室。

语言任务 Language Tasks

一、阅读理解 Reading comprehension

我有个尼泊尔同学叫哈利，骑摩托车（mótuōchē，motorcycle）摔伤了腿（tuǐ, leg）。他的几个好朋友每天都去医院照顾他，有的上午去，有的下午去，还有的晚上去。他在医院住了一个多星期。出院（chūyuàn，be discharged from hospital）以后，因为走路（zǒulù，walk）不方便，他的朋友们就去宿舍照顾他。

读后判断 True or false

1. 哈利是尼日利亚（Nigeria）人。 (　　)
2. 哈利踢球摔伤了腿。 (　　)
3. 哈利的朋友们在医院照顾他。 (　　)
4. 哈利在医院住了三个星期。 (　　)
5. 出院以后，哈利不用别人照顾了。 (　　)

二、口头表达 Oral expression

任务名称：照顾摔伤病人。

Task: Take care of the wounded.

任务要求：1. 四个学生一组，一个是摔伤病人，另外三个是病人的朋友。

2. 朋友们商量如何分工照顾摔伤的病人。

Requirements: 1. Four students work in a group. One acts as a wounded, and the other three act as the friends of the patient.

2. The friends discuss how to divide the work of taking care of the injured.

Reference words: 摔伤　严重　手术　糟糕　照顾　有的　白天　晚上　好好儿

三、书面表达 Written expression

任务名称：学习中遇到不会的问题怎么办？

Task: What should you do if you meet problems in your study?

任务要求：根据你的经验，介绍好用的解决方法，写 3—4 个句子。

Requirement: Introduce useful solutions based on your own experience, and write 3-4 sentences.

问老师 Ask the teacher	1.
	2.
上网找 Search online	1.
	2.
结论 Conclusion	

Reference words: 可以　明白　问题　问　如果……就……
从……到……　打扰　办公室

补充词汇 Supplementary Words

gǔzhé
骨折
fracture

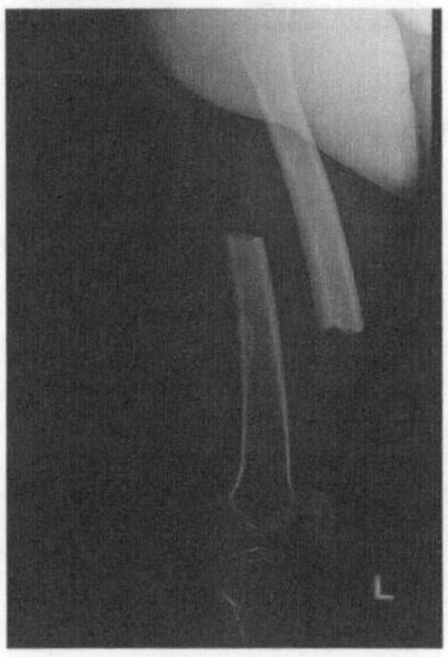

guǎizhàng
拐杖
walking stick

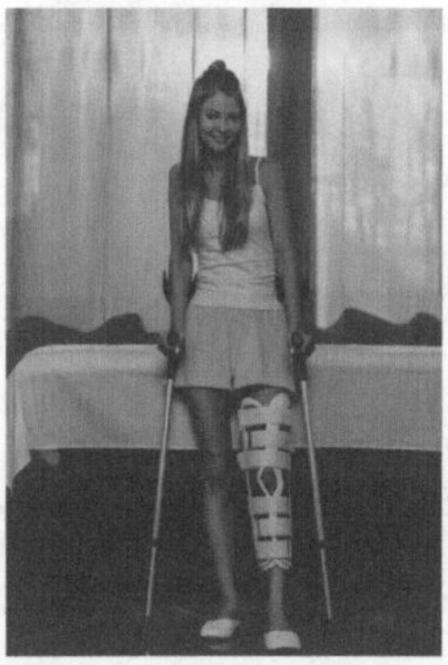

X-guāng piàn
X 光片
X-ray film

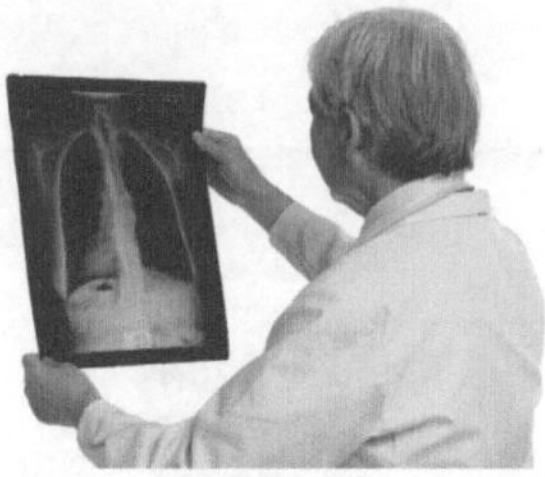

shígāo
石膏
plaster

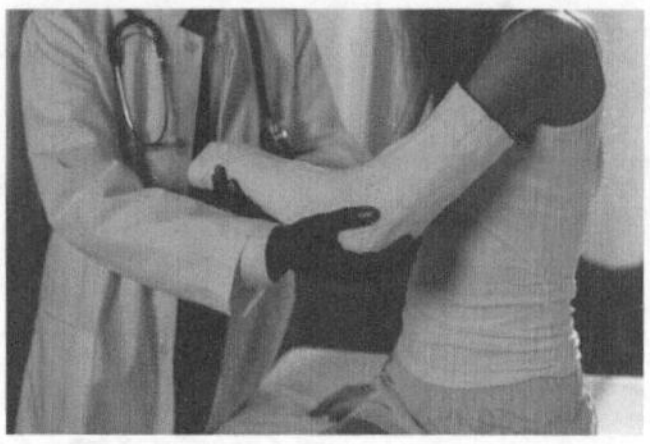

第四课
Lesson 4

Xīnzàng yǒu wèntí de rén yuè lái yuè duō

心脏 有 问题的人越来越多

More and more people have heart problems

学习目标 Learning Objectives

1. Language functions: Students can ask for the reason; students are able to express their dreams.
2. Language points: Adjective “突然”; Pivotal sentence (2) “A＋让＋B＋verb/verbal phrase”; Fixed structure “快要……了”; Fixed structure “越来越……”; Adverb “都” (2).
3. Medical knowledge: Students are expected to understand the symptoms and precautions of the cold.
4. Social culture: Students are expected to know the names of major departments in Chinese hospitals.

热身活动 Warming-up

1. 你知道感冒有什么症状吗？

Do you know the symptoms of the cold?

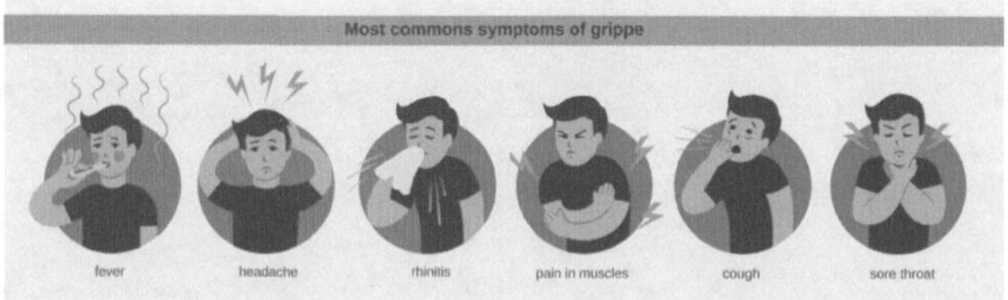

2. 你知道下列是医院的哪些科室吗？以后你最想当哪个科室的医生？

Do you know the departments of the hospital (right)? Which department of the hospital do you want to work for in the future?

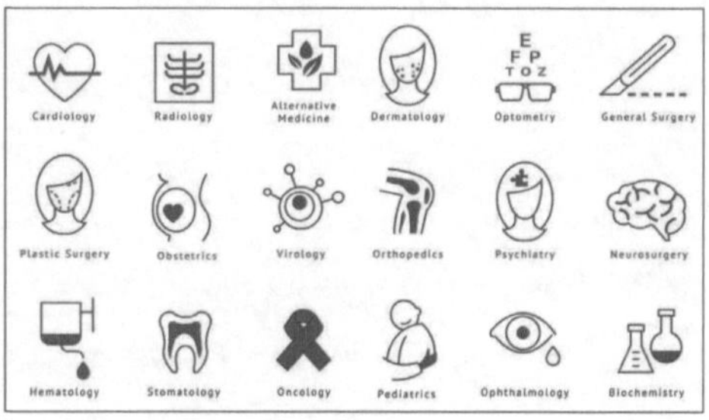

课文（一）
Text（I）

Wáng Chén shēngbìng le, Jīn Lóng hé Mǎ Dàwéi qù Wáng Chén jiā kàn tā.
（王　晨　生病　了，金龙　和马　大为　去　王　晨　家　看　他。）

Jīn Lóng: Tīngshuō nǐ shēngbìng le, wǒmen guòlai kànkan nǐ.
金龙：听说　你　生病　了，我们过来看看　你。

Wáng Chén: Wǒ méishìr, qǐng zuò. Nǐmen hē chá háishi kāfēi?
王晨：我没事儿，请　坐。你们　喝　茶　还是　咖啡？

Mǎ Dàwéi: Wǒ zǎoshang hēle yì bēi kāfēi, gěi wǒ yì bēi chá ba.
马大为：我　早上　喝了一杯　咖啡，给　我一杯　茶吧。

Jīn Lóng: Wǒ yě hē chá. Wáng Chén, nǐ zěnme tūrán shēngbìng le ne?
金龙：我也喝茶。王　晨，你怎么　突然　生病　了呢？

Wáng Chén: Shàng gè xīngqī pá shān de shíhou, xià yǔ le, wǒ méiyǒu dài sǎn, huílai jiù gǎnmào le.
王晨：上　个星期爬　山　的时候，下雨了，我没有带伞，回来就　感冒了。

Jīn Lóng: Nǐ qù yīyuàn le ma?
金龙：你去医院了吗？

Wáng Chén: Qù le, yīshēng ràng wǒ zài jiā xiūxi.
王晨：去了，医生　让　我在家休息。

Mǎ Dàwéi: Wǒ yě xiǎng zài jiā xiūxi!
马大为：我　也　想　在家休息！

Wáng Chén: Kuàiyào kǎoshì le, nǐ hǎohāor fùxí ba!
王晨：快要　考试　了，你好好儿复习吧！

(Wang Chen gets sick. Jin Long and Ma Dawei come to his home to see him.)

Jin Long: We heard you get sick. We come to see you.

Wang Chen: I'm OK. Please take a seat. What would you like to drink, tea or coffee?

Ma Dawei: I had a cup of coffee this morning. I'd like to have a cup of tea, please.

Jin Long: I also want a tea. Wang Chen, why did you suddenly get sick?

Wang Chen: When I climbed the mountain last week, it rained and I didn't have an umbrella with me. Then I got a cold after coming back.

Jin Long: Did you go to hospital?

Wang Chen: Yes. The doctor told me to have a rest at home.

Ma Dawei: I also want to rest at home!

Wang Chen: The exam is coming soon. You'd better make a good review!

生词 New words

1. 听说	tīngshuō	*v.*	to hear
2. 咖啡	kāfēi	*n.*	coffee
3. 杯	bēi	*m.*	a cup of
4. 给	gěi	*v.*	to give
5. 突然	tūrán	*adj.*	sudden
6. 上	shàng	*n.*	last
7. 带	dài	*v.*	to take
8. 伞	sǎn	*n.*	umbrella
9. 回来	huílai	*v.*	to come back
回	huí	*v.*	to return, to go back
10. 感冒	gǎnmào	*v./n.*	to catch a cold; cold
11. 让	ràng	*v.*	to let, to make (sb. do)
12. 快要	kuàiyào	*adv.*	soon, be going to

语言点 Language Points

一、形容词"突然"　Adjective"突然"

"突然"表示情况发生得快且出乎意料，常用在动词性成分前，在句中做状语。例如：

"突然" indicates that things happen quickly and unexpectedly. It is often used before a verbal element in a sentence as an adverbial. For example:

1. 你怎么突然生病了呢？
2. 今天早上突然下雨了。
3. 踢足球的时候，他突然摔了。

※ 练习：组词成句　Group words into sentences

1. 哥哥　生病　突然　了

_______________________________________。

2. 来我家　星期六　他　突然　了

_______________________________________。

3. 弟弟　了　感冒　突然

_______________________________________。

4. 请客　突然　要　美丽

_______________________________________。

二、兼语句 (2): A + 让 + B + 动词 / 动词性短语　Pivotal sentence (2): A + 让 + B + verb/verbal phrase

"让"表示指使、致使、容许或听任。在"A + 让 + B + 动词 / 动词性短语"结构中，A 是句子的主语，"让 + B + 动词 / 动词性短语"是句子的谓语，B 是"让"的宾语，同时又是后面动词 / 动词性短语的主语。否定形式常在"让"前加"不"

或"没"。例如：

"让" means to order, cause, allow or indulge. In the structure of "A + 让 + B + verb/verbal phrase", A is the subject of the sentence, "让 + B + verb/verbal phrase" is the predicate of the sentence, and B is both the object of "让" and the subject of the following "verb/verbal phrase". The negative form is often to put "不" or "没" before "让". For example:

1. 医生让我在家休息。

2. 我让金龙去看医生。

3. 老师让我们准备考试。

※ 练习：组词成句　Group words into sentences

1. 医生　休息　哥哥　在家　让

________________________________。

2. 妈妈　回微信　月亮　让

________________________________。

3. 李真　去她家　玩儿　让我们　周末

________________________________。

4. 马大为　去看电影　和他　让我　一起

________________________________。

三、固定结构"快要……了"　Fixed structure "快要……了"

"快要……了"表示某一动作行为或事件即将在较短时间内发生，也可以说"要……了"。例如：

"快要……了" indicates that an action or event is about to occur in a short time. It can also be said as "要……了". For example:

1. 快要考试了，你好好儿复习吧！

2. 快要下雨了，咱们不要去爬山了。

3. 快要上课了，我不吃早饭了。

※ 练习：请用固定结构“快要……了”完成句子　Please complete sentences with the fixed structure “快要……了”

1. 现在是晚上十点五十分，________________________________。

2. 现在是早上七点半，____________________________________。

3. 生理学我们已经学完了，________________________________。

4. 我们不要去踢足球了，__________________________________。

综合练习 Comprehensive Exercises

一、根据拼音写汉字 Write Chinese characters according to Pinyin

1. tīngshuō__________　3. tūrán__________　5. huílai__________

2. kāfēi__________　4. kuàiyào__________　6. gǎnmào__________

二、辨字组词 Discriminate between Chinese characters and make words

1. 杯________ 不________

2. 听________ 新________

3. 伞________ 来________

4. 冒________ 唱________

三、替换练习 Substitution drills

1. 你怎么突然生病了呢？

她	回家
今天	下雨
朋友	给我打电话

2. 医生 让 我 在家休息。

朋友	我	去医院看医生
妈妈	爸爸	在家做饭
老师	学生	在教室写作业

3. 快要考试了，你好好儿复习吧！

下雨	你带伞吧
做手术	你不能吃东西了
上课	我们快回教室吧

四、选词填空 Use the following words to fill in the blanks

让　听说　上　突然　回来

1. ________个周末，我朋友踢足球摔伤了。
2. 我已经到家了，你几点________？
3. 金龙怎么________去北京了？
4. 妈妈________我去买一点儿水果。
5. ________你哥哥在医院工作，是吗？

五、用所给词语完成对话 Complete the dialogues with given words

1. 美丽：妈妈，我今天晚上和朋友去看电影。

   妈妈：________________________？（回来）

2. 王晨：你喝茶还是咖啡？

   美丽：________________________。（给）

3. 医生：你哪儿不舒服？

病人：______________________________。（突然）

4. 美丽：你怎么没去上课？

金龙：______________________________。（让）

5. 王晨：已经十二点了，你怎么没去睡觉？

金龙：______________________________。（快要……了）

六、根据课文内容回答问题 Answer the following questions according to the text

1. 马大为想喝什么？
2. 王晨什么时候去爬山了？
3. 王晨怎么突然生病了呢？
4. 医生让王晨做什么？

七、根据课文内容填空 Fill in the blanks according to the text

______王晨病了，金龙和马大为去看他。王晨问他们喝茶______，马大为早上喝了______咖啡，现在想喝杯茶，金龙也想______。金龙问王晨怎么______生病了，王晨说______星期爬山的时候，下雨了，他没有______，回来就感冒了。他已经去医院了，医生__________。马大为也想在家休息，王晨说______考试了，还是好好儿复习吧。

课文（二）
Text（II）

Tóngxuémen zài tǎolùn yǐhòu de gōngzuò.
（同学们 在 讨论 以后 的 工作。）

Jīn Lóng: Jīntiān de kè zhēn yǒu yìsi.
金龙：今天的课真有意思。

Mǎ Dàwéi: Nǐmen zhīdào ma? Jīntiān gěi wǒmen shàngkè de jiàoshòu shì wǒmen de xiàozhǎng, yě shì wèi fēicháng yǒumíng de wàikē yīshēng.
马大为：你们知道吗？今天给我们上课的教授是我们的校长，也是位非常有名的外科医生。

Jīn Lóng: Wǒ yǐhòu yě xiǎng dāng yì míng wàikē yīshēng.
金龙：我以后也想当一名外科医生。

Měilì: Nǐ xiǎng qù xīnzàng wàikē háishi shénjīng wàikē?
美丽：你想去心脏外科还是神经外科？

Jīn Lóng: Xīnzàng wàikē, xiànzài xīnzàng yǒu wèntí de rén yuè lái yuè duō. Měilì, nǐ ne?
金龙：心脏外科，现在心脏有问题的人越来越多。美丽，你呢？

Měilì: Wǒ xiǎng dāng érkē yīshēng.
美丽：我想当儿科医生。

Yuèliang: Wǒ yě xǐhuan xiǎoháir, wǒ xiǎng dāng chǎnkē yīshēng.
月亮：我也喜欢小孩儿，我想当产科医生。

Měilì: Dàwéi ne? Nǐ zěnme bù shuōhuà?
美丽：大为呢？你怎么不说话？

Mǎ Dàwéi: Wǒ xiǎng dāng yuànzhǎng, nǐmen dōu kěyǐ lái wǒ de yīyuàn gōngzuò.
马大为：我想当院长，你们都可以来我的医院工作。

Jīn Lóng: Nǐ dāng yuànzhǎng de shíhou, wǒmen dōu tuìxiū le!
金龙：你 当 院长 的时候，我们 都 退休 了！

(The classmates are talking their future jobs.)

Jin Long: The class today is really interesting.

Ma Dawei: Do you know the professor of the class today is our principal and also a very famous surgeon?

Jin Long: I also want to be a surgeon in the future.

Meili: Do you want to work for the department of cardiac surgery or neurosurgery?

Jin Long: Cardiac surgery. Now, there are more and more people that have heart problems. What about you, Meili?

Meili: I want to be a paediatrician.

Yueliang: I also like kids. I want to be a obstetrician.

Meili: What about you, Dawei? Why don't you speak?

Ma Dawei: I want to be the hospital director. You all can come to work in my hospital.

Jin Long: When you become the director, we would be retired!

生词 New words

1. 有意思	yǒu yìsi	*VO*	interesting
2. 教授	jiàoshòu	*n.*	professor
3. 校长	xiàozhǎng	*n.*	principal
4. 有名	yǒumíng	*adj.*	famous
5. 外科	wàikē	*n.*	surgery
6. 当	dāng	*v.*	to serve as, to be
7. 名	míng	*m.*	used for persons
8. 心脏	xīnzàng	*n.*	heart

9. 神经	shénjīng	*n.*	neuro
10. 越来越	yuè lái yuè		more and more
11. 儿科	érkē	*n.*	pediatrics
12. 小孩儿	xiǎoháir	*n.*	kid
13. 产科	chǎnkē	*n.*	obstetrics
14. 说话	shuōhuà	*v.*	to speak, to talk
15. 院长	yuànzhǎng	*n.*	director of a hospital
16. 退休	tuìxiū	*v.*	to retire

语言点 Language Points

一、固定结构“越来越……” Fixed structure “越来越……”

“越来越……”后面一般加形容词或者心理动词，表示某种性质状态或心理状态的程度逐步加深。由于这个结构本身已经表示程度，所以它不能与其他程度副词一起使用。例如：

“越来越……” is usually followed by adjectives or psychological verbs to indicate the degree of a certain qualitative or psychological state is gradually deepening. Since this structure itself already indicates degree, it cannot be used together with other degree adverbs. For example:

1. 现在心脏有问题的人越来越多。
2. 我越来越喜欢中国了。
3. 我们小区越来越漂亮了。

※ 练习：请用固定结构"越来越……"完成句子或对话 Please complete sentences or dialogues with the fixed structure "越来越……"

1. 到了五月，天气 ________________________________。

2. 马大为学习汉语一年了，____________________________。

3. 来中国两年了，我认识的中国朋友 __________________________。

4. A：你的头还疼吗？

   B：医生，我的头 ________________________________。

二、副词"都"（2） Adverb "都" (2)

"都"可以表示已经，一般用在"都……了"结构中。例如：

"都" can indicate that someone has done something or something has been done, and is generally used in the structure of "都……了". For example:

1. 你当院长的时候，我们都退休了！
2. 都十二点了，快睡觉吧。
3. 都上课了，你怎么还在宿舍睡觉？

※ 练习：请用"都……了"和所给词语完成句子 Please use "都……了" and the given words to complete sentences

1. 他来中国 ________________________，认识了很多朋友。（十年）

2. 我学习汉语 ______________________，现在汉语越来越好。（两年）

3. 爷爷头晕 ______________________，快去医院看医生吧。（一个星期）

4. 马大为八点半到教室的时候，我们 __________________________。（上课 30 分钟）

综合练习 Comprehensive Exercises

一、根据拼音写汉字 Write Chinese characters according to Pinyin

1. yǒu yìsi________　3. yǒumíng________　5. shuōhuà________
2. jiàoshòu________　4. xiàozhǎng________　6. tuìxiū________

二、辨字组词 Discriminate between Chinese characters and make words

1. 教________ / 放________　2. 院________ / 完________　3. 孩________ / 刻________　4. 儿________ / 几________

三、替换练习 Substitution drills

1. 我以后也想当一名外科医生。

汉语老师
产科医生
儿科护士

2. 现在心脏有问题的人越来越多。

汉语课	有意思
他的头疼	严重
这门考试	难

3. 你 当院长 的时候，我们都 退休 了！

到教室	下课
打电话	点完菜
到电影院（cinema）	快看完

四、选词填空 Use the following words to fill in the blanks

有意思　有名　越来越　都　以后

1. 听说那位老师上课很________。
2. 现在有高血压的人________多。
3. 给我们上课的教授是一位非常________的外科医生。
4. 我喜欢孩子，________想当一名儿科医生。
5. ________看一晚上电影了，让眼睛休息一下吧。

五、用所给词语完成对话 Complete the dialogues with given words

1. 王晨：你以后想做什么？

   朋友：____________________________。（当）

2. 李真：____________________________。（越来越）

   美丽：是吗？我最近常常和中国朋友说话。

3. 王晨：你为什么想当心脏外科医生？

   朋友：____________________________。（越来越）

4. 妈妈：____________________________？（都……了）

   爸爸：今天太忙了，刚给病人做完手术。

5. 朋友：你的汉语很好啊！

金龙：________________。（都……了）

六、根据课文内容回答问题 Answer the following questions according to the text

1. 今天给马大为他们上课的人是谁？
2. 金龙为什么想去心脏外科？
3. 美丽想当什么医生？月亮呢？
4. 马大为以后想做什么？

七、根据课文内容填空 Fill in the blanks according to the text

金龙说今天的课________，马大为说今天给他们上课的________是他们学校的________，也是位非常________的外科医生。金龙以后也想________一名外科医生，他想去心脏外科，因为现在心脏有问题的人________。美丽想当________医生，月亮想当________医生，她们都喜欢________。马大为想当________，还让同学们都去他的医院工作。金龙说马大为当院长________，同学们________退休了！

语言任务 Language Tasks

一、阅读理解 Reading comprehension

上个星期爬山的时候，突然下雨了，我没有带伞，回来就感冒了。头很疼，不能去上课了。我去医院看了医生，医生说我不用打针（dǎzhēn，have an injection）。他给我开（kāi，prescribe）了一些药（yào，medicine），让我一天吃三次（cì，time），每次吃两片（piàn，pill）。医生还让我多穿衣服，多喝热水，多吃点儿水果，最好在家里休息两天。可是快要考试了，我要在家好好儿复习，好好儿准备。

读后判断 True or false

1. 上个星期没下雨。 ( )
2. 医生让我打针。 ( )
3. 医生给我开药了。 ( )
4. 我可以去上课了。 ( )
5. 我已经考完试了。 ( )

二、口头表达 Oral expression

任务名称：感冒后需要注意的问题。

Task: Problems needed to pay attention to after catching a cold.

任务要求：1. 两个学生一组，一个是感冒病人，一个是医生。
2. 医生询问病人的感冒症状。
3. 医生给病人开药，并告诉病人注意事项。

Requirements: 1. Two students work in a group. One acts as a patient who has a cold, the other as a doctor.
2. The doctor inquires about the patient's symptoms.
3. The doctor prescribes medicine for the patient, and then tells the patient what to pay attention to.

Reference words: 下雨 感冒 让 开药 头疼 休息 ……的时候 越来越……

三、书面表达 Written expression

任务名称：问一问你的朋友以后想当哪个科室的医生。

Task: Ask your friends which departments of the hospital they want to work for in the future.

任务要求：四个学生一组，讨论以后想当哪个科室的医生并完成下列表格。

Requirements: Four students work in a group. Discuss which departments of the hospital you want to work for in the future and complete the following table.

Reference words: 喜欢　外科　神经外科　心脏外科　眼科　儿科　产科　越来越……

同学的名字 Names of your classmates	想去的科室 The departments they want to work for	理由 Reasons

补充词汇 Supplementary Words

fù-chǎnkē
妇产科
obstetrics & gynecology

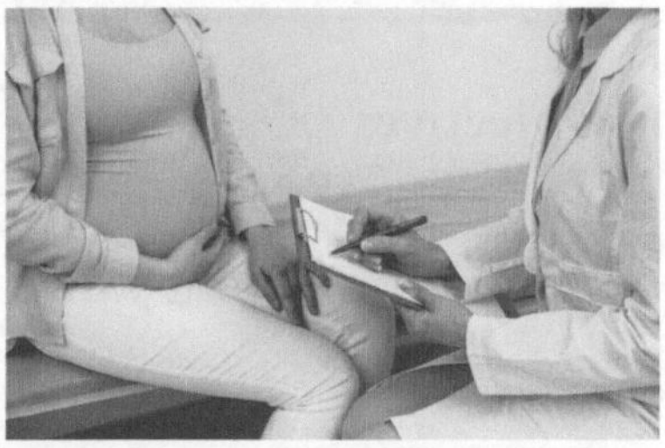

fàngshèkē
放射科
radiology

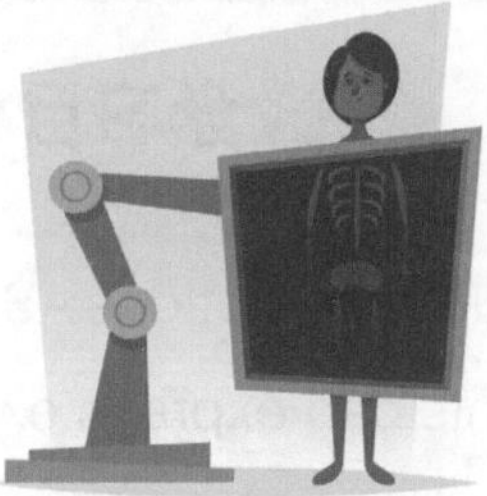

nèikē
内科
internal medicine

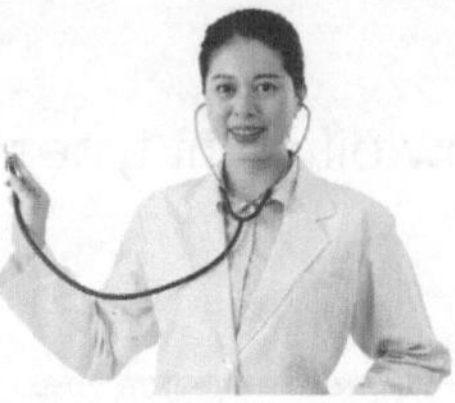

ěr-bí-hóukē
耳鼻喉科
ENT

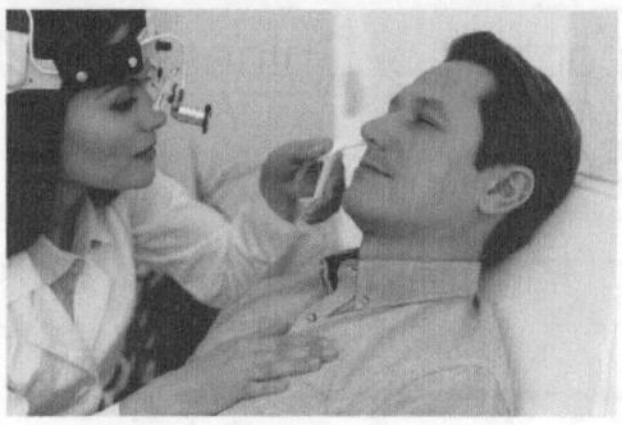

第五课
Lesson 5

Yīxuékè bǐ Hànyǔkè nán

医学课比汉语课难

Medical class is more difficult than Chinese class

学习目标 Learning Objectives

1. Language functions: Students can compare different weather; students can express exclamations.
2. Language points: Comparative sentence (1); Measure word-reduplication "AA" type; Exclamatory sentence "多（么）……啊"; Fixed structure "越……越……"; Comparative sentence (2).
3. Medical knowledge: Students are expected to understand the content of Chinese medical education.
4. Social culture: Students are expected to know different types of the climate of China.

热身活动 Warming-up

1. 你们国家一年有几个季节？你最喜欢哪个季节？
   How many seasons are there in your country? Which season is your favorite?

2. 你这学期有几门课？你觉得哪门课最难？为什么？
   How many courses do you have this semester? Which course do you think is the most difficult? Why?

课文（一）
Text（Ⅰ）

Mǎ Dàwéi hé Měilì zài tǎolùn tiānqì.
（马 大为 和美丽 在 讨论 天气。）

Mǎ Dàwéi: Jīntiān tiānqì zhēn hǎo, fēng bǐ zuótiān xiǎo.
马大为：今天天气 真 好，风 比昨天 小。

Měilì: Wēndù yě bǐ zuótiān gāo.
美丽：温度 也比昨天 高。

Mǎ Dàwéi: Nánfēi xiànzài shì shénme jìjié?
马大为：南非 现在是 什么 季节？

Měilì: Xiàtiān, wǒ de péngyou tiāntiān qù hǎi biān wánr.
美丽：夏天，我的 朋友 天天 去海 边 玩儿。

Mǎ Dàwéi: Nàlǐ dōngtiān lěng ma?
马大为：那里 冬天 冷 吗？

Měilì: Bú tài lěng, dàgài 10 dù, bǐ zhèr nuǎnhuo duō le.
美丽：不太 冷，大概10 度，比这儿 暖和 多 了。

Mǎ Dàwéi: Nǐ xǐhuan nǎ gè jìjié?
马大为：你喜欢哪个季节？

Měilì: Wǒ xǐhuan chūntiān hé qiūtiān, bù lěng yě bú rè, duō shūfu a!
美丽：我 喜欢 春天 和 秋 天，不 冷 也不热，多舒服啊！

Mǎ Dàwéi: Wǒ zuì xǐhuan xiàtiān.
马大为：我 最喜欢 夏天。

Měilì: Wèi shénme?
美丽：为 什么？

Mǎ Dàwéi: Yīnwèi xiàtiān yǒu shǔjià!
马大为：因为 夏天 有暑假！

(Ma Dawei and Meili are talking about the weather.)

Ma Dawei: The weather today is pretty good. The wind is more moderate than it was yesterday.

Meili: Yes. The temperature today is also higher than it was yesterday.

Ma Dawei: What's the season in South Africa now?

Meili: Summer. My friends go to the seaside everyday.

Ma Dawei: Is the winter cold there?

Meili: Not very cold. Around 10 Celsius. It's much warmer than here.

Ma Dawei: Which season do you like?

Meili: I like spring and autumn. It's not too cold, nor too hot. So comfortable!

Ma Dawei: I like summer the most.

Meili: Why?

Ma Dawei: Because there is summer vacation in summer!

生词 New words

1. 风	fēng	*n.*	wind
2. 比	bǐ	*prep.*	than
3. 温度	wēndù	*n.*	temperature
4. 季节	jìjié	*n.*	season
5. 夏天	xiàtiān	*n.*	summer
6. 海边	hǎi biān		seaside
7. 那里	nàlǐ	*pron.*	there
8. 冬天	dōngtiān	*n.*	winter
9. 度	dù	*m.*	degree
10. 暖和	nuǎnhuo	*adj.*	warm
11. 春天	chūntiān	*n.*	spring
12. 秋天	qiūtiān	*n.*	autumn
13. 暑假	shǔjià	*n.*	summer vacation

语言点 Language Points

一、比较句（1） Comparative sentence (1)

介词“比”表示比较，常用来表示两种事物之间的差别，一般用在下面的比较结构中：

The preposition “比” indicates comparison. It is often used to express the difference between two things, and is generally used in the following comparative structure:

A + 比 + B + adj.

1. 今天的风比昨天的小。

2. 今天的温度比昨天的高。

3. 南非比这儿暖和。

当表示两个事物之间的具体差别时，形容词后面可以带数量短语，构成下面的结构：

When expressing the specific difference between two things, the adjective can be followed by a numeral classifier phrase to form the following structure:

A + 比 + B + adj. + num.-m.

4. 今天的温度比昨天高 5 度。

5. 这个手机比那个贵 300 块。

当比较的两个事物差别很大时，形容词后面不用“很多”，而用“多了”；当差别很小时，形容词后面可以用“一点儿”。例如：

When the difference between the two things compared is very big, the adjective is not followed by “很多”, but by “多了”; when the difference is small, the adjective can be followed by “一点儿”. For example:

6. 那里不太冷，大概 10 度，比这儿暖和多了。

7. 金龙的汉语说得比马大为好一点儿。

※ 练习：组词成句　Group words into sentences

1. 这个小区　那个小区　漂亮　比

______________________________。

2. 在家住　在宿舍住　方便　比

______________________________。

3. 昨天　今天　高　比　3度

______________________________。

4. 订外卖　贵　做饭　多了　比

______________________________。

二、量词重叠"AA"式　Measure word-reduplication "AA" type

在汉语中，量词可以重叠，重叠后有"每一"的意思，表示某一范围内的所有个体都具有某种共性。例如：

In Chinese, the measure word can be reduplicated with the meaning of "every", indicating that the individuals within a certain range have something in common. For example:

1. 夏天，我的朋友天天去海边玩儿。
2. 我的朋友个个都很喜欢运动。
3. 她的衣服件件都很漂亮。

※ 练习：请用所给量词的重叠式完成句子　Please complete sentences with the reduplication of the given measure words

1. 我喜欢运动，______________________________。（天）
2. 我昨天买的苹果______________________________。（个）
3. 我喝了三杯咖啡，______________________________。（杯）
4. 这儿有很多白大褂，______________________________。（件）

三、感叹句“多（么）……啊” Exclamatory sentence “多（么）……啊”

“多（么）……啊”一般用在感叹句中，表示程度非常高，带有强烈的主观感情色彩。“多（么）”后面一般是形容词或心理动词。由于该结构本身已经表示程度很高，所以不能和程度副词连用。例如：

“多（么）……啊” is usually used in exclamatory sentences to indicate that the degree is very high with strong subjective feelings. “多（么）” is usually followed by an adjective or psychological verb. Since the structure itself expresses a high degree, it cannot be used with degree adverbs. For example:

1. 我喜欢春天和秋天，不冷也不热，多舒服啊！
2. 北京的夏天多热啊！我不喜欢。
3. 住在宿舍多方便啊！我挺喜欢的。
4. 马大为多么喜欢踢足球啊！

※ 练习：请用感叹句“多（么）……啊”完成句子 Please complete sentences with the exclamatory “多（么）……啊”

1. 我们的宿舍 ______________________________！
2. 马大为的汉语 ______________________________！
3. 李真可以住在家里，______________________________！
4. 这儿的夏天 ______________________________！

综合练习 Comprehensive Exercises

一、根据拼音写汉字 Write Chinese characters according to Pinyin

1. jìjié__________
2. nàlǐ__________
3. hǎi biān__________
4. dōngtiān__________
5. nuǎnhuo__________
6. qiūtiān__________

二、辨字组词 Discriminate between Chinese characters and make words

1. 海________ 每________
2. 秋________ 科________
3. 冬________ 疼________
4. 暖________ 爱________

三、替换练习 Substitution drills

1. 风比昨天小。

生理学	解剖学	难
今天	昨天	冷
住在宿舍	住在家里	方便

2. 不冷也不热，多舒服啊！

山上的树叶都红了	漂亮
一个苹果二十块钱	贵
他都摔伤住院了	严重

3. 我的朋友天天去海边玩儿。

天天	跑步
年年	去北京
个个	都喜欢打篮球

四、选词填空 Use the following words to fill in the blanks

比　季节　大概　海边　暖和

1. 你们国家一年有几个_______?
2. 他摔得_______上次（cì，time）严重，老师让他去医院看看。
3. 我头晕_______一个星期了。
4. 春天到了，天气比冬天_______多了。
5. 夏天的时候，大家都很喜欢去_______玩儿。

五、用所给词语完成对话 Complete the dialogues with given words

1. 美丽：______________！我们出去玩玩儿吧。（多……啊）
   月亮：虽然天气很好，但是我们要复习，不能出去玩儿。
2. 病人：我还要量血压吗？
   医生：__________________________。（天天）
3. 病人：__________________________。（比）
   医生：除了血压高，头还晕吗？
4. 大为：今天的作业多吗？
   同学：__________________________。（比）
5. 王晨：你为什么最喜欢秋天？
   同学：__________________________。（不A也不B）

六、根据课文内容回答问题 Answer the following questions according to the text

1. 今天的天气怎么样？
2. 夏天的时候，美丽的朋友天天做什么？

3. 南非冬天的天气怎么样？

4. 美丽喜欢哪个季节？

七、根据课文内容填空 Fill in the blanks according to the text

今天天气真好，风_______昨天小，_______也比昨天_______。南非现在是_______，美丽的朋友_______去_______玩儿。那里_______不太冷，_______10度，比这儿_______。马大为问美丽喜欢_______季节，美丽说她喜欢_______和秋天，__________，_______啊！马大为_______喜欢夏天，因为夏天_______！

课文（二）
Text（II）

Lǎoshī hé tóngxuémen zài liáotiānr.
（老师 和 同学们 在 聊天儿。）

lǎoshī: Nǐmen juéde Hànyǔkè nán háishi yīxuékè nán?
老师：你们 觉得汉语课难 还是医学课难？

Yuèliang: Wǒ juéde yīxuékè bǐ Hànyǔkè nán.
月亮：我觉得医学课比汉语课难。

Měilì: Duì, yīxuékè yuè xué yuè nán.
美丽：对，医学课越学越难。

Jīn Lóng: Wǒ juéde Hànyǔkè bǐ yīxuékè nán, Hànzì tài nán xiě le, tīnglì yě hěn nán.
金龙：我觉得汉语课比医学课难，汉字太难写了，听力也很难。

Yuèliang: Jīn Lóng, nǐ de Hànyǔ xué de hěn hǎo a!
月亮：金龙，你的汉语学得很好啊！

Jīn Lóng: Wǒ de Hànyǔ bǐ nǐ chà duō le, Zhōngguórén shuō de huà, wǒ hěn duō dōu bù dǒng.
金龙：我的汉语比你差多了，中国人说的话，我很多都不懂。

lǎoshī: Dàwéi, nǐ juéde nǎ mén kè nán?
老师：大为，你觉得哪门课难？

Mǎ Dàwéi: Wǒ juéde yīxuékè gēn Hànyǔkè yíyàng nán, shùxuékè zuì nán!
马大为：我觉得医学课跟汉语课一样难，数学课最难！

(The teacher and students are chatting.)

Teacher: Do you think which class is more difficult, Chinese or medical?

Yueliang: I think medical class is more difficult than Chinese class.

Meili:	Yes. Medical class is more and more difficult to learn.
Jin Long:	I think Chinese class is more difficult than medical class. Chinese characters are too hard to write. And listening is also very difficult.
Yueliang:	Jin Long, your Chinese is very good!
Jin Long:	My Chinese is much poorer than yours. I do not understand much what Chinese say.
Teacher:	Dawei, which subject do you think is difficult?
Ma Dawei:	I think medical class is as difficult as Chinese class. Math class is the most difficult!

生词 New words

1. 觉得	juéde	*v.*	to think, to feel
2. 医学课	yīxuékè	*n.*	medical course
医学	yīxué	*n.*	medical science
3. 越……越……	yuè···yuè···		the more...the more...
4. 听力	tīnglì	*n.*	listening
5. 差	chà	*adj.*	poor, bad
6. 话	huà	*n.*	words
7. 懂	dǒng	*v.*	to understand
8. 跟……一样（……）	gēn···yíyàng（···）		the same as, as...as
跟	gēn	*prep.*	with, and
一样	yíyàng	*adj.*	same
9. 数学课	shùxuékè	*n.*	math class
数学	shùxué	*n.*	mathematics

专名 Proper nouns

汉字	Hànzì	Chinese character

语言点 Language Points

一、固定结构“越……越……” Fixed structure “越……越……”

“越……越……”表示随着第一种情况的变化，后一种情况的程度逐渐加深。前后两个“越”的主语可以相同，也可以不同。例如：

“越……越……” indicates that with the change of the former situation, the degree of the latter situation gradually deepens. The subjects of the two “越” can be the same or different. For example:

1. 医学课越学越难。
2. 他家越搬越远了。
3. 我越说，妈妈越生气（shēngqì，get angry）。

※ 练习：请用固定结构“越……越……”完成对话 Please complete dialogs with the fixed structure “越……越……”

1. A：你喜欢汉语吗？

   B：______________________________。

2. A：你足球踢得怎么样？

   B：______________________________。

3. A：生理学难不难？

   B：______________________________。

4. A：快点儿爬，山上很漂亮！

   B：______________________________。

二、比较句（2） Comparative sentence (2)

"跟……一样（……）"表示两个事物比较的结果相同，否定形式是"跟……不一样"，疑问形式为"跟……一样（……）吗"或"跟……一样不一样"。"一样"的后面可以接形容词或动词。例如：

"跟……一样（……）" indicates that the two things are the same after being compared. The negative form is "跟……不一样", and the interrogative form is "跟……一样（……）吗" or "跟……一样不一样". "一样" can be followed by adjectives or verbs. For example:

1. 我觉得医学课跟汉语课一样难。
2. 哥哥做的饭跟饭店的一样好吃。
3. 我们的数学课跟你们的不一样。
4. 金龙跟马大为一样高吗？

※ 练习：组词成句 Group words into sentences

1. 生理学　数学　跟　难　一样

____。

2. 金龙的汉语　一样　跟　说得　中国人　好

____。

3. 这儿的夏天　舒服　一样　跟　春天

____。

4. 作业　今天的　多　一样　昨天　跟

____。

综合练习 Comprehensive Exercises

一、根据拼音写汉字 Write Chinese characters according to Pinyin

1. juéde________ 3. tīnglì________ 5. yíyàng________

2. Hànzì________ 4. dǒng________ 6. shùxué________

二、辨字组词 Discriminate between Chinese characters and make words

1. 觉________ / 学________

2. 力________ / 为________

3. 跟________ / 很________

4. 话________ / 说________

三、替换练习 Substitution drills

1. 医学课越学越难。

汉语课	学	有意思
雨	下	大
同学们	说	高兴

2. 我的汉语比你差多了。

今天的天气	昨天
我的听力	美丽
这次考的	上次（shàng cì，last time）

3. 我觉得 医学课 跟 汉语课 一样 难。

听	说	重要
医学院的中国学生	外国留学生	多
这个房间	那个房间	大

四、选词填空 Use the following words to fill in the blanks

觉得　懂　比　一样　听力

1. 我不认识汉字，这些字我都不________。
2. 你________数学课难不难？
3. 今天上午是________课还是数学课？
4. 你们上课学的跟我们________。
5. 医学课________汉语课难多了。

五、用所给词语完成对话 Complete the dialogues with given words

1. 大为：老师的话，你都懂了吗？
   金龙：没有，____________________。（越……越……）
2. 李真：美丽，快点儿爬。
   美丽：____________________。（越……越……）
3. 王晨：你还头晕吗？
   朋友：____________________。（比）
4. 妈妈：你觉得哪条裙子好看，红的还是蓝的？
   爸爸：____________________________。（跟……一样）

5. 家属：王医生手术做得怎么样？

护士：____________________。（verb + 得）

六、根据课文内容回答问题 Answer the following questions according to the text

1. 月亮觉得汉语课难还是医学课难？
2. 美丽觉得医学课难不难？
3. 金龙觉得汉语课难不难？
4. 金龙的汉语怎么样？

七、根据课文内容填空 Fill in the blanks according to the text

月亮觉得医学课________汉语课________，美丽也觉得医学课________。金龙________汉语课比医学课难，汉字________，________也很难。金龙觉得他的汉语比月亮的________，中国人________，他很多都________。老师问马大为________难，马大为觉得医学课________汉语课________，________课最难！

语言任务 Language Tasks

一、阅读理解 Reading comprehension

我叫美丽，是南非人。南非跟中国一样，一年也有四个季节：春、夏、秋、冬。从9月到11月是南非的春季，从12月到2月是南非的夏季。夏季最高气温为32—38度，跟济南（Jǐnán，provincial capital of Shandong）差不多，很多人都喜欢到海边去玩儿。从3月到5月是南非的秋季，从6月到8月为南非的冬季。冬季一些地方最低气温为零下（líng xià，below zero）10—12度。南非晴天很多，雨天不多，天气很好，风景（fēngjǐng，scenery）也很好。欢迎（huānyíng，welcome）你们来南非玩儿。

读后判断 True or false

1. 南非有四个季节。 （ ）
2. 在南非，12月到2月是冬季。 （ ）
3. 南非没有海。 （ ）
4. 南非的冬天不太冷。 （ ）
5. 南非天天下雨。 （ ）

二、口头表达 Oral expression

任务名称：调查所学科目的难易度。

Task: Investigate the difficulty of the subjects.

任务要求：两个学生一组，互相询问对方哪些科目难，哪些科目比较简单。

Requirements: Two students work in a group. Ask each other which subjects are difficult and which are simpler.

Reference words: 觉得　难　越……越……　跟……一样　差　懂

三、书面表达 Written expression

任务名称：你的家乡最适合旅游的季节是什么？

Task: What is the best season for traveling in your hometown?

任务要求：两个学生一组，互相询问对方家乡一年中最适合旅游的季节，并写下原因。

Requirements: Two students work in a group. Ask each other about the most suitable season for traveling in his/her hometown, and write down the reasons.

Reference words: 温度　舒服　不……也不……　山　海

季节 Seasons	原因 Reasons

补充词汇 Supplementary Words

xuě
雪
snow

wù
雾
fog

duōyún
多云
cloudy

táifēng
台风
typhoon

第六课 Lesson 6

Jīntiān shàngwǔ tā bú shì méiyǒu kè ma?

今天 上午 他不是没有课吗？

Doesn't he have classes this morning?

学习目标 Learning Objectives

1. Language functions: Students can express surprise and unexpectedness; students are able to express reasons.
2. Language points: Rhetorical question (1) "不是……吗"; Fixed structure "因为……所以……"; Adverb "再" (1); Modal verb "要" (2); Temporal noun "以前".
3. Medical knowledge: Students are expected to understand the setting of medical majors and departments in Chinese universities.
4. Social culture: Students are expected to understand the common extracurricular activities in Chinese universities.

热身活动 Warming-up

1. 你在大学里喜欢参加哪些课外活动？

   Which extracurricular activities do you like to participate in the university?

2. 你参加过哪些类型的比赛？比赛的结果怎么样？

   What types of competitions have you participated in? What was the result?

课文（一）
Text（Ⅰ）

Mǎ Dàwéi de péngyou Jímǐ lái sùshè zhǎo tā.
（马大为的朋友吉米来宿舍找他。）

Jímǐ: Mǎ Dàwéi zài sùshè ma?
吉米：马大为在宿舍吗？

Jīn Lóng: Bú zài, tā qù jiàoshì shàngkè le.
金龙：不在，他去教室上课了。

Jímǐ: Jīntiān shàngwǔ tā bú shì méiyǒu kè ma?
吉米：今天上午他不是没有课吗？

Jīn Lóng: Yīnwèi Hànyǔ lǎoshī zuótiān yǒu shìr, suǒyǐ tiáo kè le.
金龙：因为汉语老师昨天有事儿，所以调课了。

Jímǐ: Zhōngwǔ xiàkè yǐhòu, wǒ zài lái zhǎo tā ba.
吉米：中午下课以后，我再来找他吧。

Jīn Lóng: Zhōngwǔ tā yě bù yídìng huílai, Hànyǔkè jiéshù yǐhòu, tā kěnéng yào qù tǐyùguǎn duànliàn.
金龙：中午他也不一定回来，汉语课结束以后，他可能要去体育馆锻炼。

Jímǐ: Tā kě zhēn máng, xiàwǔ wǒ zài gěi tā dǎ diànhuà ba.
吉米：他可真忙，下午我再给他打电话吧。

Jīn Lóng: Tā jīntiān wàng dài shǒujī le.
金龙：他今天忘带手机了。

Jímǐ: Zhè gè mǎdàhā!
吉米：这个马大哈！

(Ma Dawei's friend Jimmy comes to the dorm to visit him.)

Jimmy: Is Ma Dawei in?

Jin Long: No. He went to class.

Jimmy: Doesn't he have class this morning?

Jin Long: The Chinese teacher didn't come because he had something to deal with yesterday, so the Chinese class is changed to today.

Jimmy: I will come to visit him when the class is over at the noon.

Jin Long: He may not come back at the noon. After the Chinese class, he may go to do exercises in the gym.

Jimmy: He is just so busy. I will call him in the afternoon.

Jin Long: He forgot to carry his cell phone today.

Jimmy: He is such a ma-da-ha! (He is so careless!)

生词 New words

1. 所以	suǒyǐ	*conj.*	so, therefore
2. 调课	tiáo kè	*VO*	to change the class time
调	tiáo	*v.*	to change, to adjust
3. 再	zài	*adv.*	again
4. 找	zhǎo	*v.*	to look for, to visit
5. 结束	jiéshù	*v.*	to finish, to be over
6. 体育馆	tǐyùguǎn	*n.*	gym
体育	tǐyù	*n.*	sports
7. 锻炼	duànliàn	*v.*	to do exercises
8. 可	kě	*adv.*	(used for emphasis) just
9. 忘	wàng	*v.*	to forget
10. 马大哈	mǎdàhā	*n./adj.*	ma-da-ha (a slang used to call someone who is very careless); careless, forgetful

语言点 Language Points

一、反问句（1）：不是……吗　Rhetorical question (1): 不是……吗

反问句"不是……吗"是用疑问的形式来表达说话人的某种观点或情绪，它比表达相同意思的陈述句语气更强烈。反问句是"无疑而问"，通常不需要对方做出回答。例如：

The rhetorical question "不是……吗" is used to express a certain point of view or emotion of the speaker in the form of a question, whose tone is stronger than the declarative sentence when expressing the same meaning. The rhetorical question is "an interrogative sentence with no question", which usually does not need an answer. For example:

1. 今天上午他不是没有课吗？
2. 你今天不是有课吗？怎么还在宿舍睡觉？
3. 明天你们不是有考试吗？怎么还不复习？

※ 练习：请用反问句"不是……吗"和所给词语完成对话　Please use the rhetorical question "不是……吗" and the given words to complete dialogues

1. 妈妈：你今天怎么不去上课？

   孩子：________________？（星期六）

2. A：幸福小区在哪儿？

   B：________________？（在你家旁边）

3. A：这个字我不认识。

   B：________________？（汉语老师）

4. A：我不认识马大为。

   B：________________？（你的同学）

二、固定结构“因为……所以……” Fixed structure“因为……所以……”

“因为……所以……”连接前后两个分句，前一分句表示原因，后一分句表示前面的原因所引起的结果。例如：

“因为……所以……” connects two clauses. The first clause indicates the reason, and the second one indicates the result caused by the reason. For example:

1. 因为汉语老师昨天有事儿，所以调课了。

2. 因为我家离医院太远了，上班不方便，所以哥哥搬家了。

3. 他因为最近工作太忙，没有好好儿休息，所以脸色不太好。

注意：（1）“因为”和“所以”可以单独使用；（2）“因为”可以用在分句主语的前面或后面，“所以”必须用在分句主语的前面。例如：

Note: (1) “因为” and “所以” can be used separately; (2) “因为” can be used before or after the subject of a clause, while “所以” must be used before the subject of a clause. For example:

4. 因为明天我有考试，（所以）今天我不能出去玩儿。

5.（因为）这个电影我已经看了，所以今天就不去了。

6. 月亮因为喜欢小孩儿，所以以后想当一名儿科医生。

※ 练习：请用固定结构“因为……所以……”完成句子 Please complete sentences with the fixed structure “因为……所以……”

1. 因为下雨了，________________。

2. 因为我是留学生，________________。

3. ________________，所以常常订外卖。

4. ________________，所以马大为天天去健身房。

三、副词“再”（1） Adverb“再”(1)

“再”可以表示动作行为的重复或继续，常用于尚未发生或经常发生的动作行为。例如：

"再" can indicate the repetition or continuation of an action, and is often used for actions that have not occurred yet or frequently occur. For example:

1. 中午下课以后，我再来找他吧。

2. 他可真忙，下午我再给他打电话吧。

3. 马大为常常运动完以后再去学习。

※ 练习：请用副词"再"完成句子 Please complete sentences with the adverb "再"

1. 老师现在不在，____________________。

2. 我还没复习完，____________________。

3. 都快上课了，____________________。

4. 今天上午我没时间，____________________。

综合练习 Comprehensive Exercises

一、根据拼音写汉字 Write Chinese characters according to Pinyin

1. duànliàn__________ 3. jiéshù__________ 5. wàng__________

2. zhǎo__________ 4. tǐyùguǎn__________ 6. suǒyǐ__________

二、辨字组词 Discriminate between Chinese characters and make words

1. 所________ 听________

2. 找________ 我________

3. 束________ 来________

4. 体________ 休________

三、替换练习 Substitution drills

1. 今天上午他不是<u>没有课</u>吗？

去医院了
去锻炼了
去爬山了

2. 因为<u>汉语老师昨天有事儿</u>，所以<u>调课了</u>。

今天下雨	我不骑自行车上班了
明天有考试	我今天要好好儿复习
我的汉语不好	我听不懂老师的话

3. <u>下午</u>我再<u>给他打电话</u>吧。

考完试	去北京玩儿
写完作业	玩儿游戏
天晴以后	去爬山

四、选词填空 Use the following words to fill in the blanks

所以　忘　结束　可　再

1. 手术_______了，病人家属请回到病房（bìngfáng，ward）。

2. 他因为最近一直熬夜复习，_______生病了。

3. 我明天______来看你。

4. 今天可能会下雨，但是我______带伞了。

5. 张医生______真忙，一天要做三台（tái，a measure word）手术。

五、用所给词语完成对话 Complete the dialogues with given words

1. 大为：你怎么感冒了？

   王晨：____________________。（因为……所以……）

2. 月亮：________________？（不是……吗）

   美丽：我忘带手机了。

3. 病人：我周二上午来找您可以吗？

   医生：________________，下午有时间。（结束）

4. 大为：今天晚上有时间吗？一起吃饭怎么样？

   吉米：今天作业很多，________________。（再）

5. 王晨：马大为昨天忘带手机，今天又忘带伞了。

   同学：________________。（可；马大哈）

六、根据课文内容回答问题 Answer the following questions according to the text

1. 今天为什么调课了？

2. 马大为中午可能要做什么？

3. 吉米打算什么时候给马大为打电话？

4. 吉米为什么不能给马大为打电话？

七、根据课文内容填空 Fill in the blanks according to the text

马大为不在宿舍，他去______了。______汉语老师昨天有事儿，______他们______了。吉米说中午下课______，他______来找马大为。金龙说中午马大为不______回来，汉语课______以后，马大为______要去体育馆______。吉米说马大为______真忙，下午他______给马大为打电话。可是马大为今天______手机了，他可真是一个______！

课文（二）
Text（II）

Mǎ Dàwéi gěi Jímǐ dǎ diànhuà.
（马 大为 给 吉米 打 电话。）

Jímǐ: Wèi, Dàwéi ma?
吉米：喂，大为 吗？

Mǎ Dàwéi: Shì wǒ, Jīn Lóng gàosu wǒ, jīntiān zǎoshang nǐ zhǎo wǒ le.
马大为：是 我，金 龙 告诉 我，今天 早上 你 找 我 了。

Jímǐ: Duì. Nǐ zhōuliù xiàwǔ yǒu kòngr ma?
吉米：对。你 周六 下午 有 空儿 吗？

Mǎ Dàwéi: Yǒu kòngr, shénme shìr?
马大为：有 空儿，什么 事儿？

Jímǐ: Zhōuliù xiàwǔ sān diǎn, yīxuéyuàn hé kǒuqiāng yīxuéyuàn yǒu lánqiú bǐsài, wǒ yǐjīng bàomíng le, nǐ yào cānjiā ma?
吉米：周六 下午 三 点，医学院 和 口腔 医学院 有 篮球 比赛，我 已经 报名 了，你 要 参加 吗？

Mǎ Dàwéi: Dāngrán! Rúguǒ wǒ cānjiā, nǐmen xuéyuàn yídìng huì shū!
马大为：当然！如果 我 参加，你们 学院 一定 会 输！

Jímǐ: Shì ma? Yǐqián nǐmen kě méiyǒu yíng!
吉米：是 吗？以前 你们 可 没有 赢！

(Ma Dawei is calling up Jimmy.)

Jimmy: Hello, is that Dawei?

Ma Dawei: It's me. Jin Long told me that you came to me this morning.

Jimmy: Yes. Do you have time on Saturday afternoon?

Ma Dawei: Yes, I do. What's up?

Jimmy: There is a basketball game between School of Medical and School of Stomatology at three o'clock on Saturday afternoon. I have signed up. Would you like to take part in?

Ma Dawei: Of course! If I participate in, your college is certain to lose!

Jimmy: Really? You never won before!

生词 New words

1. 告诉	gàosu	*v.*	to tell
2. 周六	zhōuliù	*n.*	Saturday
3. 空儿	kòngr	*n.*	free time
4. 口腔	kǒuqiāng	*n.*	oral cavity
5. 比赛	bǐsài	*n./v.*	competition; to compete
6. 报名	bàomíng	*v.*	to sign up
7. 参加	cānjiā	*v.*	to take part in
8. 输	shū	*v.*	to lose
9. 以前	yǐqián	*n.*	before
10. 赢	yíng	*v.*	to win

语言点 Language Points

一、能愿动词"要"（2） Modal verb "要" (2)

能愿动词"要"可以表示愿望或者打算，后面接动词或动词性短语。例如：

The modal verb "要" can express a wish or an intention, which is followed by a verb or verbal phrase. For example:

1. 你要参加篮球比赛吗？

2. 这周六我要去爬山。

3. 以后我要当一名心脏外科医生。

※ 练习：请用能愿动词“要”完成句子　Please complete sentences with the modal verb “要”

1. 我最近太忙了，＿＿＿＿＿＿＿＿＿＿＿＿＿＿＿＿＿＿＿＿。

2. 快考试了，＿＿＿＿＿＿＿＿＿＿＿＿＿＿＿＿＿＿＿＿＿＿。

3. 金龙感冒了，＿＿＿＿＿＿＿＿＿＿＿＿＿＿＿＿＿＿＿＿＿。

4. 明天天气很好，＿＿＿＿＿＿＿＿＿＿＿＿＿＿＿＿＿＿＿＿。

二、时间名词“以前”　Temporal noun “以前”

“以前”表示比现在或某个时间早的时间。它可以单独使用，也可以用在名词、名词性短语、动词、动词性短语或数量短语的后面。例如：

“以前” indicates a time earlier than the present or a certain time. It can be used alone or after nouns, nominal phrases, verbs, verbal phrases or numeral classifier phrases. For example:

1. 以前你们可没有赢！

2. 他的生日在护士节以前。

3. 下午三点以前我不在宿舍。

4. 来中国以前我不认识马大为。

5. 考试以前我没有时间踢足球。

6. 一周以前，这里还很热，现在已经是秋天了。

※ 练习：请用时间名词“以前”和所给词语完成对话　Please use the temporal noun “以前” and the given words to complete dialogues

1. A：你早上几点去上课？

B：＿＿＿＿＿＿＿＿＿＿＿＿＿＿＿＿。（八点）

2. A：你晚上几点睡觉？

B：______________________________。（十二点）

3. A：来中国以前，你认识他吗？

B：______________________________。（不认识）

4. A：学汉语以前，你有中国朋友吗？

B：______________________________。（没有）

综合练习 Comprehensive Exercises

一、根据拼音写汉字 Write Chinese characters according to Pinyin

1. gàosu__________ 3. bǐsài__________ 5. cānjiā__________

2. kòngr__________ 4. bàomíng__________ 6. shū__________

二、辨字组词 Discriminate between Chinese characters and make words

1. 诉________ 听________

2. 赛________ 贵________

3. 加________ 咖________

4. 空________ 穿________

三、替换练习 Substitution drills

1. 你要参加篮球比赛吗？

喝咖啡

骑共享单车

坐公共汽车去医院

2. 如果<u>我参加</u>，<u>你们学院一定会输</u>。

你没时间	我可以一个人去医院
明天下雨	我们就不去爬山了
你感冒了	就在宿舍好好儿休息吧

3. 以前<u>你们可没有赢</u>。

我不喜欢吃中国菜
这儿有一家饭店
妈妈不让我喝咖啡

四、选词填空 Use the following words to fill in the blanks

参加　输　比赛　报名　以前

1. 学校下午有篮球_______。
2. 这次（cì，time）篮球比赛我们打得不好，可能要_______了。
3. 马大为如果知道有足球比赛，一定会_______参加。
4. 吃饭_______要洗手（xǐ shǒu，wash one's hand），这是小孩儿都知道的事儿。
5. 你们学院有多少人_______比赛？

五、用所给词语完成对话 Complete the dialogues with given words

1. 病人：我什么时候做心电图？

   护士：________________________。（告诉）

2. 李真：你每天几点起床？

   美丽：________________________。（以前）

3. 王晨：你怎么也来了？

   朋友：________________________。（报名）

4. 吉米：今天下午我们和哪个学院有篮球比赛？

   大为：________________________。（口腔）

5. 月亮：你最近为什么每天都跑步？

   大为：________________________。（参加）

六、根据课文内容回答问题 Answer the following questions according to the text

1. 马大为周六下午有空儿吗？
2. 篮球比赛什么时候开始？
3. 哪两个学院比赛？
4. 马大为觉得他们学院能赢吗？

七、根据课文内容填空 Fill in the blanks according to the text

金龙________马大为今天早上吉米________他了，所以马大为给吉米回了电话。吉米告诉马大为周六下午三点，医学院和________医学院有篮球________，他已经________了，想问马大为有没有________，要不要________。马大为当然要参加，他觉得________他参加了，吉米的学院一定会________！吉米说马大为的学院________可没有________！

语言任务 Language Tasks

一、阅读理解 Reading comprehension

吉米是口腔医学院的留学生。他很高，大概一米九三。他喜欢看篮球比赛，也喜欢打篮球，天天都要去体育馆打篮球。来中国以后，他报名参加了留学生篮球队。这周六下午三点，医学院和口腔医学院有篮球比赛，吉米已经准备好了，他觉得口腔医学院一定能赢。

读后判断 True or false

1. 吉米的个子很高。 (   )
2. 吉米不喜欢看篮球比赛。 (   )
3. 吉米不常打篮球。 (   )
4. 吉米参加了留学生篮球队。 (   )
5. 这周六下午三点医学院和口腔医学院有足球比赛。 (   )

二、口头表达 Oral expression

任务名称：设计周末足球比赛的活动海报。

Task: Design a poster for the soccer match on the weekend.

任务要求：1. 四个学生一组，讨论确定周末足球比赛的时间、地点、参加人员等。

2. 将讨论结果呈现在海报上。

Requirements: 1. Four students work in a group. Discuss and determine the time, place, participants, etc. of the soccer match on the weekend.

2. Show the discussion result on the poster.

Reference words: 比赛　时间　地点（dìdiǎn，place）　参加　有空儿　要

三、书面表达 Written expression

任务名称：调查朋友周末一天的安排。

Task: Investigate a friend of his/her weekend arrangement.

任务要求：两个学生一组，互相询问周末一天的安排并完成下列表格。

Requirements: Two students work in a group. Ask each other about his/her arrangement for the weekend and complete the following table.

Reference words: 起床　看书　学汉语　打篮球　锻炼　喝咖啡　吃饭　睡觉……

姓名	上午	中午	下午	晚上

补充词汇 Supplementary Words

pīngpāngqiú
乒乓球
table tennis

yǔmáoqiú
羽毛球
badminton

páiqiú
排球
volleyball

bàngqiú
棒球
baseball

第七课 Lesson 7

Nǐ hánjià yǒu shénme dǎsuàn?

你寒假有 什么 打算?

What is your winter vacation plan?

学习目标 Learning Objectives

1. Language functions: Students can introduce their holiday arrangements and travel plans.
2. Language points: Verb-reduplication "ABAB" type; Fixed structure "……，不过……"; Modal verb "得"; Degree complement "极了"; Measure word "次"; Fixed structure "一边……一边……".
3. Social culture: Students are expected to learn about famous tourist destinations in China.

热身活动 Warming-up

1. 请说一说你的假期安排。
Please introduce your vacation plan.

2. 你知道中国的哪些旅游城市?
What tourist cities do you know in China?

课文（一）
Text（Ⅰ）

Tóngxuémen zài liáo hánjià jìhuà.
（同学们 在 聊 寒假 计划。）

Mǎ Dàwéi: Zhōngyú fàngjià le, kěyǐ fàngsōng fàngsōng le.
马大为：终于 放假 了，可以 放松 放松 了。

Jīn Lóng: Dàjiā hánjià yǒu shénme dǎsuàn?
金龙：大家寒假有 什么 打算？

Měilì: Wǒ dǎsuàn qù Hā'ěrbīn, nǐmen yào bu yào yìqǐ qù?
美丽：我 打算 去哈尔滨，你们要 不要一起去？

Jīn Lóng: Wǒ gēn nǐ yìqǐ qù, wǒ xiǎng qù kànkan Bīngxuě Jié.
金龙：我 跟你一起去，我 想 去看看 冰雪 节。

Yuèliang: Wǒ yě xiǎng qù, búguò wǒ děi huí guó, wǒ jiějie yào jiéhūn le.
月亮：我 也 想 去，不过我得回国，我姐姐要结婚了。

Mǎ Dàwéi: Hā'ěrbīn tài lěng le, wǒ yào qù Sānyà yóuyǒng.
马大为：哈尔滨太 冷 了，我要去三亚 游泳。

Yuèliang: Xiànzài shì dōngtiān, nàlǐ kěyǐ yóuyǒng ma?
月亮：现在 是 冬天，那里可以 游泳 吗？

Mǎ Dàwéi: Wǒ kàn tiānqì yùbào le, nàr jīntiān 27 dù, yóuyǒng méi wèntí.
马大为：我 看 天气 预报了，那儿今天 27 度，游泳 没 问题。

(Students are talking about their winter plans.)

Ma Dawei: The winter vacation finally begins! We can have a good relax!

Jin Long: What are your plans for the winter vacation?

Meili: I plan to visit Harbin. Would you like to go with me?

Jin Long: I'd like to. I want to see the Ice and Snow Festival.

Yueliang: Me, too. But I need to go home. My elder sister is going to get married.

Ma Dawei: Harbin is too cold. I am going to swim in Sanya.

Yueliang: It's winter now. Is there warm enough for swimming?

Ma Dawei: I have checked the weather forecast. Today it is 27 Celsius in Sanya. It's all right for swimming!

生词 New words

1. 终于	zhōngyú	*adv.*	finally
2. 放假	fàngjià	*v.*	to have a vacation
3. 放松	fàngsōng	*v.*	to relax
4. 大家	dàjiā	*pron.*	everybody
5. 寒假	hánjià	*n.*	winter vacation
6. 打算	dǎsuàn	*v.*	to plan
7. 不过	búguò	*conj.*	but
8. 得	děi	*mod.v.*	need to
9. 回国	huí guó	*VO*	to return to one's country
10. 姐姐	jiějie	*n.*	elder sister
11. 结婚	jiéhūn	*v.*	to marry, to get married
12. 游泳	yóuyǒng	*v.*	to swim
13. 天气预报	tiānqì yùbào		weather forecast
预报	yùbào	*n./v.*	forecast; to forecast
14. 那儿	nàr	*pron.*	there

专名 Proper nouns

1. 哈尔滨	Hā'ěrbīn	Harbin
2. 冰雪节	Bīngxuě Jié	Ice and Snow Festival
3. 三亚	Sānyà	Sanya

语言点 Language Points

一、动词重叠"ABAB"式 Verb-reduplication "ABAB" type

在汉语中，有的动词可以重叠，表示动作持续的时间短，或表尝试。双音节动词的重叠形式是"ABAB"式。例如：

In Chinese, some verbs can be reduplicated, indicating that the action lasts for a short time or to make a trial. The reduplication form of disyllabic verbs is "ABAB". For example:

1. 终于放假了，可以放松放松了。
2. 我太忙了，请你帮我照顾照顾我的小狗，好吗？
3. 金龙，这是我的好朋友吉米，他也喜欢踢足球，你们可以认识认识。

※ 练习：请用所给动词的重叠式完成句子 Please complete the sentences with the reduplication form of the given verbs

1. 下个星期有生理学考试，这个星期我要__________。（复习）
2. 虽然学习很忙，可是我们每天也要__________。（运动）
3. 下午有比赛，我们现在要__________。（准备）
4. 周末我不去踢球了，我要好好儿__________。（休息）

二、固定结构“……，不过……” Fixed structure “……，不过……”

“不过”连接前后两个分句，两个分句之间是转折关系，但转折的意味比“但是”轻。后一分句常补充、修正上文的意思。“……，不过……”多用在口语中。例如：

“不过” connects two clauses. There is a transitional relation between the two clauses, but the transitional tone is lighter than “但是”. The latter clause usually means to supplement or amend the above text. “……，不过……” is often used in spoken Chinese. For example:

1. 我也想去，不过我得回国，我姐姐要结婚了。
2. 哥哥很喜欢做饭，不过常常没时间做。
3. 汉语课很难，不过我觉得医学课更难。

※ 练习：请用“不过”完成句子 Please complete sentences with “不过”

1. 晚上我想去看电影，__________________________。
2. 我想和朋友去哈尔滨玩儿，______________________。
3. 坐出租车有点儿贵，__________________________。
4. 我想买这条蓝裙子，__________________________。

三、能愿动词“得” Modal verb “得”

能愿动词“得”（děi）表示情理上、事实上或意志上需要、应该。它不能单独回答问题，一般用在口语中。例如：

The modal verb “得” (děi) indicates a need or necessity in reason, fact or will. It cannot answer questions alone, and is usually used in spoken Chinese. For example:

1. 我得回国，我姐姐要结婚了。
2. 明天考试，我今天得复习复习。
3. 七点五十五了，我得去上课了。

注意：其否定形式是“不用”，不说“不得”。例如：

Note: Its negative form is “不用”, not “不得”. For example:

4. 明天有考试，但是我不用复习，因为我已经复习完了。

5. A：明天就比赛了，你好好儿准备一下吧。

B：不用，我们一定会赢。

6. A：你最近脸色不好，得好好儿休息一下。

B：不用，后天要考试了，我还没复习好。

※ 练习：请用能愿动词“得”和所给词语完成句子 Please use the modal verb “得” and the given words to complete sentences

1. 马大为感冒了，________________。（医院）

2. 下雨了，________________。（回家）

3. 金龙生病了，________________。（休息）

4. 明天有比赛，________________。（准备）

综合练习 Comprehensive Exercises

一、根据拼音写汉字 Write Chinese characters according to Pinyin

1. jiéhūn________ 3. yóuyǒng________ 5. fàngsōng________

2. dǎsuàn________ 4. zhōngyú________ 6. yùbào________

二、辨字组词 Discriminate between Chinese characters and make words

1. 寒________ 赛________

2. 假________ 锻________

3. 姐________ 婚________

4. 预________ 舒________

三、替换练习 Substitution drills

1. 终于放假了，可以<u>放松放松</u>了。

休息休息
锻炼锻炼
运动运动

2. 我也想去，不过我得<u>回国</u>。

准备考试
上班
照顾病人

3. 我姐姐要<u>结婚</u>了。

搬家
回国
做手术

四、选词填空 Use the following words to fill in the blanks

得　打算　不过　终于　结婚

1. 听说你下个月要_______了？
2. 医生说我_______在家休息一个星期。
3. 手术已经做完了，_______病人还要好好儿休息一个月才行。
4. 你_______什么时候去看医生？
5. 生理学_______考完了，我们可以放松放松了。

五、用所给词语完成对话 Complete the dialogues with given words

1. 朋友：你寒假有什么打算？

   大为：______________________________。（放松放松）

2. 病人：医生，我的病大概多长时间能好？

   医生：______________________________。（……，不过……）

3. 病人：医生，请问我多长时间量一次（cì，time）血压？

   医生：______________________________。（得 děi）

4. 朋友：明天天气怎么样？

   月亮：______________________________。（天气预报）

5. 医生：你手术后恢复（huīfù，recover）得不错，明天就可以回家了。

   病人：______________________________。（终于）

六、根据课文内容回答问题 Answer the following questions according to the text

1. 寒假谁要去哈尔滨？
2. 金龙为什么要去哈尔滨？
3. 月亮寒假有什么打算？
4. 马大为寒假打算怎么放松放松？

七、根据课文内容填空 Fill in the blanks according to the text

终于放假了，同学们打算在寒假________。美丽打算去________，金龙要和她一起去，因为金龙想去看看__________。月亮也想去，她得回国，因为她姐姐__________结婚__________。马大为觉得哈尔滨_______，他要去三亚________。天气________说，今天三亚 27 度，游泳________。

课文（二）
Text（II）

Měilì hé Yuèliang zài shìpín liáotiānr.
（美丽和 月亮 在 视频 聊天儿。）

Měilì: Yuèliang, nǐ dào jiā le ma? Lùshang shùnlì ma?
美丽：月亮，你到家了吗？ 路上 顺利吗？

Yuèliang: Gāng dào jiā, hěn shùnlì. Nǐ zài Hā'ěrbīn zěnmeyàng?
月亮：刚 到家，很顺利。你在哈尔滨怎么样？

Měilì: Hā'ěrbīn hěn lěng, búguò piàoliang jí le!
美丽：哈尔滨很 冷，不过 漂亮 极了！

Yuèliang: Nàlǐ xià xuě le ma?
月亮：那里下雪了吗？

Měilì: Xià xuě le, zhè shì wǒ dì-yī cì kànjiàn xuě. Wǒmen yìbiān kàn xuě, yìbiān chī bīngjīlíng, kāixīn jí le!
美丽：下雪了，这是我第一次看见 雪。我们一边看雪，一边吃冰激凌，开心极了！

Yuèliang: Shénme? Xià xuě tiān chī bīngjīlíng?
月亮：什么？下 雪 天 吃冰激凌？

Měilì: Lái Bīngchéng, dāngrán yào chī bīngjīlíng!
美丽：来 冰城，当然 要 吃冰激凌！

Yuèliang: Zhēn hǎo, míngnián hánjià wǒ yě yào qù.
月亮：真 好，明年 寒假我也要去。

(Meili and Yueliang are chatting by video.)

Meili: Yueliang, do you reach home? Is everything OK on the road?

Yueliang: I just arrived. Everything is OK. How are you doing in Harbin?

Meili: Harbin is very cold. But it's extremely beautiful!

Yueliang: Does it snow there?

Meili: It snows. This is the first time that I see the snow. We enjoy the snow while eating ice cream. We are so happy!

Yueliang: What? Eating ice cream in a snowy day?

Meili: Since we come to the Icy City, of course, we would eat ice cream!

Yueliang: So good. I will also visit the city in the winter vacation next year.

生词 New words

1. 路上	lùshang	*n.*	on the road
2. 顺利	shùnlì	*adj.*	smooth
3. 极	jí	*adv.*	extremely
4. 下雪	xià xuě	*VO*	to snow
雪	xuě	*n.*	snow
5. 第一	dì-yī	*num.*	first
第	dì	*pref.*	before numerals to form ordinal numbers
6. 次	cì	*m.*	time
7. 一边……一边……	yìbiān···yìbiān···		while
一边	yìbiān	*adv.*	at the same time
8. 冰激凌	bīngjīlíng	*n.*	ice cream
9. 开心	kāixīn	*adj.*	happy
10. 明年	míngnián	*n.*	next year

专名 Proper nouns

冰城	Bīngchéng	Ice City

语言点 Language Points

一、程度补语"极了"　Degree complement "极了"

"极了"经常用在形容词或心理动词后面做程度补语，表示最高程度，一般用在口语中。例如：

"极了" is often used as a degree complement after adjectives or psychological verbs to indicate the highest degree, it is usually used in spoken Chinese. For example:

1. 哈尔滨很冷，不过漂亮极了！
2. 骑共享单车去方便极了！
3. 这个电影马大为喜欢极了，每年都要看一次。

※ 练习：请用程度补语"极了"完成对话　Please complete the dialogues with the degree complement "极了"

1. A：王医生，你工作忙吗？

   B：________________________________。

2. A：你的汉语怎么样？

   B：________________________________。

3. A：你们的数学课难不难？

   B：________________________________。

4. A：这儿春天的天气怎么样？

   B：________________________________。

二、量词"次"　Measure word "次"

"次"是动量词，用来计量可以重复出现的动作行为。例如：

"次" is a verb-measure word used to measure actions that can appear repeatedly. For example:

1. 这是我第一次看见雪。

2. 这个星期我参加了一次篮球比赛。

3. 今年我搬了两次家。

※ 练习：请用量词“次”完成对话 Please complete dialogues with the measure word “次”

1. 医生：手术后病人去卫生间了吗？

   家属：________________________。

2. 大为：这个饭店的菜做得太好吃了！

   金龙：________________________。

3. 美丽：你不认识他吗？

   月亮：________________________。

4. 学生：对不起，老师，我没听见。

   老师：________________________。

三、固定结构“一边……一边……” Fixed structure “一边……一边……”

“一边……一边……”连接两个表并列关系的分句，表示两个动作同时进行。前后两个分句的主语可以一样，也可以不一样。例如：

“一边……一边……” is used to connect two paratactic clauses, indicating that the two actions are performed at the same time. The subjects of the two clauses can be the same or different. For example:

1. 我们一边看雪，一边吃冰激凌，开心极了！

2. 我们一边吃饭，一边聊天儿（liáotiānr，chat）。

3. 老师一边说，我们一边写。

※ 练习：请用固定结构“一边……一边……”和所给词语完成句子 Please use the fixed structure “一边……一边……” and the given words to complete sentences

1. 护士不能________________。（工作、聊天儿）
2. 马大为在体育馆________________。（锻炼、打电话）
3. 周末我喜欢和朋友________________。（喝咖啡、聊天儿）
4. 我们不要________________。（开车、看手机）

综合练习 Comprehensive Exercises

一、根据拼音写汉字 Write Chinese characters according to Pinyin

1. shùnlì________　　3. dì________　　5. xuě________
2. cì________　　4. kāixīn________　　6. jí________

二、辨字组词 Discriminate between Chinese characters and make words

1. 次________ / 冷________　　2. 第________ / 算________　　3. 边________ / 过________　　4. 顺________ / 题________

三、替换练习 Substitution drills

1. 我们一边看雪，一边吃冰激凌。

看电影	吃爆米花（bàomǐhuā，popcorn）
写作业	听歌儿
喝咖啡	聊天儿

2. 哈尔滨很冷，不过漂亮极了！

汉语很难	有意思
我很累	开心
宿舍很小	方便

3. 这是我第一次看见雪。

来中国
做手术
搬家

四、选词填空 Use the following words to fill in the blanks

第一　暖和　明年　开心　顺利

1. 医生，我爸爸这次手术_______吗？
2. 马上要当爸爸了，王东_______极了！
3. 三亚冬天也有 20 度，比哈尔滨_______多了。
4. 我是_______次来北京，我觉得北京漂亮极了！
5. 哈尔滨冬天太冷了，_______我不会再来了。

五、用所给词语完成对话 Complete the dialogues with given words

1. 朋友：________________________________？（顺利）

　病人：很顺利，医生告诉我下周就可以出院（chūyuàn，be discharged from hospital）了。

2. 朋友：你现在在做什么？

大为：____________________。（一边……一边……）

3. 金龙：外科医生的工作怎么样？

医生：____________________。（极了）

4. 王晨：你会做饭吗？

朋友：____________________。（次）

5. 大为：哈尔滨冬天那么冷，你为什么要去哈尔滨？

朋友：哈尔滨冬天很冷，____________________。（不过）

六、根据课文内容回答问题 Answer the following questions according to the text

1. 月亮现在在哪儿？
2. 美丽觉得哈尔滨怎么样？
3. 美丽以前见过雪吗？
4. 美丽为什么觉得开心极了？

七、根据课文内容填空 Fill in the blanks according to the text

月亮回国了，美丽打电话问她路上是不是________，月亮说她________到家，路上很顺利。美丽告诉月亮哈尔滨很冷，________漂亮________！美丽在哈尔滨________看见雪，她和金龙一边看雪，吃________，开心________！

语言任务 Language Tasks

一、阅读理解 Reading comprehension

哈尔滨，也叫“冰城”，是中国东北（northeast）有名的城市（chéngshì，city）。那儿冬天的温度很低，1 月平均（píngjūn，average）温度在 –20°C 左右。每年冬天，那儿的冰雪节吸引（xīyǐn，attract）很多游客（yóukè，tourist）来参观（cānguān，visit）。人们一边吃冰激凌，一边参加冰上运动，开心极了！

读后判断 True or false

1. 哈尔滨在中国的南方。（ ）
2. 哈尔滨 1 月最低温度 24°C 左右。（ ）
3. 哈尔滨每年冬天都有冰雪节。（ ）
4. 冬天的哈尔滨有很多游客。（ ）
5. 人们一边吃冰激凌，一边参加冰上运动。（ ）

二、口头表达 Oral expression

任务名称：旅途小药箱。

Task: Traveling medicine chest.

任务要求：1. 三个学生一组，讨论旅途需要哪些常备药品，可查询词典找到相应的汉语表达。
2. 分角色，一个是药店工作人员，另外两个是前来购药的顾客。
3. 去药店购买旅途所需的药物，向药店工作人员说明需求，询问价格。

Requirements: 1. Three students work in a group. Discuss which regular medicines are needed when traveling. You can look up the dictionary for the corresponding Chinese.

2. Work in roles: One student acts as the staff of the pharmacy, and the other two as the customers who come to buy medicine.
3. The two customers go to the pharmacy to buy the medicine needed for the trip, explain their demand to the staff of the pharmacy, and ask about the price.

Reference words: 终于　打算　得　不过　路上　顺利

三、书面表达 Written expression

任务名称：同学们的寒假安排。

Task: Arrangements of the students' winter vacation.

任务要求：调查班上同学们各自的寒假安排，并完成下列表格。

Requirement: Investigate the winter vacation arrangements of your classmates and complete the following table.

Reference words：寒假　打算　旅行（lǚxíng，travel）　顺利　次　路上

同学的名字	寒假打算

第八课
Lesson 8

Nǐ qùguo kǒuqiāng yīyuàn ma?

你去过 口腔 医院 吗？

Have you ever been to the stomatological hospital?

学习目标 Learning Objectives

1. Language functions: Students can introduce process; students can talk about their favorite taste.
2. Language points: Aspectual particle “过”; Fixed structure “先……然后……”; Fixed structure “一……就……”; Fixed structure “不但……而且……”.
3. Medical knowledge: Students are expected to understand the consultation process of the stomatological hospital.
4. Social culture: Students are expected to understand China’s takeaway-economy.

热身活动 Warming-up

1. 这是什么地方？你去过吗？

What is this place? Have you ever been there?

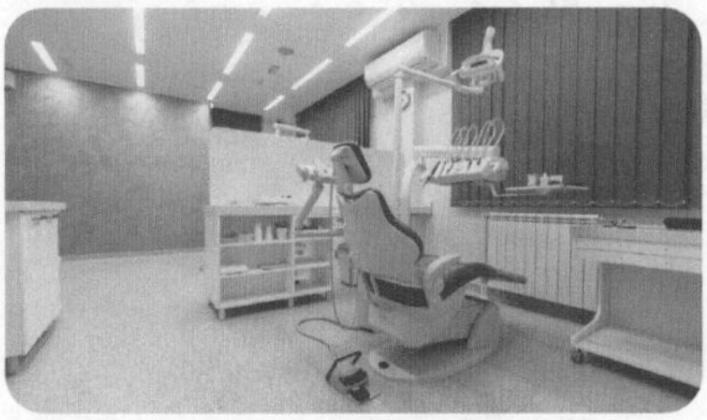

2. 你知道口腔医院有哪些科室吗？

Do you know what departments there are in the stomatological hospital?

课文（一）
Text（I）

Měilì hé Lǐ Zhēn zài liáotiānr.
（美丽和李真在聊天儿。）

Měilì: Nǐ qùguo kǒuqiāng yīyuàn ma?
美丽：你去过口腔医院吗？

Lǐ Zhēn: Qùguo, jiù zài zánmen xuéxiào běimén fùjìn. Nǐ yá téng ma?
李真：去过，就在咱们学校北门附近。你牙疼吗？

Měilì: Bú shì, wǒ de yátào xūyào tiáozhěng, wǒ xiǎng míngtiān qù kànkan.
美丽：不是，我的牙套需要调整，我想明天去看看。

Lǐ Zhēn: Nǐ zhīdào zěnme guàhào ma?
李真：你知道怎么挂号吗？

Měilì: Bù zhīdào. Lái Zhōngguó yǐhòu, wǒ méi qù yīyuàn kànguo bìng.
美丽：不知道。来中国以后，我没去医院看过病。

Lǐ Zhēn: Nǐ kěyǐ xiān zài shǒujī shàng guàhào, ránhòu dàishàng hùzhào qù qǔ hào.
李真：你可以先在手机上挂号，然后带上护照去取号。

Měilì: Nǐ juéde wǒ yí gè rén qù, xíng ma?
美丽：你觉得我一个人去，行吗？

Lǐ Zhēn: Búyòng dānxīn, fēnzhěntái de hùshi huì bāngzhù nǐ.
李真：不用担心，分诊台的护士会帮助你。

Měilì: Hǎo de, wǒ míngtiān yì qǐchuáng jiù qù.
美丽：好的，我明天一起床就去。

(Meili and Li Zhen are chatting.)

Meili: Have you been to the stomatological hospital?

Li Zhen: Yes. It's near the north gate of our college. Do you have a toothache?

Meili: No. My tooth socket need to be adjusted. I want to have it checked tomorrow.

Li Zhen: Do you know how to register?

Meili: No. I haven't seen the doctor since I came to China.

Li Zhen: You can register online via your mobile phone, and then go to the hospital to take your queue number with your passport.

Meili: Do you think it's OK that I go to the hospital alone?

Li Zhen: Don't worry. The nurse on the redirect stand will help you.

Meili: OK. I will go tomorrow as soon as I get up.

生词 New words

1. 过	guo	*part.*	an aspectual particle to indicate the action has occurred
2. 北门	běimén	*n.*	north gate
北	běi	*n.*	north
3. 附近	fùjìn	*n.*	nearby
4. 牙	yá	*n.*	tooth
5. 牙套	yátào	*n.*	tooth socket
6. 需要	xūyào	*v.*	to need
7. 调整	tiáozhěng	*v.*	to adjust
8. 挂号	guàhào	*v.*	to register
9. 看病	kànbìng	*v.*	to see a doctor
10. 然后	ránhòu	*conj.*	then
11. 护照	hùzhào	*n.*	passport
12. 取号	qǔ hào	*VO*	to take a queue number

13. 担心	dānxīn	*v.*	to worry
14. 分诊台	fēnzhěntái	*n.*	redirect stand
分诊	fēnzhěn	*v.*	to make a triage
15. 帮助	bāngzhù	*v.*	to help
16. 一……就……	yī…jiù…		as soon as

语言点 Language Points

一、动态助词"过" Aspectual particle "过"

动态助词"过"用在动词后，表示过去的经验或经历。其否定式是"没（有）+ 动词 + 过"，疑问式是"动词 + 过（+ 宾语）+ 没有 / 吗"或"动词 + 没 + 动词 + 过（+ 宾语）"。例如：

The aspectual particle "过" is used after the verb to express past experience or experiences. The negative form is "没（有）+ verb + 过", and the interrogative form is "verb + 过（+ object）+ 没有 / 吗" or "verb + 没 + verb + 过（+ object）". For example:

1. 你去过口腔医院吗？
2. 来中国以后，我没去医院看过病。
3. 你订没订过外卖？

※ 练习：回答问题 Answer questions

1. 你去过哈尔滨吗？

________________________________。

2. 你去过金龙说的饭馆吗？

________________________________。

3. 你参加过篮球比赛吗？

________________________________。

4. 来中国以前，你学没学过汉语？

________________________________。

二、固定结构“先……然后……” Fixed structure “先……然后……”

“先……然后……”连接表示承接关系的分句，表示动作行为或事件发生的先后顺序。例如：

“先……然后……” connects the clauses of the continuing relationship, indicating the sequence of actions or events. For example:

1. 你可以先在手机上挂号，然后带上护照去取号。
2. 我想先学习汉语，然后学习医学。
3. 下课以后，我先去吃饭，然后回宿舍写作业。

※ 练习：请用固定结构“先……然后……”回答问题 Please answer questions with the fixed structure “先……然后……”

1. 周末你有什么打算？

________________________________。

2. 这个寒假你有什么打算？

________________________________。

3. 下课以后，你要做什么？

________________________________。

4. 晚上你在宿舍都做什么？

________________________________。

三、固定结构“一……就……” Fixed structure “一……就……”

“一……就……”连接两个表示承接关系的分句，表示一个动作行为紧接着另一个动作行为发生。两个动作行为的主语可以一样，也可以不一样。如果主语不一样，两个主语要分别出现在“一”和“就”之前。例如：

“一……就……” connects two clauses of the continuing relationship, indicating that one action is closely followed by another. The subject of the two actions can be the same or different. If the subjects are different, the two subjects should be put before “一” and “就” respectively. For example:

1. 我明天一起床就去。
2. 我打算一放假就回国。
3. 老师一说下课，马大为就去吃饭了。

※ 练习：完成句子　Complete sentences

1. 同学们一考完试 ______________________________。
2. 美丽一下课 ______________________________。
3. 金龙一来中国 ______________________________。
4. 王医生一到办公室，护士 ______________________________。

综合练习 Comprehensive Exercises

一、根据拼音写汉字 Write Chinese characters according to Pinyin

1. dānxīn__________	3. yá__________	5. fùjìn__________
2. ránhòu__________	4. bāngzhù__________	6. guo__________

二、辨字组词 Discriminate between Chinese characters and make words

1. 附________ 付________
2. 牙________ 呀________
3. 担________ 但________
4. 病________ 疼________

三、替换练习 Substitution drills

1. 你去过口腔医院吗？

参加	篮球比赛
量	血压
见	雪

2. 你可以先在手机上挂号，然后带上护照去取号。

写作业	去玩儿游戏
去量血压	去做心电图
报名	去参加比赛

3. 我明天一起床就去。

考完试	回国
写完作业	去游泳
下课	给你打电话

四、选词填空 Use the following words to fill in the blanks

需要　调整　担心　挂　过

1. 您好，请问您哪儿不舒服？要_______什么号？
2. 别_______，医生说手术很顺利。
3. 病人在医院_______照顾。
4. 你要回国？那我们的寒假计划要_______一下了。
5. 我去医院看_______，医生说我的病不太严重。

五、用所给词语完成对话 Complete the dialogues with given words

1. 美　丽：请问卫生间在哪儿？

   服务员：______________________________。（先……然后……）

2. 医生：______________________________？（过）

   病人：量过，血压不太高。

3. 妈妈：______________________________？（一……就……）

   王晨：今天太累了，我想先睡一会儿。

4. 美丽：你去口腔医院做什么？

   朋友：__________________________。（调整）

5. 美丽：我没去中国的医院看过病。

   朋友：别担心，__________________。（帮助）

六、根据课文内容回答问题 Answer the following questions according to the text

1. 口腔医院在哪儿？
2. 美丽为什么要去口腔医院？
3. 去口腔医院看病要先做什么？

4. 美丽担心什么？

七、根据课文内容填空 Fill in the blanks according to the text

美丽的牙套需要________，她想明天去________医院看看。来中国以后，她没去________口腔医院。李真告诉美丽，去口腔医院前可以先在手机上________，然后带上________去________，分诊台的护士会________她。美丽说明天一起床________去。

课文（二）
Text（II）

Jímǐ hé Mǎ Dàwéi zài liáotiānr.
（吉米和马 大为 在 聊天儿。）

Jímǐ: Zhōngwǔ yìqǐ qù shítáng chīfàn ba.
吉米：中午 一起去食堂 吃饭吧。

Mǎ Dàwéi: Shítáng li búdàn rén duō, érqiě hěn chǎo, wǒ zhōngwǔ dǎsuàn dìng wàimài.
马大为：食堂 里不但 人 多，而且很 吵，我 中午 打算 订外卖。

Jímǐ: Nǐ dìngguo wàimài ma?
吉米：你 订过 外卖 吗？

Mǎ Dàwéi: Wǒ jīngcháng dìng wàimài.
马大为：我 经常 订 外卖。

Jímǐ: Wǒ méi dìngguo, nǐ néng gěi wǒ tuījiàn jǐ gè diàn ma?
吉米：我 没 订过，你 能 给 我 推荐几个店 吗？

Mǎ Dàwéi: Dāngrán kěyǐ. Wǒ zhīdào hěn duō yòu piányi yòu hǎochī de diàn, nǐ xǐhuan shénme cài?
马大为：当然 可以。我 知道 很 多 又 便宜 又 好吃的 店，你喜欢 什么 菜？

Jímǐ: Wǒ xǐhuan là de.
吉米：我 喜欢 辣的。

Mǎ Dàwéi: Zánmen liǎ kǒuwèi chàbuduō, wǒ xiànzài fā gěi nǐ.
马大为：咱们 俩 口味 差不多，我 现在 发给 你。

Jímǐ: Tài bàng le, jīntiān zhōngwǔ wǒ jiù dìng.
吉米：太 棒 了，今天 中午 我就 订。

(Jimmy and Ma Dawei are chatting.)

Jimmy: Let's go to have lunch in canteen this noon.

Ma Dawei: The canteen is not only crowded, but also very noisy. I plan to order takeaway this noon.

Jimmy: Have you ordered takeaway?

Ma Dawei: I often order takeaway.

Jimmy: I have never ordered takeaway. Can you recommend me any restaurants?

Ma Dawei: Of course. I know many cheap and good restaurants. What kind of dishes do you like to eat?

Jimmy: I like spicy food.

Ma Dawei: Our taste are similar. I am sending you the names of the restaurants I like.

Jimmy: Great. I will order this noon.

生词 New words

1. 食堂	shítáng	*n.*	canteen
2. 不但……而且……	búdàn…érqiě…		not only...but also...
不但	búdàn	*conj.*	not only
而且	érqiě	*conj.*	but (also), and that
3. 吵	chǎo	*adj.*	noisy
4. 经常	jīngcháng	*adv.*	often
5. 推荐	tuījiàn	*v.*	to recommend
6. 店	diàn	*n.*	shop, store
7. 便宜	piányi	*adj.*	cheap
8. 辣	là	*adj.*	spicy
9. 俩	liǎ	*num.-m.*	two, a pair

10. 口味	kǒuwèi	*n.*	taste
11. 差不多	chàbuduō	*adj.*	similar
12. 棒	bàng	*adj.*	great

语言点 Language Points

固定结构"不但……而且……"　Fixed structure "不但……而且……"

"不但……而且……"连接两个表示递进关系的分句，后一分句比前一分句在意思上更进一层。前后两个分句的主语可以一样，这时候主语一般在前一分句"不但"之前。前后两个分句的主语也可以不一样，这时候两个主语一般分别在"不但"和"而且"之后。例如：

"不但……而且……" connects two clauses of the progressive relationship. The latter clause is more progressive in meaning than the previous one. The subject of the two clauses can be the same. In this case, the subject is usually put before the "不但" in the previous clause. The subject of the two clauses can also be different. In this case, the two subjects are usually put after "不但" and "而且" respectively. For example:

1. 食堂里不但人多，而且很吵。
2. 李真家不但很大，而且很漂亮。
3. 不但数学很难，而且医学也很难。

※ 练习：请用固定结构"不但……而且……"造句　Please make sentences with the fixed structure "不但……而且……"

1. 会做饭　做得很好吃

______________________________。

2. 喜欢打篮球　打得很好

________________________________。

3. 马大为去　金龙也去

________________________________。

4. 去过　去过很多次

________________________________。

综合练习 Comprehensive Exercises

一、根据拼音写汉字 Write Chinese characters according to Pinyin

1. jīngcháng________ 3. chǎo________ 5. tuījiàn________

2. piányi________ 4. kǒuwèi________ 6. là________

二、辨字组词 Discriminate between Chinese characters and make words

1. 荐________ 在________

2. 吵________ 少________

3. 推________ 住________

4. 棒________ 极________

三、替换练习 Substitution drills

1. 食堂里不但人多，而且很吵。

今天	雨很大	风也很大
熬夜	让人又累又困	伤身体（shēntǐ，body）
游泳	锻炼身体	能减肥（jiǎnféi，lose weight）

2. 你能<u>给我推荐几个店</u>吗？

> 给我挂一个口腔医院的号
> 爬快一点儿
> 一回家就写作业

3. <u>咱们俩口味</u>差不多。

> 咱们俩的爱好（àihào，hobby）
> 这两天的温度
> 我们的寒假计划（jìhuà，plan）

四、选词填空 Use the following words to fill in the blanks

订　俩　差不多　推荐　便宜

1. 这两个病房（bìngfáng，ward）大小________。
2. 您好，我要________一个房间。
3. 我们________都当了心脏外科医生。
4. 我想去看牙，你能给我________一家好的口腔医院吗？
5. 这家饭店的菜又好吃又________。

五、用所给词语完成对话 Complete the dialogues with given words

1. 朋友：这里的医生怎么样？

   病人：________________________________。（不但……而且……）

2. 孩子：________________________？（能）

妈妈：你先写完作业。

3. 朋友：你看天气预报了吗？明天天气怎么样？

大为：________________________。（差不多）

4. 医生：你哪儿不舒服？

病人：________________________。（经常）

5. 朋友：你喜欢什么菜？我喜欢辣的。

王晨：________________________。（俩）

六、根据课文内容回答问题 Answer the following questions according to the text

1. 马大为和吉米中午打算去哪儿吃饭？
2. 马大为觉得食堂怎么样？
3. 马大为订过外卖吗？
4. 吉米喜欢什么口味的菜？马大为呢？

七、根据课文内容填空 Fill in the blanks according to the text

马大为觉得在______吃饭______人多，而且很______，所以他经常在网上（wǎng shang，online）______外卖。他知道很多又便宜______好吃的店。吉米没订______外卖，他喜欢吃______的菜。他们______口味______，马大为就给他______了几个又又______的店。

语言任务 Language Tasks

一、阅读理解 Reading comprehension

东山大学口腔医院离学校不太远，就在学校北门附近，走路十分钟就到了。因为需要调整牙套，我差不多每个月都要去一次。每次去我都会先在手机上挂号，然后带上护照去取号。如果有不明白的地方，我一点儿也不会担心，分诊台的护士会帮助我。

读后判断 True or false

1. 东山大学口腔医院离学校北门不远。 (　　)
2. "我"在东山大学口腔医院工作。 (　　)
3. "我"经常去口腔医院。 (　　)
4. 去口腔医院挂号不用护照。 (　　)
5. 去口腔医院看病很方便。 (　　)

二、口头表达 Oral expression

任务名称：你去过口腔医院吗？

Task: Have you ever been to the stomatological hospital?

任务要求：调查班里的同学最近三年去看过几次牙医，分别是什么原因，并完成下面的表格。

Requirement: Investigate how many times your classmates have seen the dentist in the last three years and why, and complete the following table.

Reference words: 口腔医院　经常　次　调整　牙套　差不多

序号 No.	姓名 Name	次数 Times	原因 Reasons
1			
2			

（续表）

序号 No.	姓名 Name	次数 Times	原因 Reasons
3			
4			

三、书面表达 Written expression

任务名称："订外卖"还是"去食堂"？

Task: "Ordering takeaway" or "going to the canteen"?

任务要求：请和同学们讨论一下"订外卖"和"去食堂"的优缺点，并完成下面的表格。

Requirement: Please discuss the advantages and disadvantages of "ordering takeaway" and "going to the canteen" with your classmates, and complete the following table.

Reference words: 方便　离……近　便宜　贵　又……又……
干净（gānjìng，clean）时间　钱　快
麻烦（máfan，troublesome）忙　工作
健康（jiànkāng，healthy）胖（pàng，fat）越来越……

	订外卖 Ordering takeaway	去食堂 Going to the canteen
优点 Advantages		
缺点 Disadvantages		
选择和原因 Your choice and reasons		

补充词汇 Supplementary Words

bá yá
拔牙
tooth extraction

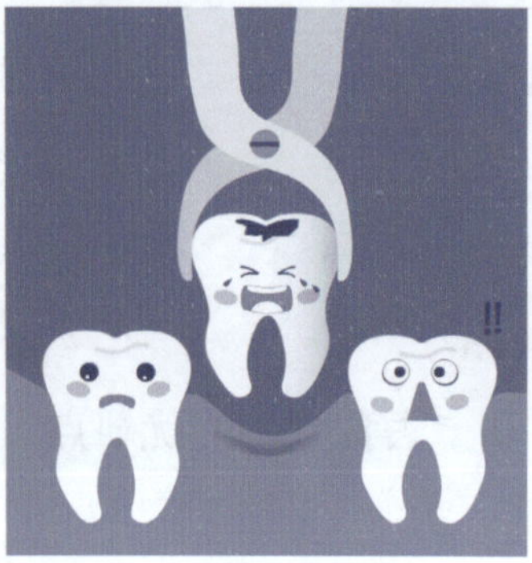

xǐ yá
洗牙
toothwash

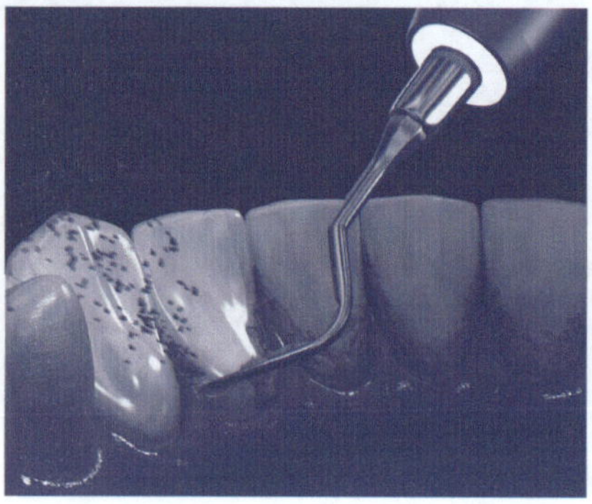

zhòng yá
种牙
tooth implantation

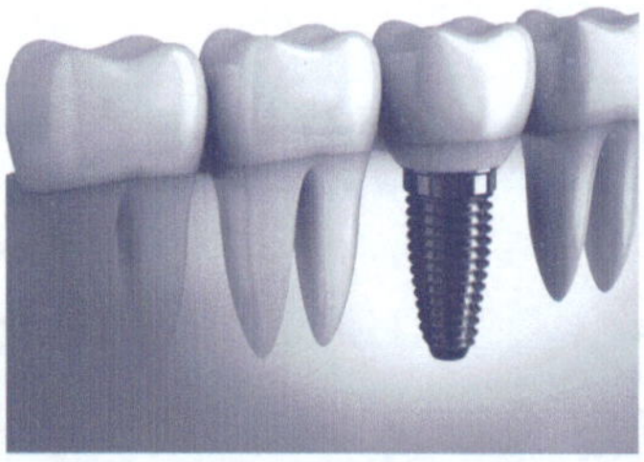

bǔ yá
补牙
tooth filling

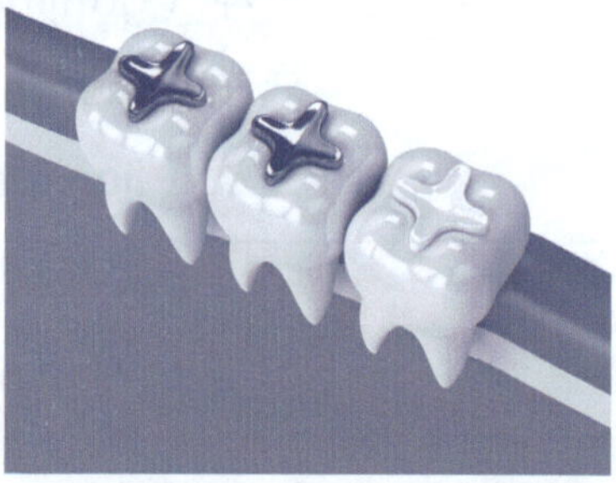

第九课 Lesson 9

Shǒushù shì Wáng dàifu zuò de

手术 是 王 大夫做的

Dr. Wang performed the surgery

学习目标 Learning Objectives

1. Language functions: Students learn to express their concern and greetings when visiting patients; students can explain the postoperative precautions of patients.
2. Language points: "是……的"-sentence; Expressions for approximate number (1); Imperative sentence (3); Fixed structure "多 + V / VP"; Adverb "按时"; Fixed structure "要是……就……".
3. Medical knowledge: Students are expected to understand general postoperative precautions.
4. Social culture: Students are expected to understand what Chinese people should pay attention to when visiting patients and the relevant cultural taboos.

热身活动 Warming-up

1. 去医院看望病人时你会选择带什么礼物？

What gift do you choose when visiting a patient in the hospital?

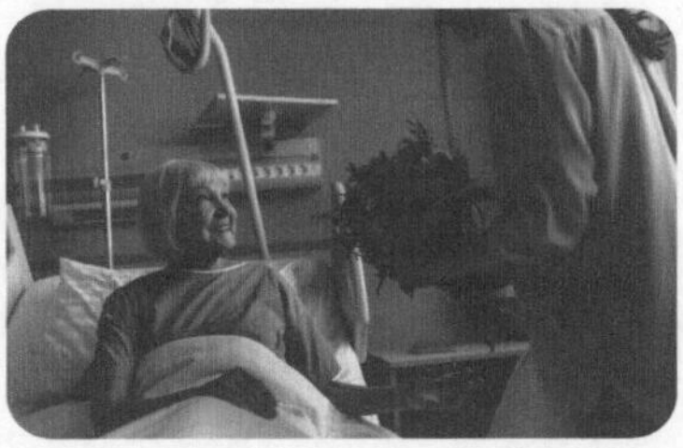

2. 病人手术后在饮食上一般要注意什么？

What should the patient pay attention to on diet after surgery?

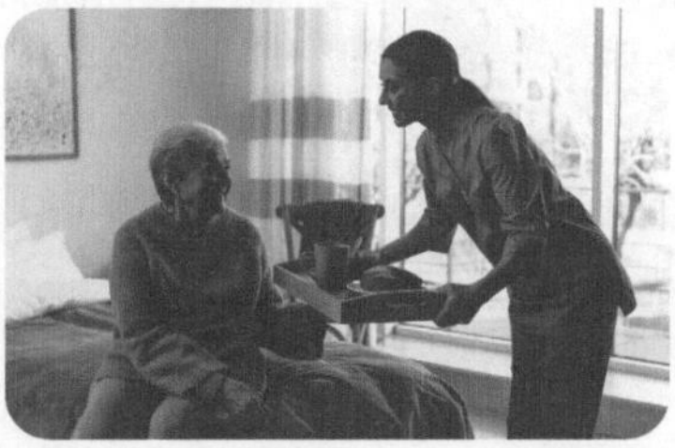

课文（一）
Text（I）

Liú lǎoshī zuòle shǒushù, tā de péngyou lái yīyuàn kàn tā.
（刘 老师 做了 手术，她的 朋友 来 医院 看 她。）

péngyou: Nǐ xiànzài gǎnjué zěnmeyàng?
朋友：你现在感觉 怎么样？

Liú lǎoshī: Hǎo yìdiǎnr le, xièxie nǐ lái kàn wǒ. Nǐ jiā lí yīyuàn zhème yuǎn, nǐ shì zěnme lái de?
刘老师：好一点儿了，谢谢你来看 我。你家离医院 这么 远，你是怎么来的？

péngyou: Wǒ shì dǎchē lái de, hěn fāngbiàn. Nǐ de shǒushù shì shénme shíhou zuò de?
朋友：我 是 打车来的，很 方便。你的 手术 是 什么 时候 做 的？

Liú lǎoshī: Qiántiān zuò de, shì gè xiǎo shǒushù.
刘老师：前天 做 的，是个 小 手术。

péngyou: Tīng wǒ érzi shuō, xiāohuà wàikē de Lǐ zhǔrèn hěn yǒumíng, shǒushù shì tā zuò de ma?
朋友：听 我儿子说，消化 外科的李主任 很 有名，手术 是他做的吗？

Liú lǎoshī: Bú shì, shì Wáng dàifu zuò de, tā de shuǐpíng yě hěn gāo.
刘老师：不 是，是 王 大夫做的，他的 水平 也很 高。

péngyou: Wǎnshang shéi zài yīyuàn zhàogù nǐ?
朋友：晚上 谁 在 医院 照顾 你？

Liú lǎoshī: Wǒ zhàngfu hé nǚ'ér.
刘老师：我 丈夫 和女儿。

péngyou: Shénme shíhou néng chūyuàn?
朋友：什么 时候 能 出院？

Liú lǎoshī: Hái yào sān-sì tiān.
刘老师：还 要 三 四 天。

(Ms. Liu had a surgery and her friend comes to the hospital to visit her.)

Friend: How do you feel?

Ms. Liu: Better. Thank you for coming to see me. Your home is so far from the hospital. How do you come?

Friend: I come by taxi. It's very convenient. When did you have the surgery?

Ms. Liu: The day before yesterday. It's a minor surgery.

Friend: I heard from my son that Director Li of digestive surgery is very famous. Did he do the surgery?

Ms. Liu: No. It was Dr. Wang that did the surgery. The level of his technique is also very high.

Friend: Who takes care of you in the hospital at night?

Ms. Liu: My husband and daughter.

Friend: When are you discharged from hospital?

Ms. Liu: Three to four days later.

生词 New words

1. 感觉	gǎnjué	*v./n.*	to feel; feeling
2. 打车	dǎchē	*v.*	to take a taxi
3. 前天	qiántiān	*n.*	the day before yesterday
4. 儿子	érzi	*n.*	son
5. 消化	xiāohuà	*v.*	to digest
6. 主任	zhǔrèn	*n.*	director
7. 大夫	dàifu	*n.*	doctor
8. 水平	shuǐpíng	*n.*	level

9. 丈夫	zhàngfu	*n.*	husband
10. 女儿	nǚ'ér	*n.*	daughter
11. 出院	chūyuàn	*v.*	to discharge from hospital

专名 Proper nouns

刘	Liú	a Chinese surname

语言点 Language Points

一、"是……的"句　"是……的"-sentence

在汉语中，"是……的"句可以用来强调已经发生的动作行为的施事、时间、地点、方式等。"是"用在要强调的部分之前，有时候可以省略。否定式为"不是……的"，否定式中的"是"不能省略。例如：

In Chinese, the "是……的"-sentence can be used to emphasize the agent, time, place, manner, etc. of the action that has occurred. "是" is used before the part to be emphasized, and sometimes it can be omitted. The negative form is "不是……的", and "是" in the negative form cannot be omitted. For example:

1. 手术是王大夫做的，不是李主任做的。
2. 你家离医院这么远，你（是）怎么来的？
3. 你的手术（是）什么时候做的？
4. 我不是开车来的。

※ 练习：回答问题　Answer questions

1. 你是什么时候来中国的？

______________________________。

2. 你是怎么来的？

______________________________。

3. 你是和谁一起来的？

______________________________。

4. 你的衣服是在哪儿买的？

______________________________。

二、概数表达法（1） Expressions for approximate number (1)

在汉语中，相邻的两个数字连用可以表示概数。但是，“九十”只表示具体的数字“90”，不表示概数。例如：

In Chinese, two adjacent numbers can be used together to represent approximate numbers. However, “九十” only refers to the specific number “90”, not the approximate number. For example:

1. 还要三四天才能出院。
2. 这件衣服五六百块。
3. 他哥哥今年二十七八岁。

※ 练习：请用相邻两个数字连用表概数的方式回答问题 Please answer questions by using the approximate number of two adjacent numbers

1. 这条裙子多少钱？

______________________________。

2. 你每天运动多长时间？

______________________________。

3. 你有多少个中国朋友？

______________________________。

4. 你认识多少个汉字？

________________________________。

综合练习 Comprehensive Exercises

一、根据拼音写汉字 Write Chinese characters according to Pinyin

1. nǚ'ér__________ 3. gǎnjué__________ 5. dǎchē__________

2. chūyuàn__________ 4. zhǔrèn__________ 6. shǔipíng__________

二、辨字组词 Discriminate between Chinese characters and make words

1. 消________ 海________

2. 任________ 住________

3. 主________ 王________

4. 夫________ 天________

三、替换练习 Substitution drills

1. 你的手术是什么时候做的？

你	怎么去口腔医院
早饭	谁做
你的衣服	在哪儿买

2. 手术是他做的吗？

外卖	你订
伞	你带过来
手术	前天做

3. 还要<u>三四天</u>才能<u>出院</u>。

一两个小时（xiǎoshí，hour）	写完作业
坐三四个小时	到家
调整两三次	摘（zhāi，take off）牙套

四、选词填空 Use the following words to fill in the blanks

感觉　是　打车　出院　水平

1. 我是_______来口腔医院的。
2. 手术以后你_______怎么样？
3. 我_______早上量的血压。
4. 李大夫做手术的_______很高。
5. 大夫，我什么时候能_______？

五、用所给词语完成对话 Complete the dialogues with given words

1. 朋友：____________________________？（是……的）

   病人：手术是昨天做的。
2. 朋友：你的丈夫是做什么的？

   艺文：____________________________。（大夫）
3. 爸爸：这么晚了，你是怎么回来的？

   女儿：____________________________。（打车）
4. 医生：你哪里不舒服？

   病人：____________________________。（感觉）

5. 朋友：你什么时候能出院？

吉米：________________。（概数，approximate number）

六、根据课文内容回答问题 Answer the following questions according to the text

1. 刘老师现在在哪儿？
2. 刘老师的朋友是怎么来医院的？
3. 刘老师的手术是什么时候做的？是谁做的？
4. 刘老师什么时候能出院？

七、根据课文内容填空 Fill in the blanks according to the text

刘老师的朋友去医院看她。朋友的家______医院很远，她是______来的。刘老师做了个小手术，手术不是______做的，是王大夫做的，他的______很高。晚上，刘老师的______和______在医院照顾她。她现在感觉______了，三四天以后就能______了。

课文（二）
Text（II）

Liú lǎoshī chūyuàn qián hé Wáng dàifu jiāoliú.
（刘老师 出院 前和 王 大夫交流。）

Wáng dàifu: Dāokǒu hái téng ma?
王大夫：刀口 还疼 吗？

Liú lǎoshī: Hái yǒudiǎnr téng.
刘老师：还有点儿 疼。

Wáng dàifu: Ràng wǒ kàn yíxià. Huīfù de búcuò, jīntiān jiù kěyǐ chūyuàn le.
王大夫：让 我看一下。恢复得不错，今天就可以出院 了。

Liú lǎoshī: Wáng dàifu, chūyuàn yǐhòu, xūyào zhùyì shénme?
刘老师：王 大夫，出院 以后，需要注意什么？

Wáng dàifu: Bié chī liáng de, là de, yě bié jùliè yùndòng, yào duō xiūxi,
王大夫：别吃凉 的、辣的，也别剧烈运动，要多休息，

duō hē shuǐ, ànshí chī yào.
多喝水，按时吃药。

Liú lǎoshī: Shénme shíhou lái fùchá?
刘老师：什么 时候来复查？

Wáng dàifu: Liǎng gè xīngqī yǐhòu. Yàoshi fùtòng, ǒutù, jiù mǎshàng
王大夫：两 个星期以后。要是 腹痛、呕吐，就 马上

lái yīyuàn.
来医院。

Liú lǎoshī: Hǎo de, xièxie Wáng dàifu.
刘老师：好的，谢谢 王 大夫。

(Ms. Liu talks with Dr. Wang before being discharged from hospital.)

Dr. Wang: Does your cut still feel achy?

Ms. Liu: Still a little achy.

Dr. Wang: Let me have a look. Your cut recovers well. You could be discharged from hospital today.

Ms. Liu: Dr. Wang, what do I need to pay attention to after leaving hospital?

Dr. Wang: Don't eat anything cold or spicy. Don't do strenuous exercise. You need to have more rest, drink more water and take medicine on time.

Ms. Liu: When shall I come back to have a second test?

Dr. Wang: Two weeks later. If you have a stomachache or vomit, come to hospital immediately.

Ms. Liu: OK. Thank you, Dr. Wang.

生词 New words

1. 刀口	dāokǒu	*n.*	cut
2. 恢复	huīfù	*v.*	to recover
3. 注意	zhùyì	*v.*	to pay attention to
4. 别	bié	*adv.*	don't
5. 凉	liáng	*adj.*	cool
6. 剧烈	jùliè	*adj.*	violent, strenuous, fierce
7. 按时	ànshí	*adv.*	on time
8. 药	yào	*n.*	medicine
9. 复查	fùchá	*v.*	to recheck, to reexamine
10. 要是……就……	yàoshi…jiù…		if, suppose
要是	yàoshi	*conj.*	if
11. 腹痛	fùtòng	*n./adj.*	stomachache, abdominal pain

腹	fù	*n.*	abdomen, stomach
痛	tòng	*adj.*	painful, sore
12. 呕吐	ǒutù	*v.*	to vomit

语言点 Language Points

一、祈使句（3） Imperative sentence (3)

副词"别"表示劝阻、阻止某人做某事。例如：

The adverb "别" indicates to dissuade or stop someone from doing something. For example:

1. 别吃凉的、辣的，也别剧烈运动。
2. 你感冒了，别喝太多咖啡。
3. 别订外卖了，我们去食堂吃饭吧。

※ 练习：请用副词"别"和所给词语完成句子　Please use the adverb "别" and the given words to complete sentences

1. 你生病了，______________________________。（去上班）
2. 你感冒了，______________________________。（去上课）
3. 太晚了，________________________________。（看电影）
4. 你刚做完手术，__________________________。（运动）

二、固定结构"多 + V/VP"　Fixed structure "多 + V/VP"

形容词"多"用在动词或动词性短语前，表示数量大或数量增加，与"少"相对。例如：

The adjective "多" is used in front of a verb or verbal phrase to indicate a large or increased number. It is opposite to "少". For example:

1. 你要多休息，多喝水，按时吃药。
2. 你生病了，要少喝咖啡，多喝水。
3. 你身体（shēntǐ，body）不好，要多锻炼。

※ 练习：选出"多"在句子中的位置　Choose the position of "多" in sentences

1. A 想学好 B 汉语，C 要 D 说。
2. A 医生 B 让我 C 运动 D。
3. 你 A 感冒了 B，C 要 D 喝水。
4. 汉字 A 太难了，B 我一定 C 要 D 写。

三、副词"按时"　Adverb "按时"

"按时"表示按照约定或规定的时间做某事。例如：

The adverb "按时" indicates to do something at an agreed or stipulated time. For example:

1. 你要按时吃药。
2. 你是学生，要按时上课。
3. 你刚做完手术，一定要按时吃饭、休息。

※ 练习：请用副词"按时"和所给词语完成句子　Please use the adverb "按时" and the given words to complete sentences

1. 好的，明天早上八点见，我会 ______________。（到）
2. 医生让病人 ______________。（吃药）
3. 金龙每天都 ______________。（起床、睡觉）

4. A：他怎么又生病了？

B：______________。（休息）

四、固定结构“要是……就……” Fixed structure “要是……就……”

“要是……就……”连接表假设关系的两个分句，其中前一分句提出假设，后一分句说明在这种情况下会出现的结果。例如：

“要是……就……” connects two clauses that express a hypothetical relationship. The first clause proposes a hypothesis, and the second clause describes the results that will appear in this case. For example:

1. 要是腹痛、呕吐，就马上来医院。
2. 要是生病了，你就别来上课了。
3. 要是下雨了，我就打车去上班。

※ 练习：请用固定结构“要是……就……”回答问题 Please answer questions with the fixed structure “要是……就……”

1. 星期六你去爬山吗？

__________________________________。

2. 寒假你要去哈尔滨吗？

__________________________________。

3. 明天你要参加篮球比赛吗？

__________________________________。

4. 周末咱们一起去健身房锻炼吧？

__________________________________。

综合练习 Comprehensive Exercises

一、根据拼音写汉字 Write Chinese characters according to Pinyin

1. fùchá__________　3. bié__________　5. zhùyì__________
2. ànshí__________　4. yàoshi__________　6. liáng__________

二、辨字组词 Discriminate between Chinese characters and make words

1. 烈________ 热________
2. 凉________ 京________
3. 刀________ 力________
4. 药________ 荐________

三、替换练习 Substitution drills

1. 你别<u>吃凉的、辣的</u>。

喝咖啡
摔伤了
担心

2. 要是<u>腹痛、呕吐</u>，就<u>马上来医院</u>。

你不想去食堂	订外卖吧
你明天有时间	来我家玩儿吧
你没有课	来我们学校看看吧

3. 你要多<u>休息</u>，多<u>喝水</u>。

运动	锻炼
听	想
看书	学习

四、选词填空 Use the following words to fill in the blanks

恢复　注意　要是　按时　剧烈

1. 医生告诉我手术后要________休息。
2. 你别忘了________吃药。
3. 你的刀口________得怎么样了？
4. 你________感觉不舒服，就马上来医院。
5. 手术以后不要________运动。

五、用所给词语完成对话 Complete the dialogues with given words

1. 病人：大夫，手术以后要注意什么？

   医生：________________________。（别）

2. 病人：________________________？（要是）

   医生：你得马上来医院。

3. 朋友：你还需要去医院复查吗？

   病人：________________________。（按时）

4. 学生：老师，怎么学好汉语呀？

   老师：________________________。（多）

5. 大夫：手术后已经三四天了，现在刀口还疼吗？

   病人：________________________。（恢复）

六、根据课文内容回答问题 Answer the following questions according to the text

1. 刘老师的刀口恢复得怎么样？
2. 刘老师什么时候能出院？
3. 出院以后，刘老师需要注意什么？
4. 刘老师什么时候来医院复查？

七、根据课文内容填空 Fill in the blanks according to the text

刘老师手术后恢复得________，今天就可以出院了。医生告诉她出院以后不能吃________、辣的，也________剧烈运动，要________休息，________吃药，两个星期以后来医院________。________腹痛、呕吐，就要________来医院。

语言任务 Language Tasks

一、阅读理解 Reading comprehension

一般（yìbān，general）病人做完手术以后要注意休息，别熬夜；别做剧烈运动，也不要走太长时间；要注意按时吃药、换（huàn，change）药；别吃凉的、辣的，可以多吃蔬菜（shūcài，vegetable）、水果；别抽烟、喝酒（jiǔ，wine）；要按时来医院复查。

读后判断 True or false

1. 术后病人要注意休息。（ ）
2. 术后病人可以踢足球锻炼身体。（ ）
3. 术后病人可以吃冰激凌。（ ）
4. 术后病人要按时吃药、按时复查。（ ）

5. 术后病人可以多吃蔬菜、水果。 ( )

二、口头表达 Oral expression

任务名称：阑尾炎手术后需要注意的问题。

Task: Problems should be paid attention to after the appendectomy.

任务要求：1. 两个学生一组，一个是病人，一个是医生。病人做完阑尾炎手术，明天就可以出院了。

2. 病人询问医生出院后需要注意哪些问题。

3. 医生告诉病人手术后需要注意的问题。

Requirements: 1. Two students work in a group. One acts as a patient, the other as a doctor. The patient will be discharged from hospital tomorrow after the appendectomy.

2. The patient asks the doctor what needed to pay attention to after being discharged from hospital.

3. The doctor tells the patient what to pay attention to after the operation.

Reference words: 刀口 恢复 有点儿 注意 疼 复查 腹痛 呕吐 要是……就…… 多 + V/VP 不能

三、书面表达 Written expression

任务名称：带什么礼物去看望病人？

Task: What gifts do you carry when visiting patients?

任务要求：请和同学们讨论一下去看望病人时怎样挑选礼物、哪些可以带、哪些不能带，并完成下面的表格。

Requirement: Please discuss with your classmates how to choose gifts, which gifts are suitable and which are not for visiting patients, and complete the following table.

Reference words: 不但……而且…… 恢复 别 要是 感觉 推荐 差不多 需要

可以带的礼物 Suitable gifts	不可以带的礼物 Unsuitable gifts

补充词汇 Supplementary Words

yūndǎo
晕倒
faint

jīngjué
惊厥
convulsion

fùxiè
腹泻
diarrhea

xuànyùn
眩晕
dizziness

第十课 Lesson 10

Tā zhèngzài zuò shǒushù ne

他 正在 做 手术 呢

He is performing the operation now

学习目标 Learning Objectives

1. Language functions: Students can describe the current action or state; students are able to express their requests; students can describe appearance.
2. Language points: Fixed structure "正在……（呢）"; Expressions for approximate number (2); Compound directional complement; Adverb "好"; Adjective-reduplication "AA" type; Adverb "全".
3. Medical knowledge: Students are expected to understand the contents of medical records written by Chinese doctors.
4. Social culture: Students are expected to learn about Chinese birthday custom.

热身活动 Warming-up

1. 你认为病历有什么用？病历上面可能包含哪些内容？
What do you think is the use of medical records? What contents might a medical record contain?

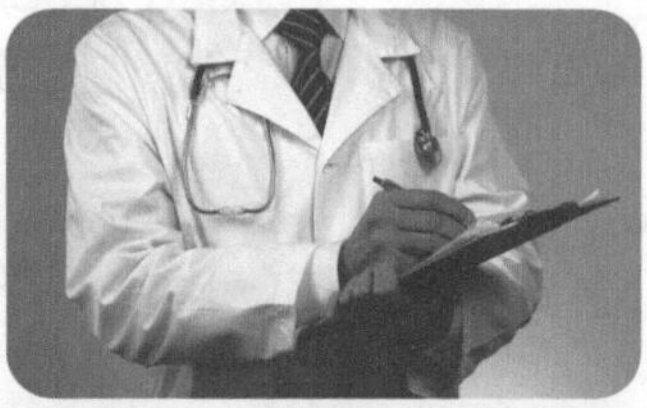

2. 你怎么庆祝生日？
How do you celebrate your birthday?

课文（一）
Text（Ⅰ）

Wàikē zhǔrèn Liú Wén gěi Wáng Dōng bàngōngshì dǎ diànhuà.
（外科 主任 刘 文 给 王 东 办公室 打 电话。）

Liú zhǔrèn: Wǒ shì Liú Wén. Wáng Dōng yīshēng zài bàngōngshì ma?
刘主任：我是刘文。王 东 医生 在 办公室 吗？

Lǐ yīshēng: Liú zhǔrèn nín hǎo, Wáng yīshēng bú zài, tā zhèngzài zuò shǒushù ne.
李医生：刘 主任 您 好，王 医生 不 在，他 正在 做 手术 呢。

Liú zhǔrèn: Dàgài shénme shíhou zuòwán?
刘主任：大概 什么 时候 做完？

Lǐ yīshēng: Shíyī diǎn zuǒyòu.
李医生：十一点 左右。

Liú zhǔrèn: Nǐ xiànzài máng shénme ne?
刘主任：你现在 忙 什么 呢？

Lǐ yīshēng: Wǒ zhèngzài xiě bìnglì.
李医生：我 正在 写 病历。

Liú zhǔrèn: Wǒmen zhèngzài kāihuì, xiǎng kànkan wǔ chuáng bìngrén de bìnglì, nǐ néng zhǎodào ma?
刘主任：我们 正在 开会，想 看看 五 床 病人 的 病历，你 能 找到 吗？

Lǐ yīshēng: Wǒ zhǎo yíxià. Zhǎodào le, jiù zài Wáng yīshēng de zhuōzi shàng.
李医生：我 找 一下。找到 了，就在 王 医生 的 桌子 上。

Liú zhǔrèn: Wǒ zài huìyìshì, qǐng bāngmáng ná guòlai, xièxie.
刘主任：我在会议室，请 帮忙 拿过来，谢谢。

Lǐ yīshēng: Hǎo de, wǒ xiànzài gěi nín sòng guòqu.
李医生：好 的，我现在给您 送 过去。

(Liu Wen, the director of the surgical department, is calling up Wang Dong.)

Director Liu: This is Liu Wen. Is Dr. Wang Dong in the office?

Dr. Li: Hello, Director Liu, Dr. Wang is not in the office. He is performing the surgery.

Director Liu: When will he probably finish?

Dr. Li: Around eleven.

Director Liu: What are you busy with?

Dr. Li: I'm writing medical records.

Director Liu: We are having a meeting in the conference room and want to see the medical records of the patient of bed No.5. Can you find it?

Dr. Li: Let me try. I find it. It's on Dr. Wang's desk.

Director Liu: Please bring it over to us. Thank you.

Dr. Li: OK. I will take it to you right now.

生词 New words

1. 正在	zhèngzài	*adv.*	right in the middle of (doing sth.), in the process of
正	zhèng	*adv.*	right, just
在	zài	*adv.*	in the process of
2. 呢	ne	*part.*	used at the end of a statement to indicate an action or a situation is continuing
3. 左右	zuǒyòu	*n.*	around, about
4. 忙	máng	*v.*	to be busy with
5. 写病历	xiě bìnglì	*VO*	to write medical records
病历	bìnglì	*n.*	clinical case, medical records
6. 开会	kāihuì	*v.*	to have a meeting
7. 会议室	huìyìshì	*n.*	conference room

会议	huìyì	*n.*	conference
8. 帮忙	bāngmáng	*v.*	to help
9. 拿	ná	*v.*	to bring, to take
10. 送	sòng	*v.*	to give, to send
11. 过去	guòqu	*v.*	after a verb to indicate a motion away from the speaker

专名 Proper nouns

刘文	Liú Wén	a Chinese name

语言点 Language Points

一、固定结构"正在……（呢）" Fixed structure "正在……（呢）"

"正在……（呢）"表示动作行为的进行或者状态的持续。与它相似的语言形式还有"正……呢""在……呢""……呢"。例如：

"正在……(呢)" indicates the progress of the action or the continuity of the state. The structures similar to it include "正……呢" "在……呢" "……呢". For example:

1. 他正在做手术呢。
2. 我正写病历呢。
3. 我们在开会呢。
4. 你现在忙什么呢？

※ 练习：组词成句　Group words into sentences

1. 马大为　锻炼　呢　正在

______________________。

2. 做手术　正　王医生　呢

______________________________。

3. 妈妈　做饭　在　呢

______________________________。

4. 月亮　呢　买衣服

______________________________。

二、概数表达法（2）　Expressions for approximate number (2)

方位名词“左右”用在数量（名）结构后面表示概数，意思是比某一数量稍多或稍少。例如：

The locative noun “左右” is used after the numeral-measure word (noun) structure to indicate the approximate number, meaning that it is slightly more or less than a certain number. For example:

1. 刘主任：王医生大概什么时候做完手术？

   李医生：十一点左右。

2. A：你打算什么时候回国？

   B：明年五月左右。

3. 这件衣服八百块左右。

※ 练习：请用表达概数的“左右”完成对话　Please complete dialogues with “左右” to express the approximate number

1. A：昨天晚上你几点睡觉的？

   B：______________________________。

2. A：你们学校有多少个留学生？

   B：______________________________。

3. A：坐出租车去要多长时间？

B：________________________________。

4. A：在这家饭店吃饭一个人要多少钱？

B：________________________________。

三、复合趋向补语　Compound directional complement

由趋向动词"来""去"与其他趋向动词"上""下""进""出""回""起""过"合成的复合趋向动词，放在动词后补充说明动作的方向，这样的补语叫复合趋向补语。例如：

Compound directional verbs composed of directional verbs "来" and "去" with other directional verbs "上" "下" "进" "出" "回" "起" and "过" are placed after the verb to supplement the direction of the action. Such complements are called compound directional complements. For example:

1. 刘主任：请帮忙拿过来，谢谢。

   李医生：好的，我现在给您送过去。

2. 马大为的白大褂我给他拿回来了。

3. 金龙已经爬上去了。

如果动词所带的宾语是处所名词，那么要放在"来""去"的前面。例如：

If the object of the verb is a locative noun, it should be placed before "来" and "去". For example:

4. 他已经跑回宿舍去了。

5. 爸爸今天没开车，他是走回家来的。

如果动词所带的宾语是其他名词，那么放在"来""去"的前面或后面都可以。例如：

If the object of the verb is other kind of noun, it can be placed before or after "来" and "去". For example:

6. 哥哥买回来一个手机。/ 哥哥买回一个手机来。

※ 练习：组词成句　Group words into sentences

1. 带回来　美丽　一杯咖啡　给我

______________________________________。

2. 昨天　开　我没有　回来　车

______________________________________。

3. 哥哥的车　家　回　开　已经　了　来

______________________________________。

4. 伞　金龙　了　宿舍　回　拿　去

______________________________________。

综合练习 Comprehensive Exercises

一、根据拼音写汉字 Write Chinese characters according to Pinyin

1. bāngmáng__________　3. ná__________　5. zhèngzài__________

2. zuǒyòu__________　4. guòqu__________　6. sòng__________

二、辨字组词 Discriminate between Chinese characters and make words

1. 送________ 远________　2. 议________ 汉________　3. 正________ 五________　4. 拿________ 伞________

三、替换练习 Substitution drills

1. 他 正在 做手术 呢。

老师	上课
女儿	睡觉
我	和朋友说话

2. 王医生 十一点 左右 做完手术 。

我	二十一号	回国
你	一个星期	复查一次
我们	十号	放寒假

3. 我现在给您 送过去 。

带回来
放进去
找出来

四、选词填空 Use the following words to fill in the blanks

拿　帮忙　送　过去　正在

1. 你明天有空儿________我去上班吗？
2. 你去医院复查别忘了________病历。
3. 我________口腔医院挂号呢。
4. 谢谢你________照顾我家小孩儿。
5. 马大为的伞我给他带________吧。

五、用所给词语完成对话 Complete the dialogues with given words

1. 护士：请问您上次复查是什么时候？

 病人：________________________。（左右）

2. 朋友：我们去踢足球吧。

 金龙：________________________。（正在……呢）

3. 大为：下雨了，我没带伞。

 朋友：你在哪儿？________________________。（过去）

4. 医生：你头晕多长时间了？

 病人：________________________。（大概）

5. 朋友：________________________？（帮忙）

 吉米：不用，已经有人来照顾我了。我过两天就可以出院了。

六、根据课文内容回答问题 Answer the following questions according to the text

1. 王医生为什么不在办公室？
2. 王医生的手术什么时候结束？
3. 李医生现在在忙什么？
4. 刘主任为什么打这个电话？

七、根据课文内容填空 Fill in the blanks according to the text

刘主任打电话找王医生，可是王医生________做手术________，十一点________能做完。李医生________写病历。刘主任正在会议室________，想看看五床病人的病历。病历就在王医生的________上，李医生现在帮刘主任送________。

课文（二）
Text（II）

Jīn Lóng hé Měilì zài kàn shǒujī shàng de zhàopiàn.
（金龙和美丽在看手机上的照片。）

Měilì: Nǐ zài kàn shénme ne? Zhème gāoxìng.
美丽：你在看什么呢？这么高兴。

Jīn Lóng: Kàn shǒujī li cún de zhàopiàn.
金龙：看手机里存的照片。

Měilì: Shénme zhàopiàn? Ná guòlai wǒ yě kànkan. Zhè shì Wáng Chén zài tī qiú, hǎo shuài a!
美丽：什么照片？拿过来我也看看。这是王晨在踢球，好帅啊！

Jīn Lóng: Duì, tā tī de hěn hǎo.
金龙：对，他踢得很好。

Měilì: Zhè gè gèzi gāogāo de, shòushòu de nánháir shì shéi? Liǎn shàng quán shì dàngāo.
美丽：这个个子高高的、瘦瘦的男孩儿是谁？脸上全是蛋糕。

Jīn Lóng: Shì wǒ. Shàng gè xīngqīliù wǒ péngyou guò shēngrì, wǒmen yìqǐ chī wǎnfàn le.
金龙：是我。上个星期六我朋友过生日，我们一起吃晚饭了。

Měilì: Zhàopiàn shàng zěnme méiyǒu Mǎ Dàwéi? Tā méi qù ma?
美丽：照片上怎么没有马大为？他没去吗？

Jīn Lóng: Dāngrán qù le, kěshì tā hēzuì le, dāngshí zhèngzài shāfā shàng shuìjiào ne.
金龙：当然去了，可是他喝醉了，当时正在沙发上睡觉呢。

(Jin Long and Meili are looking at pictures in the cell phone.)

Meili: What are you looking at? Why so happy?

Jin Long: I'm looking at pictures saved in my cell phone.

Meili: What pictures? Pass me over. I also want to see. This is Wang Chen playing soccer. So amazing!

Jin Long: Yes. He plays very well.

Meili: Who is this tall and slim boy? There is cake cream all over his face.

Jin Long: It's me. Last Saturday, my friend celebrated his birthday and we had dinner together.

Meili: Why Ma Dawei is not in the picture? Didn't he go there?

Jin Long: Of course he went there. But he was drunk at that time and sleeping on the couch.

生词 New words

1. 存	cún	*v.*	to save
2. 照片	zhàopiàn	*n.*	picture, photo
3. 好	hǎo	*adv.*	very
4. 帅	shuài	*adj.*	handsome, amazing
5. 个子	gèzi	*n.*	height
6. 瘦	shòu	*adj.*	thin
7. 男孩儿	nánháir	*n.*	boy
8. 脸	liǎn	*n.*	face
9. 全	quán	*adv.*	all, whole
10. 蛋糕	dàngāo	*n.*	cake
11. 晚饭	wǎnfàn	*n.*	dinner
12. 醉	zuì	*v.*	to be drunk
13. 当时	dāngshí	*n.*	at that time, then
14. 沙发	shāfā	*n.*	couch

语言点 Language Points

一、副词“好” Adverb “好”

副词“好”用在形容词之前，表示程度深，多带有感叹语气，后面常常有语气词“啊”相呼应。例如：

The adverb “好” is used in front of an adjective to express a deep degree, usually with an exclamation tone, and often followed by the mood particle “啊”. For example:

1. 这是王晨在踢球，好帅啊！
2. 今天的作业好多啊！
3. 汉语课好难啊！

※ 练习：请用“好 + adj.”完成句子 Please complete sentences with “好 + adj.”

1. 今天 39 度，________________！
2. 我昨天去了学校附近的饭店，________________！
3. 寒假我和朋友去哈尔滨玩儿了，那儿________________！
4. 什么？一件衣服 5000 块钱，________________！

二、形容词重叠“AA”式 Adjective-reduplication “AA” type

在汉语中，部分单音节形容词可以重叠，表示程度深或者带有喜爱的感情色彩，其后常常加“的”。例如：

In Chinese, some monosyllabic adjectives can be reduplicated, expressing a deep degree, or a sentimental color of appreciation. It is often followed by “的”. For example:

1. 这个个子高高的、瘦瘦的男孩儿是谁？
2. 美丽的宿舍大大的，很漂亮。
3. 我现在想喝一杯热热的咖啡。

※ 练习：请用所给形容词的重叠式完成句子　Please complete sentences with the reduplication of the given adjectives

1. 你的脸 ______________________，是不是不舒服？（红）

2. 王晨是一个 ______________________ 的男孩儿。（高、帅）

3. 这件衣服 ______________________，是谁的？（小）

4. 月亮今天穿了一条 ______________________ 的裙子。（大）

三、副词"全"　Adverb "全"

副词"全"表示所有的都包括在内。例如：

The adverb "全" means all are included. For example:

1. 他的脸上全是蛋糕。

2. 我们学院的学生全都学习医学。

3. 昨天的手术，病人的家人全来了。

※ 练习：请用副词"全"和所给词语完成句子　Please use the adverb "全" and the given words to complete sentences

1. 参加篮球比赛的 ______________________________。（男孩子）

2. 金龙的同学 ______________________________。（外国留学生）

3. 这个寒假同学们 ______________________________。（回国）

4. 下（next）个星期 ______________________________。（考完）

综合练习 Comprehensive Exercises

一、根据拼音写汉字 Write Chinese characters according to Pinyin

1. dàngāo________　3. zuì________　5. zhàopiàn________

2. wǎnfàn________　4. dāngshí________　6. quán________

二、辨字组词 Discriminate between Chinese characters and make words

1. 沙________ 少________　2. 帅________ 师________　3. 全________ 会________　4. 醉________ 辣________

三、替换练习 Substitution drills

1. 王晨好帅啊！

医院里的人	多
刀口	疼
头	晕

2. 这个个子高高的、瘦瘦的男孩儿是谁？

凉凉的、绿绿的	东西	是什么
黑黑的、小小的	水果	叫什么
大大的、红红的	苹果	是在哪儿买的

3. 这个男孩儿脸上 全是 蛋糕 。

马大为手机里	朋友的照片
学校健身房里	人
这条路上	共享单车

四、选词填空 Use the following words to fill in the blanks

醉　全　瘦　高　帅

1. 你是不是喝________了？需要我送你回家吗？
2. 我女儿很________，这条裙子有没有小号的？
3. 爸爸的个子比我________一点儿。
4. 妈妈做的________是我爱吃的菜。
5. 打篮球的那个男孩儿你认识吗？好________啊！

五、用所给词语完成对话 Complete the dialogues with given words

1. 美丽：你觉得这件衣服怎么样？

   朋友：______________________________。（好 + adj.）

2. 朋友：______________________________？（形容词重叠"AA"式）

   大为：他是我的哥哥。

3. 朋友：你恢复得怎么样？

   病人：______________________________。（全）

4. 医生：你感觉头晕以后有没有量血压？

   病人：______________________________。（当时）

5. 妈妈：今天晚上出去吃饭别喝太多酒（jiǔ，wine）。

儿子：________________________。（醉）

六、根据课文内容回答问题 Answer the following questions according to the text

1. 金龙在看什么？
2. 照片里有谁？
3. 照片是什么时候拍（pāi，take a picture）的？
4. 马大为为什么没在照片里？

七、根据课文内容填空 Fill in the blanks according to the text

金龙正在看________呢，美丽也想看看。美丽觉得照片里正在踢球的王晨________！有一张（zhāng，a measure word）照片是________星期六金龙朋友过生日的时候拍（pāi）的，照片里金龙脸上________蛋糕。拍照片的时候马大为喝________了，________沙发上睡觉呢，所以照片里没有他。

语言任务 Language Tasks

一、阅读理解 Reading comprehension

王东医生正在医院二楼会议室开会。这时候，一个个子高高的、瘦瘦的男孩儿来医院找他，说有重要的东西要给王医生。医院的工作人员（gōngzuò rényuán，staff）告诉他，王东医生十二点半左右结束会议。如果着急（zháojí，worry）的话，工作人员可以帮忙把东西给王医生送过去。男孩儿想了想，决定（juédìng，decide）在会议室外面等王医生。工作人员让男孩儿坐在沙发上等。

读后判断 True or false

1. 王东医生正在做手术。 （ ）
2. 找王医生的男孩儿又高又瘦。 （ ）
3. 王医生十二点半左右结束会议。 （ ）
4. 工作人员可以帮忙把东西送到会议室里去。 （ ）
5. 男孩儿最后决定坐在沙发上等王医生。 （ ）

二、口头表达 Oral expression

任务名称：记录那一刻。

Task: Record that moment.

任务要求：1. 三个学生一组，每人携带至少两张生活照片（包含人物），并依次展示自己带来的照片。

2. 展示照片的学生可以简单介绍一下照片的拍摄背景，如拍摄时间、人物、地点、事件等，并回答他人的相关问题。

3. 选出自己最满意的一张照片，并说明原因。

Requirements: 1. Three students work in a group. Each student should carry at least two life photos (including people) to the class and show the photos in turn.

2. The student who shows the pictures can briefly introduce the background of the pictures, such as when, who, where and why the pictures are taken, and answer the relevant questions raised by others.

3. Choose the photo you are most satisfied with and explain why.

Reference words: 正在 大概 左右 是……的 拿 好（adv.） 当时

三、书面表达 Written expression

任务名称：小小病历，大大用途。

Task: Small medical record, great use.

任务要求：请和同学们讨论一下病历里应该包含哪些信息。

Requirement: Please discuss with your classmates about what information should be included in the medical record.

Reference words: 不但……而且……　个子　需要　注意　复查　按时　药

病历内容
1. 2. 3. 4. 5. ……

补充词汇 Supplementary Words

B chāo
B 超
B-ultrasound

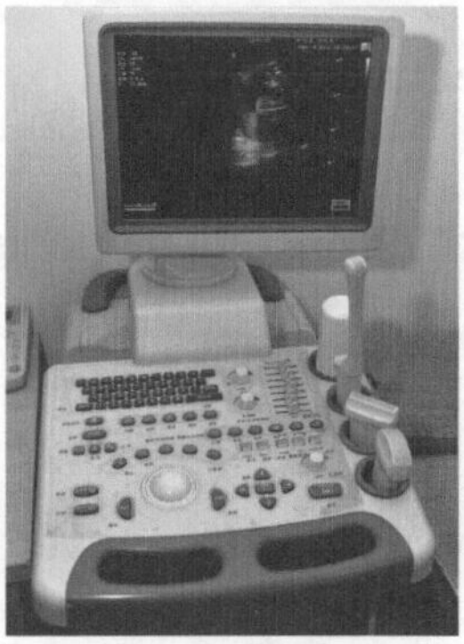

xiōngtòu
胸透
chest X-ray

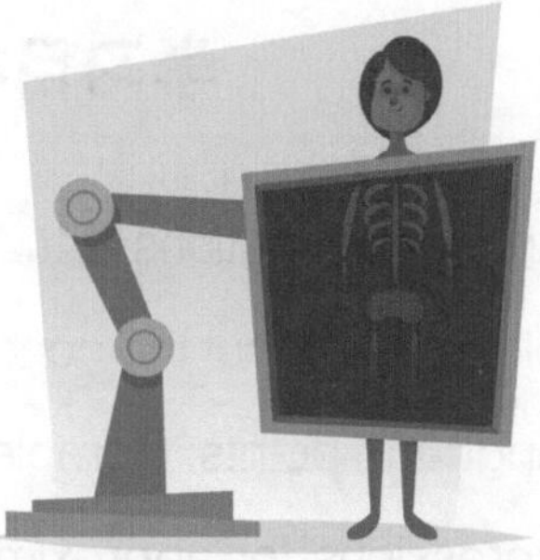

CT
CT
captive test

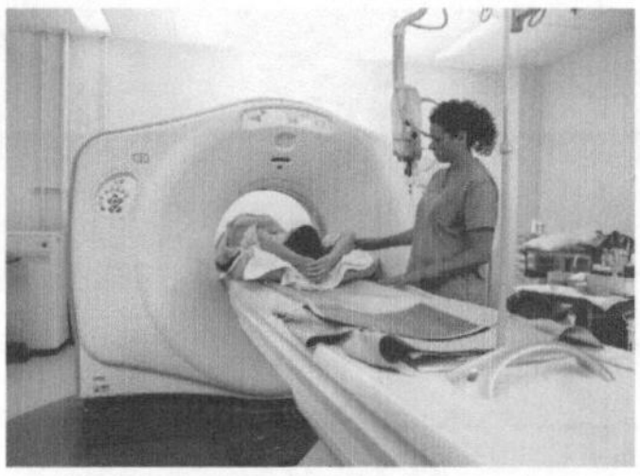

wèijìng
胃镜
gastroscope

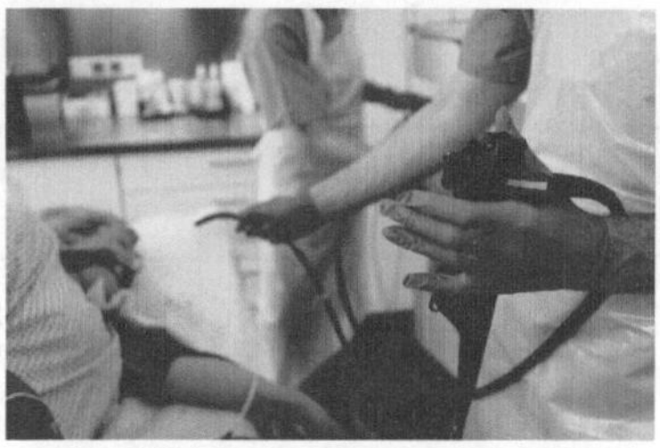

第十一课 Lesson 11

Tā yǐjīng dǎle wǔ tiān diàozhēn le

她已经打了五天 吊针 了

She has been put on drips for five days

学习目标 Learning Objectives

1. Language functions: Students can express their concern; students are able to ask about the condition; students are able to express their praise.
2. Language points: Complement of duration; Fixed structure “快……了”; Expressions for approximate number (3); Adverb “才” (1); Adverb “怪不得”.
3. Medical knowledge: Students are expected to know about the treatment and nursing of acute cholecystitis.
4. Social culture: Students are expected to learn about the way Chinese people express their praise.

热身活动 Warming-up

1. 你知道下面这个器官用汉语怎么说吗？它有什么作用？
Do you know the Chinese name of this organ? What is its function?

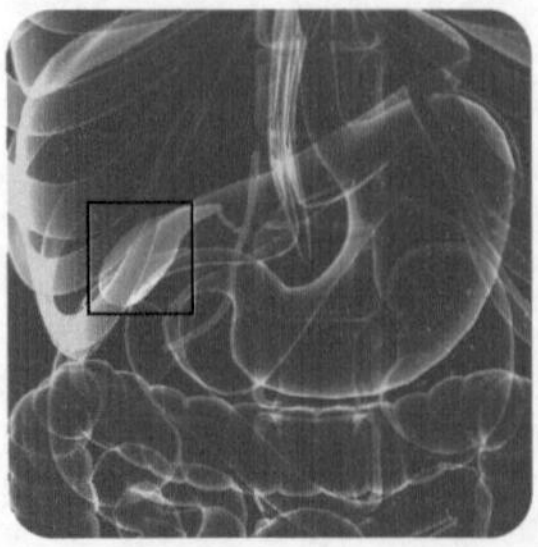

2. 请跟大家分享一下你认为有效的汉语学习方法。
Please share with us what you think is an effective way to learn Chinese.

课文（一）
Text（Ⅰ）

Lǎoshī hé Měilì zài liáo Yuèliang de qíngkuàng.
（老师 和 美丽 在 聊 月亮 的 情况。）

lǎoshī: Yuèliang zhè jǐ tiān zěnme yìzhí qǐngjià?
老师：月亮 这几天 怎么 一直 请假？

Měilì: Tā shēngbìng le, bìngle yí gè xīngqī le.
美丽：她 生病 了，病了一个星期了。

lǎoshī: Shénme bìng?
老师：什么 病？

Měilì: Tā déle jíxìng dǎnnángyán, měi tiān dōu yào qù yīyuàn dǎ diàozhēn.
美丽：她得了急性 胆囊炎，每 天 都 要 去医院 打 吊针。

lǎoshī: Xiànzài zěnmeyàng le?
老师：现在 怎么样 了？

Měilì: Tā yǐjīng dǎle wǔ tiān diàozhēn le, yīshēng shuō rúguǒ wǔ tiān hòu téngtòng hái bù huǎnjiě, jiù xūyào zuò shǒushù.
美丽：她已经打了五 天 吊针 了，医生 说 如果五天 后 疼痛 还不缓解，就需要做 手术。

lǎoshī: Zhème yánzhòng?
老师：这么 严重？

Měilì: Búguò, zuótiān tā shuō bú tài téng le, kuài hǎo le.
美丽：不过，昨天 她说 不太 疼 了，快 好 了。

lǎoshī: Xīwàng tā zǎorì kāngfù.
老师：希望 她早日康复。

(The teacher and Meili are talking about Yueliang.)

Teacher: Why does Yueliang always ask for leave these days?

Meili: She has been sick for a week.

Teacher: What's the matter?

Meili: She got acute cholecystitis and has to go to the hospital to have infusions everyday.

Teacher: How is she now?

Meili: She has been put on drips for five days. The doctor says if the pain isn't be relieved after five days, she needs to have an operation.

Teacher: Is that serious?

Meili: But yesterday, she said she didn't feel too painful and was about to recover.

Teacher: Wish she will get well soon.

生词 New words

1. 请假	qǐngjià	*v.*	to ask for leave
2. 得	dé	*v.*	to get, to have
3. 急性	jíxìng	*adj.*	acute
……性	…xìng	*suf.*	used to form mounds and adjectives
4. 胆囊炎	dǎnnángyán	*n.*	cholecystitis
胆囊	dǎnnáng	*n.*	cholecyst
5. 打吊针	dǎ diàozhēn	*VO*	to be put on a drip
吊针	diàozhēn	*n.*	infusion
6. 疼痛	téngtòng	*adj.*	painful
7. 缓解	huǎnjiě	*v.*	to relieve
8. 希望	xīwàng	*v.*	to hope, to wish
9. 早日	zǎorì	*adv.*	soon
10. 康复	kāngfù	*v.*	to recover

语言点 Language Points

一、时量补语 Complement of duration

时量补语用在动词后，补充说明动作持续的时间。如果动词后带宾语，时量补语一般放在动词和宾语中间，构成"V 了 + 时量补语 + O"的结构。如果宾语是人称代词，时量补语往往置于宾语之后。例如：

The complement of duration is used after the verb to supplement the duration of the action. If the verb is followed by an object, the complement of duration is usually placed between the verb and the object, forming the structure of "V 了 + complement of duration + O". If the object is a personal pronoun, the complement of duration is often placed after the object. For example:

1. 她已经打了五天吊针了。
2. 她生病了，病了一个星期了。
3. 马大为学了一年汉语了，现在汉语越说越好。
4. 我等了她一个小时。

※ 练习：组词成句 Group words into sentences

1. 我 一个小时 打了 篮球 了

______________________________。

2. 金龙 两个小时 锻炼 了

______________________________。

3. 王医生 七年 医学 学了

______________________________。

4. 马大为 等了 半天 王晨

______________________________。

二、固定结构“快……了” Fixed structure “快……了”

“快……了”表示动作行为或事件即将在较短时间内发生，中间可以是动词性成分，也可以是表示具体时间的名词性成分。例如：

“快……了” indicates that the action or event will occur in a short time. The part between “快” and “了” can be a verbal element or a nominal element that represents a specific time. For example:

1. 昨天她说不太疼了，快好了。
2. 我们快考完试了。
3. 同学们快放假了。
4. 快八点了，我们去教室吧。

※ 练习：请用固定结构“快……了”完成句子 Please complete sentences with the fixed structure “快……了”

1. ______________________________，我们去哈尔滨玩儿吧。
2. ______________________________，睡觉吧。
3. ______________________________，我们要好好儿准备。
4. ______________________________，我得复习。

综合练习 Comprehensive Exercises

一、根据拼音写汉字 Write Chinese characters according to Pinyin

1. huǎnjiě__________ 3. zǎorì__________ 5. xīwàng__________

2. qǐngjià__________ 4. kāngfù__________ 6. téngtòng__________

二、辨字组词 Discriminate between Chinese characters and make words

1. 康________ 瘦________
2. 胆________ 脸________
3. 吊________ 员________
4. 急________ 忘________

三、替换练习 Substitution drills

1. 她病了一个星期了。

忙	一天
找	一晚上
学	一上午

2. 她的病快好了。

我的作业	做完
暑假	结束
护士节	到

3. 如果五天后疼痛还不缓解，就需要做手术。

你不想去食堂吃饭	订外卖吧
你累了	在家好好儿休息吧
你不忙	写一下病历吧

四、选词填空 Use the following words to fill in the blanks

希望　得　疼痛　生病　康复

1. 医生说我________了阑尾炎。
2. 吃了药以后，________有没有缓解一点儿？
3. 我________早一点儿放假。
4. ________了要好好儿休息。
5. 祝你早日________！

五、用所给词语完成对话 Complete the dialogues with given words

1. 朋友：你最近怎么这么开心？

   美丽：________________________________。（快……了）

2. 医生：你头疼多久了？

   病人：________________________________。（V 了 + 时量补语）

3. 病人：放心吧，刀口已经不疼了。

   朋友：________________________________。（早日）

4. 病人：大夫，我怎么了？

   医生：________________________________。（得）

5. 朋友：你的阑尾炎好点儿了吗？

   病人：________________________________。（打吊针）

六、根据课文内容回答问题 Answer the following questions according to the text

1. 月亮最近为什么一直请假？
2. 月亮得了什么病？

3. 月亮需要做手术吗？

4. 月亮现在好点儿了吗？

七、根据课文内容填空 Fill in the blanks according to the text

月亮这几天一直______，她______了一个星期了。她______了急性胆囊炎，挺______的。她已经______了五天吊针了，医生说______五天后疼痛______不缓解，就需要做手术。老师______她早日康复。

课文（二）
Text（II）

Mǎ Dàwéi zài Wáng Chén jiā zuòkè.
（马大为在王晨家做客。）

Wáng Chén māma: Nǐ xué Hànyǔ xuéle duō cháng shíjiān le?
王晨妈妈：你学汉语学了多长时间了？

Mǎ Dàwéi: Wǒ shì cóng qùnián jiǔ yuè kāishǐ xué de, xuéle bàn nián duō le.
马大为：我是从去年九月开始学的，学了半年多了。

Wáng Chén māma: Cái bàn nián duō, shuō de zhème hǎo, nǐ zhēn cōngming! Hái yào xué duō jiǔ?
王晨妈妈：才半年多，说得这么好，你真聪明！还要学多久？

Mǎ Dàwéi: Hái yào xué yì nián duō.
马大为：还要学一年多。

Wáng Chén māma: Nǐ xǐhuan xuéxí Hànyǔ ma?
王晨妈妈：你喜欢学习汉语吗？

Mǎ Dàwéi: Tèbié xǐhuan. Wǒ yǐjīng rènshi sānbǎi duō gè Hànzì le. Suīrán yǒudiǎnr nán, dànshì hěn yǒu yìsi.
马大为：特别喜欢。我已经认识三百多个汉字了。虽然有点儿难，但是很有意思。

Wáng Chén māma: Nǐ jīngcháng shuō Hànyǔ ma?
王晨妈妈：你经常说汉语吗？

Mǎ Dàwéi: Duì, wǒ jiāole hěn duō Zhōngguó péngyou, hái jīngcháng gēn chūzūchē sījī liáotiānr.
马大为：对，我交了很多中国朋友，还经常跟出租车司机聊天儿。

Wáng Chén māma:　Guàibude nǐ de Hànyǔ shuō de zhème biāozhǔn.
王晨妈妈：怪不得你的汉语说得这么标准。

(Ma Dawei visits Wang Chen's home.)

Wang Chen's mother: Hong long have you been learning Chinese?

Ma Dawei: I started learning Chinese from last September and have been learning it for more than half a year.

Wang Chen's mother: Just in more than half a year can you speak Chinese so well. You are so smart! How long will you continue to learn Chinese?

Ma Dawei: More than one year.

Wang Chen's mother: Do you like learning Chinese?

Ma Dawei: Very much. I have known over three hundred Chinese characters. Although the language a little difficult, it's very interesting.

Wang Chen's mother: Do you often speak Chinese?

Ma Dawei: Yes, I make many Chinese friends and I also often chat with taxi drivers.

Wang Chen's mother: No wonder you speak Chinese so standardly!

生词 New words

1. 去年	qùnián	*n.*	last year
2. 开始	kāishǐ	*v.*	to start
3. 才	cái	*adv.*	just
4. 聪明	cōngming	*adj.*	smart
5. 久	jiǔ	*adj.*	long
6. 交朋友	jiāo péngyou	*VO*	to make friends with sb.
交	jiāo	*v.*	to associate with, to make friends with

7. 司机	sījī	*n.*	driver
8. 聊天儿	liáotiānr	*v.*	to chat
9. 怪不得	guàibude	*adv.*	no wonder
10. 标准	biāozhǔn	*adj.*	standard

语言点 Language Points

一、概数表达法（3） Expressions of approximate number (3)

"多"用在数量词后，表示不确定的零数。

"多" is used after a numeral measure word to indicate an uncertain fraction.

第一种结构是：数词 + 多 + 量词（+ 名词）。数词是十位以上的整数，"多"表示整位数以下的零数。例如：

The first structure is: numeral + 多 + measure word (+ noun). Numerals are integers with more than ten digits, and "多" refers to fractions of less than ten. For example:

1. 我已经认识三百多个汉字了。
2. 王晨的哥哥三十多岁。
3. 我们学院有三十多名教授。

第二种结构是：数词 + 量词 + 多（+ 名词）。数词是个位数或者带个位数的多位数，"多"表示个位数以下的零数。例如：

The second structure is: numeral + measure word + 多 (+ noun). Numerals are single digits or multi digits with single digits, and "多" represents fractions less than ten. For example:

4. 王医生做了两个多小时（xiǎoshí，hour）手术了。
5. 我学了四个多月汉语。

6. 这些水果三十一块多。

※ 练习：请用“多”完成句子　Please complete sentences with “多”

1. 我们是老朋友，认识二十 ______________________。
2. 星期天我们爬山爬了五 ______________________。
3. 我们医学院有六百 ______________________。
4. 我早上吃了两 ______________________。

二、副词“才”（1）　Adverb “才” (1)

副词“才”出现在表示数量、时间的词语之前，表示数量少或时间早。例如：

The adverb “才” is used before the words indicating quantity and time, indicating small quantity or early time. For example:

1. 才半年多，说得这么好，你真聪明！
2. 才六点他就到教室了。
3. 你今天怎么才吃了半碗米饭？

※ 练习：完成句子　Complete sentences

1. 这个手机才 _______________，很便宜。
2. 现在才 _______________，你别着急（zháojí，hurry）。
3. 我是今年开始学习汉语的，才 _______________。
4. 我们是新朋友，才 _______________。

三、副词“怪不得”　Adverb “怪不得”

副词“怪不得”表示突然醒悟，明白了原因，不再感到奇怪，前后常常有表明原因的语句。例如：

The adverb “怪不得” means that one suddenly wakes up, understands the reason, and no longer feels strange. There are often statements indicating reasons before or after the adverb. For example:

1. A：我交了很多中国朋友，还经常跟出租车司机聊天儿。

   B：怪不得你的汉语说得这么标准。

2. 王晨感冒了，怪不得他今天没来上课。

3. 他最近血压一直很高，怪不得他经常说头晕。

※ 练习：请用副词“怪不得”完成对话　Please complete dialogues with the adverb “怪不得”

1. A：老王生病了，在医院。

   B：________________________________。

2. A：王东的家离医院太远了！

   B：________________________________。

3. A：昨天晚上下雪了！

   B：________________________________。

4. A：马大为昨天晚上喝醉了。

   B：________________________________。

综合练习 Comprehensive Exercises

一、根据拼音写汉字 Write Chinese characters according to Pinyin

1. cōngming________　　3. liáotiānr________　　5. sījī________

2. biāozhǔn________　　4. kāishǐ________　　6. guàibude________

二、辨字组词 Discriminate between Chinese characters and make words

1. 标________ 杯________

2. 怪________ 恢________

3. 久________ 又________

4. 交________ 校________

三、替换练习 Substitution drills

1. 我 才 学了半年多汉语。

我们	认识一个星期
会议	开始十分钟
我昨晚	睡了四个小时（xiǎoshí，hour）

2. 我已经认识三百 多 个汉字 了。

他已经头晕一个	星期
他哥哥已经三十	岁
我已经喝了十	杯咖啡

3. 怪不得 你的汉语说得这么标准。

你找王医生做手术

好久没见到他了

你没有休息时间

四、选词填空 Use the following words to fill in the blanks

久　交　开始　才　聪明

1. 你还要在中国学习多______？
2. 这个孩子又______又漂亮。
3. 我已经______了三个中国朋友了。
4. 我做手术的刀口又______疼了。
5. 我______打了一天吊针，还要打三天呢。

五、用所给词语完成对话 Complete the dialogues with given words

1. 老师：你来中国多久了？

   大为：____________________。（才）

2. 朋友：____________________？（开始）

   美丽：我是去年开始学习汉语的。

3. 病人：我得了阑尾炎，刚做完手术。

   朋友：____________________。（怪不得）

4. 医生：你量血压了吗？

   病人：量了，高压____________________。（num. + 多）

5. 朋友：____________________？（标准）

   金龙：因为我每天和中国朋友聊天儿。

六、根据课文内容回答问题 Answer the following questions according to the text

1. 马大为是从什么时候开始学习汉语的？

2. 马大为的汉语怎么样？

3. 马大为喜欢学习汉语吗？

4. 马大为的汉语为什么说得很标准？

七、根据课文内容填空 Fill in the blanks according to the text

马大为学了________汉语了，他是从去年九月________学的，还要学习________。他特别喜欢学习汉语，现在已经认识________个汉字了。他觉得汉语________有点儿难，________很有意思。他________了很多中国朋友，还经常和出租车________一起________。

语言任务 Language Tasks

一、阅读理解 Reading comprehension

急性胆囊炎是一种常见的急性消化道疾病（xiāohuàdào jíbìng，digestive tract disease）。发病（fābìng，attack）的时候会感到腹痛、恶心（ěxin，nausea）、呕吐，还可能会发烧（fāshāo，have a fever）。出现了这样的情况（qíngkuàng，situation），要马上去医院看医生。病人情况如果严重的话，就需要做手术。

急性胆囊炎病人要注意平时（píngshí，in normal times）多吃水果、蔬菜（shūcài，vegetable），少吃油腻（yóunì，oily）的食物；多运动，少生气（shēngqì，get angry）。

读后判断 True or false

1. 急性胆囊炎是消化道疾病。 （ ）

2. 得了急性胆囊炎可能会感到恶心、呕吐。 (　　)

3. 急性胆囊炎病人不需要做手术。 (　　)

4. 急性胆囊炎病人不能吃油腻的食物。 (　　)

5. 得了急性胆囊炎，平时应该多锻炼身体。 (　　)

二、口头表达 Oral expression

任务名称：看望病人。

Task: Visiting a patient.

任务要求：1. 两个学生一组，一个是急性胆囊炎病人，一个是看望病人的朋友。

2. 朋友询问病人的病情。

3. 朋友表达对病人的关心。

Requirements: 1. Two students work in a group. One acts as a patient with acute cholecystitis, and the other as a friend who visits the patient.

2.The friend inquires about the patient's condition.

3.The friend expresses his/her concern for the patient.

Reference words: 刀口　恢复　有点儿　注意　疼　腹痛　呕吐　要是……就……　不能　手术　久　开始　得　生病　急性胆囊炎　早日　康复

三、书面表达 Written expression

任务名称：比一比谁说的话好听。

Task: Compare whose expression sounds nicer.

任务要求：通过讨论、查词典，收集表示赞扬的句子并列在下面的表格中。

Requirement: Discussing with your classmates and looking up the dictionary to collect sentences expressing praise, and list them in the following table.

Reference words: 聪明　标准　好　棒　好（*adv.*）　帅　漂亮　水平　高　有意思

表达赞扬的句子 Sentences expressing praise
1. 2. 3. 4. 5. ……

补充词汇 Supplementary Words

pínèi zhùshè
皮内注射
intradermal injection

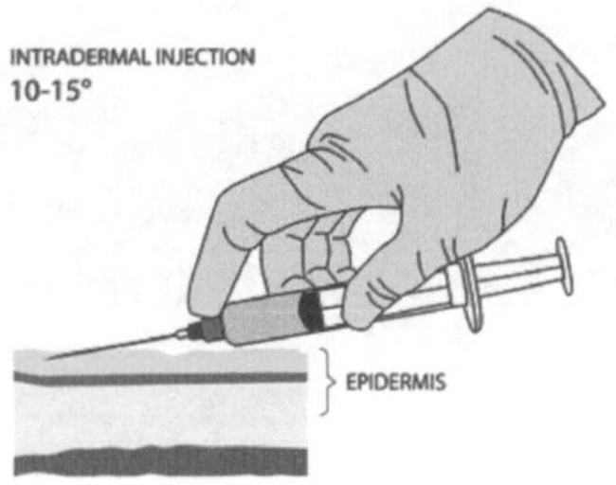

píxià zhùshè
皮下注射
subcutaneous injection

jīròu zhùshè
肌肉注射
intramuscular injection

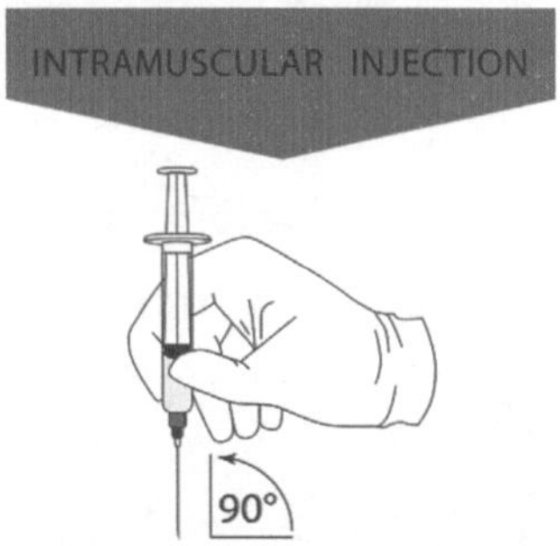

jìngmài zhùshè
静脉注射
intravenous injection

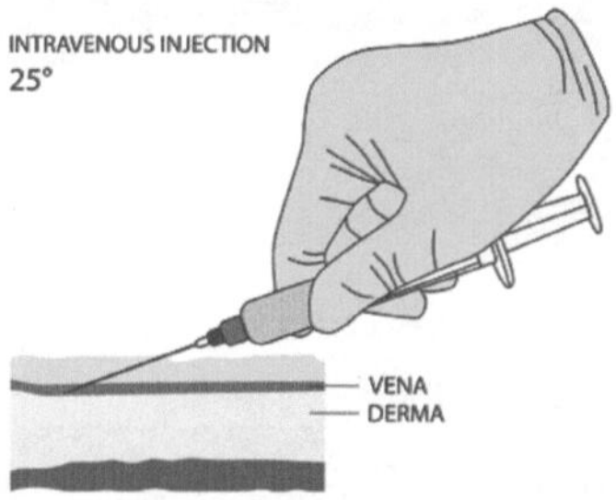

第十二课 Lesson 12

Tā zuòguo liǎng cì shǒushù le

他做过两次手术了

He had two operations

学习目标 Learning Objectives

1. Language functions: Students can explain reasons; students are able to describe the specific situation.
2. Language points: Verbal structure used as attributive; Verb "对了"; Verbal phrase "不到"; Verbal quantification complement; Adverb "又"; Modal verb "应该" (1); Aspectual particle "着" (1).
3. Medical knowledge: Students are expected to understand the precautions after intestinal polyp operation.
4. Social culture: Students are expected to have a brief knowledge of the tourism resources in Xinjiang, China.

热身活动 Warming-up

1. 在你的家乡，有什么常见的水果？

What common fruits are there in your hometown?

2. 你知道肠息肉手术吗？

Do you know the operation for intestinal polyps?

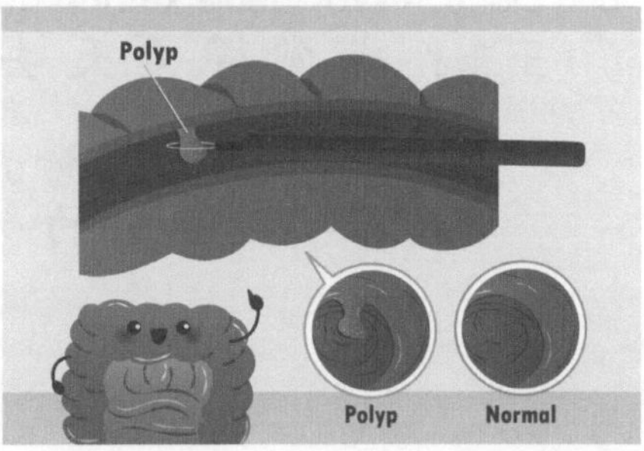

课文（一）
Text（I）

Wáng Dōng hé tóngshì zài bàngōngshì liáotiānr.
（王 东 和 同事 在 办公室 聊天儿。）

Lǐ yīshēng: Wáng yīshēng, zhè shì wǒ zài wǎng shang mǎi de Xīnjiāng pútao.
李医生：王 医生，这是我在网 上 买的新疆 葡萄。

Nǐ cháng yíxià, tèbié tián.
你尝 一下，特别甜。

Wáng Dōng: Xièxie, zhēn tián. Duìle, nǐ qùguo Xīnjiāng ma?
王东：谢谢，真 甜。对了，你去过 新疆 吗？

Lǐ yīshēng: Méi qùguo, tài yuǎn le.
李医生：没 去过，太 远 了。

Wáng Dōng: Zuò fēijī bú dào wǔ gè xiǎoshí, tǐng fāngbiàn de.
王东：坐飞机不到 五 个 小时，挺 方便 的。

Lǐ yīshēng: Nǐ qùguo ma?
李医生：你去过吗？

Wáng Dōng: Wǒ qùguo sān cì le. Nàlǐ tài měi le, nǐ yídìng yào qù kànkan.
王东：我 去过 三 次了。那里太美了，你一定要 去看看。

Lǐ yīshēng: Shénme jìjié qù zuì hǎo?
李医生：什么 季节去最好？

Wáng Dōng: Wǒ juéde xiàtiān qù zuì hǎo, búdàn jǐngsè piàoliang, érqiě yǒu hěn duō hǎochī de shuǐguǒ.
王东：我觉得夏天去最好，不但景色 漂亮，而且有很 多 好吃的 水果。

(Wang Dong and his colleague are chatting in the office.)

Dr. Li: Dr. Wang, this is the Xinjiang grape that I bought online. Have a taste. It's very sweet.

Wang Dong: Thanks. Really sweet. By the way, have you been to Xinjiang?

Dr. Li: No. It's too far.

Wang Dong: It takes less than five hours by plane. It's pretty convenient.

Dr. Li: Have you been there?

Wang Dong: I have been there three times. There is so beautiful. You must have a look.

Dr. Li: Which season is the best for visiting Xinjiang?

Wang Dong: I think summer is the best. Besides the beautiful scenery, there are also many delicious fruits there in summer.

生词 New words

1. 网上	wǎng shang		online
2. 葡萄	pútao	*n.*	grape
3. 尝	cháng	*v.*	to taste
4. 甜	tián	*adj.*	sweet
5. 对了	duìle	*v.*	by the way
6. 飞机	fēijī	*n.*	aircraft, plane
7. 不到	bú dào	*VP*	less than
8. 小时	xiǎoshí	*n.*	hour
9. 美	měi	*adj.*	beautiful
10. 景色	jǐngsè	*n.*	scenery

专名 Proper noun

新疆	Xīnjiāng	a provincial administrative region in China

语言点 Language Points

一、动词性结构做定语　Verbal structure used as attributive

在汉语中，有些动词、动词性短语、主谓短语可以做定语。例如：

In Chinese, some verbs, verbal phrases and subject predicate phrases can be used as attributives. For example:

1. 这是我在网上买的新疆葡萄。
2. 金龙写的汉字很好看。
3. 这是爸爸给我买的手机。

※ 练习：选词填空　Choose words to fill in blanks

说的汉语　买的手机　过生日的照片　做手术的刀口

1. 爷爷 ________________ 很小，不太疼，别担心。
2. 马大为 ________________ 很标准。
3. 快来看，这些是王晨 ________________。
4. 月亮 ________________ 是红色的。

二、动词“对了”　Verb “对了”

动词“对了”用于句首，常表示突然想起某事。例如：

The verb “对了” is used at the beginning of a sentence. It often indicates that something suddenly comes one's mind. For example:

1. 谢谢，真甜。对了，你去过新疆吗？
2. 周末我们去踢足球吧。对了，马大为去不去？
3. 今天没有作业，太好了！对了，你知道明天汉语老师调课了吗？

※ 练习：请用动词“对了”完成句子　Please complete sentences with the verb “对了”

1. 下个星期我们放假。对了，________________?

2. 我牙疼，想去口腔医院看看。对了，________________?

3. 马大为不在宿舍。对了，________________?

4. 咱们去上课吧。对了，________________?

三、动词性短语“不到”　Verbal phrase “不到”

“不到”后加数量词时，表示少于、不足。例如：

“不到” is followed by the numeral-measure word, it means less than or insufficient. For example:

1. 坐飞机不到五个小时，挺方便的。

2. 金龙学汉语不到一年，可是汉语说得真不错。

3. 这件衣服不到 200 块，很便宜。

※ 练习：请用动词性短语“不到”完成句子　Please complete sentences with the verbal phrase “不到”

1. 我认识的汉字不太多，________________。

2. 昨天的手术做得很快，________________。

3. 图书馆离这儿不远，________________。

4. 我订的外卖不贵，________________。

四、动量补语　Verbal quantification complement

动量补语用在动词后，可以补充说明动作进行的次数。如果动词后带宾语，动量补语一般放在动词和宾语中间，构成“V 过 + 动量补语 + O”的结构。如果宾语是人称代词，动量补语往往置于宾语之后。例如：

The verbal quantification complement is used after the verb to supplement the frequency of the action. If the verb is followed by an object, the verbal quantification complement is usually placed between the verb and the object, forming the structure of "V 过 + verbal quantification complement + O". If the object is a personal pronoun, the verbal quantification complement is often placed after the object. For example:

1. 我去过三次了。
2. 金龙的爸爸去过两次北京。
3. 我很喜欢这个电影，看过三次。
4. 我见过她三次。

※ 练习：选出下列词语在句子中的位置　Choose the correct position of the following words in the sentences

1. 上个星期 A，B 我 C 去了 D 新疆。　（一次）
2. 马大为 A 昨天 B 订了 C 外卖 D。　（两次）
3. 美丽的牙套需要 A 调整，B 今天 C 要去 D 口腔医院。　（一次）
4. 我 A 太喜欢 B 哈尔滨了，已经 C 去过 D 了。　（三次）

综合练习 Comprehensive Exercises

一、根据拼音写汉字 Write Chinese characters according to Pinyin

1. pútao________　3. fēijī________　5. měi________
2. cháng________　4. xiǎoshí________　6. jǐngsè________

二、辨字组词 Discriminate between Chinese characters and make words

1. 尝________ 常________
2. 甜________ 话________
3. 机________ 几________
4. 景________ 影________

三、替换练习 Substitution drills

1. 这是<u>我在网上买的</u><u>新疆葡萄</u>。

马大为推荐的	外卖店
美丽打算去的	地方
姐姐做的	宫保鸡丁

2. <u>坐飞机</u>不到<u>五个小时</u>。

骑车	半个小时
这件衣服	两百块钱
我们学院的留学生	三百个

3. 我<u>去</u>过<u>三次北京</u>了。

看	两次电影
吃	一次烤鸭
参加	两次篮球比赛

四、选词填空 Use the following words to fill in the blanks

网上　尝　对了　不到　景色

1. 你做完手术还________三天，不能出院。
2. 你的手机真漂亮！________，我也买了一个新手机。
3. ________说得了急性胆囊炎可能会腹痛和呕吐。
4. 我已经________过了，这个菜真的很辣。
5. 冬天的哈尔滨________真是太美了！

五、用所给词语完成对话 Complete the dialogues with given words

1. 儿子：妈妈，这葡萄真甜，你从哪儿买的？

   妈妈：________________________________。（是……的）

2. 同学：我想去哈尔滨玩儿，什么时候去最好？

   美丽：冬天，__________________________。（不但……而且……）

3. 朋友：我要去买点儿东西，你去吗？

   大为：我昨天去了。______________________。（对了）

4. 家属：________________________________？（次）

   医生：一天三次，我已经告诉你丈夫了。

5. 家属：请问这个手术要做多长时间啊？

   护士：这是个小手术，_____________________。（不到）

六、根据课文内容回答问题 Answer the following questions according to the text

1. 李医生在哪儿买的葡萄？
2. 坐飞机到新疆需要多长时间？
3. 王东去过新疆吗？那儿怎么样？
4. 什么季节去新疆最好？为什么？

七、根据课文内容填空 Fill in the blanks according to the text

李医生在_______买的_______特别_______，王东问他_______新疆吗，他说没有，因为______。王东说坐飞机______五个小时，______方便的。王东去过______了，那里太______了，让李医生一定要去看看。李医生想知道______季节去最好，王东觉得______最好，不但______漂亮，而且有很多______的水果。

课文（二）
Text（II）

Wàikē zhǔrèn hé Wáng Dōng zài cháfáng.
（外科 主任 和 王 东 在 查房。）

wàikē zhǔrèn: Bìngrén shénme qíngkuàng?
外科主任： 病人 什么 情况？

Wáng Dōng: Chángxīròu, zuótiān xiàwǔ zuò de shǒushù.
王东： 肠息肉，昨天 下午 做的 手术。

bìngrén: Wǒ yǐqián yě zuòguo liǎng cì chángxīròu shǒushù.
病人： 我 以前也 做过 两 次 肠息肉 手术。

wàikē zhǔrèn: Shì bu shì xīròu yòu zhǎng chūlai le?
外科主任： 是不是息肉又 长 出来了？

bìngrén: Shì.
病人： 是。

wàikē zhǔrèn: Jiǎnchá de jiéguǒ zěnmeyàng?
外科主任： 检查 的结果 怎么样？

Wáng Dōng: Xīròu tǐng duō, yǒu jǐ kē bǐjiào dà, yǐjīng qiēchú le.
王东： 息肉挺 多，有几颗比较大，已经 切除了。

wàikē zhǔrèn: Yīnggāi dǎ jǐ tiān xiāoyánzhēn. Kāi le ma?
外科主任： 应该 打几天 消炎针。开 了 吗？

Wáng Dōng: Zhèng dǎzhe ne.
王东： 正 打着 呢。

(The director of the surgical department and Wang Dong are making the rounds of the wards.)

Director: What's the matter with the patient?

Wang Dong: Intestinal polyps. He had the operation yesterday afternoon.

Patient: I have had intestinal polyps operation for two times.

Director: Did the polyps grow again?

Patient: Yes.

Director: How about the result of the examination?

Wang Dong: The polyps are pretty many. And some that are quite big have been removed.

Director: He should have antiphlogistic injections for several days. Have you prescribed?

Wang Dong: He is having the injection.

生词 New words

1. 情况	qíngkuàng	*n.*	matter, situation
2. 肠息肉	chángxīròu	*n.*	intestinal polyps
息肉	xīròu	*n.*	polyp
3. 长	zhǎng	*v.*	to grow, to come into being
4. 出来	chūlai	*v.*	to come out
5. 检查	jiǎnchá	*v.*	to test, to check
6. 结果	jiéguǒ	*n.*	result
7. 颗	kē	*m.*	usually used for sth. small and roundish
8. 比较	bǐjiào	*adv.*	pretty
9. 切除	qiēchú	*v.*	to cut off
10. 应该	yīnggāi	*mod.v.*	should
11. 打针	dǎzhēn	*v.*	to have an injection
12. 消炎针	xiāoyánzhēn	*n.*	antiphlogistic injection
消炎	xiāoyán	*v.*	to diminish inflammation

13. 开	kāi	*v.*	to prescribe
14. 着	zhe	*part.*	aspectual particle added to a verb or an adjective to indicate a continued action or state, often with the particle “呢” at the end of the sentence

语言点 Language Points

一、副词“又” Adverb “又”

副词“又”表示同一个动作行为重复发生，一般用于已经发生的事情。例如：

The adverb “又” refers to the repetition of the same action, which is usually used to describe things that have already happened. For example:

1. 是不是息肉又长出来了？
2. 她的牙又疼了！
3. 昨天早上美丽又去口腔医院了。

又 VS 再

“又”和“再”都是副词，都表示动作行为的重复，但是“又”一般用于已经发生的事情，“再”一般用于尚未发生的事情。

“又” and “再” are adverbs, both of which indicate the repetition of actions, but “又” is usually used to describe things that have already happened, and “再” is usually used to describe things that have not yet happened.

※ 练习：请选择“再”或“又”填空　Please select “再” or “又” to fill in the blanks

1. 马大为现在不在宿舍，你下午______来吧。

2. 昨天下雪了，今天______下雪了。

3. 新疆的葡萄很好吃，我今天______买了一点儿。

4. 哈尔滨太漂亮了，我打算明年______去一次。

二、能愿动词“应该”（1） Modal verb “应该” (1)

能愿动词“应该”表示需要做某事，后面一般加动词性成分。例如：

The modal verb “应该” indicates that something needed to be done, usually followed by a verbal component. For example:

1. 病人应该打几天消炎针。
2. 你感冒了，应该好好儿休息。
3. 美丽，你的牙套应该调整了。

※ 练习：请用能愿动词“应该”完成句子　Please complete sentences with the modal verb “应该”

1. 下雪了，______________________________。
2. 快考试了，____________________________。
3. 星期六有比赛，________________________。
4. 都七点五十了，________________________。

三、动态助词“着”（1） Aspectual particle “着” (1)

“着”用在动词后，表示动作正在进行或者状态正在持续。例如：

“着” is used after the verb to indicate that the action is in progress or the state is continuing. For example:

1. 正打着（消炎针）呢。
2. A：马大为，你在哪儿？

   B：我正爬着山呢。
3. 这位穿着白大褂的教授是我们的生理学老师。

※ 练习：请用动态助词“着”完成对话　Please complete dialogues with the aspectual particle “着”

1. A：你们学完生理学了吗？

B：________________________________。

2. A：你今天量血压了吗？

B：________________________________。

3. A：你现在去体育馆锻炼吗？

B：________________________________。

4. A：王医生怎么不在办公室？

B：________________________________。

综合练习 Comprehensive Exercises

一、根据拼音写汉字 Write Chinese characters according to Pinyin

1. qíngkuàng__________　3. jiǎnchá__________　5. bǐjiào__________

2. zhǎng__________　4. jiéguǒ__________　6. yīnggāi__________

二、辨字组词 Discriminate between Chinese characters and make words

1. 情________ 晴________
2. 结________ 给________
3. 较________ 校________
4. 该________ 刻________

三、替换练习 Substitution drills

1. 是不是<u>息肉</u>又<u>长出来了</u>？

头	晕
刀口	疼
马大为	找不到教室了

2. 你应该<u>打几天消炎针</u>。

按时吃药
早点儿回家
多交朋友

3. <u>病人</u>正<u>打</u>着<u>消炎针</u>呢。

我	打	吊针
王医生	做	手术
汉语老师	上	课

四、选词填空 Use the following words to fill in the blanks

应该　又　结果　比较　着

1. 下午病人_______呕吐了两次。

2. 都晚上十一点了，孩子们_______睡了吧？

3. 你的肠息肉有几颗______大，最好（had better）做手术切除。

4. 检查的______不太好。

5. 我正吃______饭呢，你有什么事儿啊？

五、用所给词语完成对话 Complete the dialogues with given words

1. 妈妈：______________。（应该）

   孩子：我已经写完作业了。

2. 同学：______________？（出来）

   美丽：还没有，下周才能知道。

3. 医生：你不是上周刚出院吗？

   病人：______________。（又）

4. A：这几条裙子哪条好看？

   B：______________。（比较）

5. 病人：请问，王医生在吗？

   护士：不在，______________。（着）

六、根据课文内容回答问题 Answer the following questions according to the text

1. 病人什么情况？
2. 病人以前做过肠息肉手术吗？做过几次？
3. 病人的检查结果怎么样？
4. 病人正在做什么？

七、根据课文内容填空 Fill in the blanks according to the text

外科主任问病人的______怎么样，王东说是______，昨天下午________。病人说他________做过________手术，可是息肉________出来了。病人检查的________是息肉挺多，有几________比较大，已经________了。主任说________打几天消炎针，王东已经给他开了，________呢。

语言任务 Language Tasks

一、阅读理解 Reading comprehension

做完肠息肉手术要注意什么？第一，手术后一段时间内（nèi，within）不能吃饭和喝水。医生同意（tóngyì，agree）病人吃饭以后，可以吃一些鸡蛋、青菜等容易（róngyì，easy）消化的食物，也可以吃苹果等水果，但最好不要喝牛奶，更不能吃辣的和喝酒。第二，手术后一周内不能活动，要多休息，注意伤口，按时吃药和打针。第三，肠息肉切除后，两到四周内要注意避免（bìmiǎn，avoid）过度（guòdù，excessive）的活动。术后一般不会复发（fùfā，recur），恢复期间也要定期去医院做复查。此外，做过肠息肉手术以后，每年要复查一次肠镜（chángjìng，colonoscopy），来观察（guānchá，observe）息肉有没有复发。

读后判断 True or false

1. 肠息肉手术以后可以吃饭。（ ）
2. 肠息肉手术以后不能吃鸡蛋。（ ）
3. 做完肠息肉手术还需要打针。（ ）
4. 做完肠息肉手术不能跑步。（ ）

5. 做完肠息肉手术以后不需要复查。 (　　)

二、口头表达 Oral expression

任务名称：肠息肉手术后需要注意的问题。

Task: Problems needed to notice after the intestinal polyp surgery.

任务要求：1. 两个学生一组，一个扮演刚做完肠息肉切除手术的病人，一个扮演护士。

2. 病人询问护士需要注意哪些问题。

3. 护士告诉病人手术后需要注意的问题。

Requirements: 1. Two students work in a group. One acts as a patient who has just had an intestinal polypectomy, and the other as a nurse.

2. The patient asks the nurse what should pay attention to after the surgery.

3. The nurse tells the patient what to pay attention to after the surgery.

Reference words: 准备　以后　能 / 不能　不用　又　切除　按时　药　打针　消炎　复查

三、书面表达 Written expression

任务名称：你去过哪儿？

Task: Where have you been?

任务要求：三个学生一组讨论自己去过哪些地方旅行、什么时候去的、怎么去的、那儿怎么样等，然后根据讨论内容完成下列表格。

Requirement: Three students work in a group to discuss where you have visited, when and how you went there, and how is there, and then complete the following table according to the discussion.

Reference words: V + 过　次　季节　飞机　方便　不到　景色　不但……而且……

去过哪儿 （几次）	什么时候 去的	怎么去的	景色怎么样	……

补充词汇 Supplementary Words

zhuāfàn
抓饭
Xinjiang Rice

náng
馕
nang

yángròuchuànr
羊肉串儿
mutton shashlik

hāmìguā
哈密瓜
Hami melon

第十三课
Lesson 13

Qǐng bǎ hūjiàolíng guānshang
请 把呼叫铃 关上
Please turn off the call bell

学习目标 Learning Objectives

1. Language functions: Students can ask various questions; students can express how to prevent somebody from doing something.
2. Language points: 把-sentence (1); Conjunction “那”; Adverb “还” (2); Numeral-measure word “一会儿” (1); Numeral-measure word “一会儿” (2); Subject-predicate predicate sentence; Adverb “还是” (1).

热身活动 Warming-up

1. 我们在哪儿会看到这个？它有什么作用？

Where can we see this gadget? What is its function?

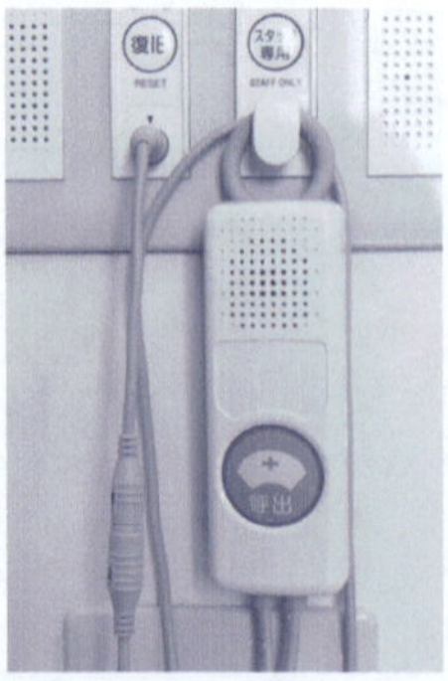

2. 如果一天不用手机，你的生活会有哪些不便？

What inconveniences will you meet if you don’t use your mobile phone for one day?

课文（一）
Text（I）

Hùshi zài jiāojiē bān cháfáng.
（护士 在 交 接班 查房。）

hùshi: Qǐng dàjiā bǎ chuānghu dǎkāi, bǎ zhuōzi shàng de dōngxi shōushi gānjìng.
护士：请 大家把 窗户 打开，把桌子 上 的东西 收拾 干净。

bìngrén 1: Hǎo de. Qǐngwèn jīntiān shì nǎ wèi yīshēng cháfáng, Zhāng yīshēng háishi Wáng yīshēng?
病人1：好 的。请问 今天是哪位 医生 查房， 张 医生 还是 王 医生？

hùshi: Zhāng yīshēng. Èr chuáng qǐng bǎ hūjiàolíng guānshang, búyào suíbiàn àn.
护士：张 医生。二 床 请把呼叫铃 关上，不要 随便 按。

bìngrén 2: Bù hǎoyìsi, gāngcái bù xiǎoxīn pèngle tā yíxià.
病人2：不好意思，刚才不小心 碰了它一下。

bìngrén 3: Hùshi, qǐngwèn jīntiān wǒ shénme shíhou kěyǐ chūyuàn?
病人3：护士，请问 今天 我 什么 时候可以出院？

hùshi: Nǐ xiān bǎ dōngxi shōushi hǎo, yīshēng cháfáng de shíhou huì gàosu nǐ chūyuàn shíjiān.
护士：你先 把东西 收拾 好， 医生 查房 的 时候 会 告诉你 出院 时间。

bìngrén 3: Nà jīntiān zǎoshang wǒ hái xūyào dǎzhēn ma?
病人3：那今天 早上 我还需要 打针 吗？

hùshi: Wǒ yíhuìr qù hùshizhàn kàn yíxià.
护士：我一会儿去护士站 看一下。

bìngrén 3:　Hǎo de,　xièxie nín.
病人 3：好 的，谢谢您。

(The nurse is making the rounds of the wards for shift change.)

Nurse: Please open the windows and tide up the desks.

Patient 1: OK. Could you please tell me which doctor will make the rounds of the wards today, Dr. Zhang or Dr. Wang?

Nurse: Dr. Zhang. Bed No.2, please turn off the call bell and don't press it at random.

Patient 2: Sorry. I just by accident hit it.

Patient 3: Miss, when shall I be discharged from hospital today?

Nurse: You pack up first. When the doctor makes the rounds of the wards, he will tell you the time.

Patient 3: Then, do I need to have injections this morning?

Nurse: I will go to check at the nurse station after a while.

Patient 3: OK, thank you.

生词 New words

1. 把	bǎ	*prep.*	used to shift the object ahead of the verb, which must be reduplicated or accompanied by some other word or expression
2. 窗户	chuānghu	*n.*	window
3. 打开	dǎkāi	*v.*	to open
4. 收拾	shōushi	*v.*	to tide up
5. 干净	gānjìng	*adj.*	clean
6. 查房	cháfáng	*v.*	to make the rounds of the wards
7. 呼叫铃	hūjiàolíng	*n.*	call bell
8. 关	guān	*v.*	to turn off, to close

9. 上	shàng	*v.*	used after a verb to indicate the result of an action
10. 随便	suíbiàn	*adj.*	random
11. 按	àn	*v.*	to press
12. 不小心	bù xiǎoxīn	*AP*	careless, by accident
小心	xiǎoxīn	*adj.*	careful
13. 碰	pèng	*v.*	to hit, to touch, to bump
14. 它	tā	*pron.*	it
15. 那	nà	*conj.*	then
16. 一会儿	yíhuìr	*num.-m.*	a little while
17. 护士站	hùshizhàn	*n.*	nurse station

专名 Proper nouns

张	Zhāng	a Chinese surname

语言点 Language Points

一、"把"字句（1） 把-sentence (1)

"把"字句是汉语特有的句式。它表示主语对宾语施加某一动作行为，致使宾语发生了变化。

把-sentence is a special sentence pattern in Chinese. It indicates that the subject changes the object by applying an action on the object.

该句式的基本结构是：主语＋把＋宾语＋动词＋其他成分。这里的"其他成分"可以是结果补语。例如：

The basic structure of this sentence pattern is: subject + 把 + object + verb + other component. The "other component" here can be the resultative complement. For example:

1. 请大家把窗户打开，把桌子上的东西收拾干净。

2. 二床请把呼叫铃关上。

3. 你先把东西收拾好。

如果句中有否定词或能愿动词，必须把它们放在"把"的前面。例如：

If there is a negative word or modal verb in the sentence, it must be put before "把". For example:

4. 我没有把门关上。

5. 请不要把呼叫铃打开。

6. 你应该先把号挂上。

※ 练习：组词成句 Group words into sentences

1. 我的房间 把 收拾干净了 妈妈

________________________________。

2. 我 做完了 把 今天的作业

________________________________。

3. 金龙 看完 把 那本书 没

________________________________。

4. 应该 把 病历 你 带过来

________________________________。

二、连词"那" Conjunction "那"

连词"那"表示顺着上文的语意，引出应有的结果或做出判断，相当于"那么"。这里的"上文"通常指对话或自己提出的问题或假设。例如：

The conjunction "那" indicates to introduce the expected result or make a judgment according to the meaning of the above text, which is equivalent to "那么". The "above text" here usually refers to the dialogue or the questions or assumptions raised by the speaker himself/herself. For example:

1. A：你先把东西收拾好，医生查房的时候会告诉你出院时间。

   B：那今天早上我还需要打针吗？

2. A：今天晚上没有作业，太好了！

   B：那我们去打篮球吧！

3. 王老师不在办公室，那我去问我的中国朋友吧。

※ 练习：请用连词"那"和所给词语完成对话　Please use the conjunction "那" and the given words to complete dialogues

1. A：明天我们没有课。

   B：______________________________。（玩儿）

2. A：下雨了。

   B：______________________________。（别去踢足球）

3. A：大家都说三亚很漂亮。

   B：______________________________。（旅游，lǚyóu，travel）

4. A：我的牙套得调整了。

   B：______________________________。（口腔医院）

三、副词"还"（2）　Adverb "还" (2)

副词"还"表示某一行为动作继续进行。例如：

The adverb "还" indicates that a certain action continues. For example:

1. 那今天早上我还需要打针吗？
2. 今天中午你还订外卖吗？
3. 马大为昨天去打篮球了，今天他还去。

※ 练习：请用副词"还"完成句子 Please complete sentences with the adverb "还"

1. 这家饭店的菜太好吃了，我 ____________________。

2. 他今天打了一针，明天 ____________________。

3. 王医生今天上午做了一个手术，下午 ________________。

4. 这些葡萄太好吃了，我 ____________________。

四、数量词"一会儿"（1） Numeral-measure word "一会儿" (1)

数量词"一会儿"在句中可以做时间状语，表示在很短的时间之内。例如：

The numeral-measure word "一会儿" can be used as an adverbial of time in a sentence, indicating a short time. For example:

1. 我一会儿去护士站看一下。
2. 一会儿见！
3. 一会儿打完球我们一起去吃饭吧。

※ 练习：请用数量词"一会儿"完成对话 Please complete dialogues with the numeral-measure word "一会儿"

1. A：你什么时候到？

   B：____________________。

2. A：你现在去食堂吃饭吗？

   B：____________________。

3. A：都十二点了，你还不睡觉吗？

   B：____________________。

4. A：快上课了，咱们去教室吧。

   B：____________________。

综合练习 Comprehensive Exercises

一、根据拼音写汉字 Write Chinese characters according to Pinyin

1. chuānghu________　3. shōushi________　5. suíbiàn________

2. dǎkāi________　4. gānjìng________　6. xiǎoxīn________

二、辨字组词 Discriminate between Chinese characters and make words

1. 窗________ 突________
2. 收________ 放________
3. 拾________ 给________
4. 净________ 凉________

三、替换练习 Substitution drills

1. 请大家把<u>窗户</u><u>打开</u>。

作业	写完
手机	关上
衣服	洗（xǐ，wash）干净

2. 那<u>今天早上我还需要打针吗</u>？

今天我还要上课吗
明天我们还去爬山吗
寒假你还打算去哈尔滨吗

3. 我一会儿 去护士站看一下。

去问问老师
去超市（chāoshì，supermarket）买葡萄
来拿检查结果

四、选词填空 Use the following words to fill in the blanks

干净　那　随便　一会儿　小心

1. 我们________去看电影，你去不去？
2. 刚下过雨，你骑车________一点儿，不要摔了。
3. 做完手术不能________吃东西，要先问问医生。
4. 我朋友要来看我，我得把房间收拾________。
5. 我下午出院，________上午还要打针吗？

五、用所给词语完成对话 Complete the dialogues with given words

1. 儿子：妈妈，我去学校了。

   妈妈：好，你________________________________吗？（把）

2. 美丽：房间里有点儿冷。

   月亮：________________________________。（上）

3. 病人：检查结果什么时候能出来？

   护士：________________________________。（一会儿 + V）

4. 金龙：听说新疆的夏天景色特别美。

   大为：________________________________。（那）

5. 病人：______________________________？（还）

护士：对，下午还要打针。

六、根据课文内容回答问题 Answer the following questions according to the text

1. 护士让大家做什么？
2. 护士让二床病人做什么？
3. 三床病人什么时候可以出院？
4. 今天早上三床病人还需要打针吗？

七、根据课文内容填空 Fill in the blanks according to the text

护士请病人把________打开，________收拾干净。一床病人想知道今天是哪位医生________，张医生________王医生，护士告诉他是张医生。护士请二床病人把呼叫铃________，不要________按。二床病人说________，刚才________碰了它一下。三床病人问护士今天________可以出院，护士让他先________东西________，医生查房的时候会告诉他出院时间。三床病人问今天早上________打针吗，护士说她________去护士站________。

课文（二）
Text（II）

Lǐ Zhēn zài shǒujī wéixiūdiàn xiū shǒujī.
（李真 在 手机 维修店 修 手机。）

Lǐ Zhēn: Shīfu nín hǎo, wǒ bǎ shǒujīpíng shuāi le, máfan nín bāng wǒ kàn yíxià.
李真：师傅您好，我把手机屏摔了，麻烦您帮我看一下。

gōngzuò rényuán: Qǐng tián yíxià wéixiūdān. Hái néng kāijī ma?
工作人员：请 填 一下维修单。还 能 开机吗？

Lǐ Zhēn: Néng.
李真：能。

gōngzuò rényuán: Qǐng děng yíhuìr.
工作人员：请 等 一会儿。

Lǐ Zhēn: Hǎo de.
李真：好 的。

Gōngzuò rényuán jiǎnchá shǒujī.
（工作 人员 检查 手机。）

gōngzuò rényuán: Shǒujī wǒ kànguo le, méiyǒu dà wèntí, huàn gè píng jiù kěyǐ.
工作人员：手机我看过了，没有大问题，换个屏就可以。

Lǐ Zhēn: Xiànzài néng huàn ma?
李真：现在 能 换 吗？

gōngzuò rényuán: Zhè gè xínghào de shǒujīpíng diàn li méiyǒu, děi děng sān-sì tiān.
工作人员：这 个 型号 的 手机屏 店 里没有，得 等 三四 天。

Lǐ Zhēn: Xūyào duōshao qián?
李真：需要 多少 钱？

gōngzuò rényuán: Yìqiān èr.
工作人员：1200。

Lǐ Zhēn: Zhème guì! Nà wǒ bù xiū le, wǒ háishi zài mǎi yí gè xīn de ba.
李真：这么 贵！那我不修了，我还是再买 一个新的吧。

(Li Zhen comes to have her mobile phone repaired at a mobile phone repair shop.)

Li Zhen: Excuse me, Shifu, I broke the screen of my phone. Please have a look for me.

Staff: Please fill in the repair sheet. Can it start up?

Li Zhen: Yes.

Staff: Please wait a moment.

Li Zhen: OK.

(The staff checks the phone.)

Staff: I have checked the phone. There is no big problem with it. It just needs a new screen.

Li Zhen: Can you change the screen now?

Staff: We don't have the screen of this type in our shop. You need to wait three to four days.

Li Zhen: How much is it?

Staff: 1200.

Li Zhen: So expensive! I don't want to have it repaired. I'd rather buy a new one!

生词 New words

1. 师傅	shīfu	*n.*	form of address for any stranger
2. 手机屏	shǒujīpíng	*n.*	mobile screen

屏	píng	*n.*	screen
3. 麻烦	máfan	*v./adj.*	to bother, excuse me; troublesome
4. 帮	bāng	*v.*	to help
5. 人员	rényuán	*n.*	staff
6. 维修单	wéixiūdān	*n.*	repair sheet
维修	wéixiū	*v.*	to maintain, to repair
单	dān	*n.*	sheet, list
7. 开机	kāijī	*v.*	to start up
8. 换	huàn	*v.*	to change
9. 型号	xínghào	*n.*	type
10. 修	xiū	*v.*	to repair
11. 还是	háishi	*adv.*	expressing a preference for an alternative

语言点 Language Points

一、数量词"一会儿"(2)　Numeral-measure word "一会儿" (2)

数量词"一会儿"用在动词后做时量补语，表示很短的时间。例如：

The numeral-measure word "一会儿" is used after a verb as a complement of duration to measure time, indicating a very short time. For example:

1. 请等一会儿。
2. 我们看一会儿电影再去吃饭吧。
3. 今天下课以后我想运动一会儿。

※ 练习：请用数量词“一会儿”完成句子 Please complete sentences with the numeral-measure word “一会儿”

1. 我快写完了，请你 ______________________________。

2. 你脸色不太好，快 ______________________________。

3. 太困了，我要 ______________________________。

4. 我现在不想写作业，______________________________。

二、主谓谓语句 Subject-predicate predicate sentence

在汉语中，主谓短语可以做谓语，这样的句子叫主谓谓语句。例如：

In Chinese, subject-predicate phrases can be used as predicates, and such sentences are called subject-predicate predicate sentences. For example:

1. 手机我看过了。
2. 这个型号的手机屏店里没有。
3. 这门课我们学过。

※ 练习：选择合适的短语完成句子 Choose the right phrase to complete sentences

天气很好　　我吃过　　马大为没有参加　　工作很忙

1. 医生 ______________。

2. 明天 ______________。

3. 这种葡萄 __________。

4. 昨天的篮球比赛 ________________。

三、副词“还是”（1） Adverb “还是” (1)

副词“还是”表示经过比较和思考之后做出某种选择。例如：

The adverb “还是” indicates to make a choice after comparison and thinking. For example:

1. 这么贵！那我不修了，我还是再买一个新的吧。

2. 我今天不想做饭，还是订外卖吧。

3. 今天天气不好，还是别去运动了，在家休息吧。

※ 练习：请用副词“还是”完成对话　Please complete dialogues with the adverb “还是”

1. A：买这条蓝裙子吧，很好看。

   B：有点儿贵，______________________。

2. A：我的牙很疼，想去药店（pharmacy）买点儿药。

   B：____。

3. A：我们去饭店吃怎么样？

   B：______________________。

4. A：周末咱们去看电影吧。

   B：______________________。

综合练习 Comprehensive Exercises

一、根据拼音写汉字 Write Chinese characters according to Pinyin

1. shīfu__________　3. bāng__________　5. huàn__________

2. máfan__________　4. xiū__________　6. háishi__________

二、辨字组词 Discriminate between Chinese characters and make words

1. 麻________ 床________
2. 修________ 候________
3. 换________ 晚________
4. 单________ 果________

三、替换练习 Substitution drills

1. 这个型号的手机屏 店里没有。

那个电影	大家都想看
这个手术	张医生做过
这件事儿	我们都不知道

2. 请 等 一会儿。

休息
放松
坐

3. 我还是 再买一个新的吧。

去医院看医生吧
把病历给您送过去吧
夏天去新疆吧

四、选词填空 Use the following words to fill in the blanks

麻烦	填	换	还是	一会儿

1. 检查结果还没出来，你等_______再来吧。
2. _______您帮我拿一下那本书。
3. 先_______一下维修单吧。
4. 我不想做饭，_______去外面吃吧。
5. 这件衣服太大了，您帮我_______小号的吧。

五、用所给词语完成对话 Complete the dialogues with given words

1. A：师傅，您店里有这个型号的手机屏吗？

   B：______________________________。（主谓谓语句）
2. A：月亮，我的外卖到了，__________________？（麻烦）

   B：好的，我一会儿就去拿。
3. 维修人员：手机怎么了？

   马大为：____________________。（把）
4. 女儿：爸爸，__________________。（一会儿）

   爸爸：好，我在楼下等你。
5. 病人：我好多了，现在就可以出院了吧？

   护士：____________________________。（还是）

六、根据课文内容回答问题 Answer the following questions according to the text

1. 李真的手机怎么了？

2. 工作人员让李真做什么？

3. 现在能换手机屏吗？为什么？

4. 李真决定（juédìng，decide）修手机吗？为什么？

七、根据课文内容填空 Fill in the blanks according to the text

李真______手机屏______了，______工作人员______她看一下。工作人员请李真______维修单，李真说手机还能______。李真等了______，工作人员说手机______，没有大问题，______就可以。但是，这个______的手机屏店里没有，______三四天，而且需要1200元。李真说______，那她不修了，她______再买一个新的吧。

语言任务 Language Tasks

一、阅读理解 Reading comprehension

手机让我们的生活（shēnghuó，life）越来越方便，比如（for example）手机支付让我们出门不用带钱。手机还可以帮助我们学习很多新东西，让我们和朋友的联系（liánxì，contact）更方便。所以，人们用手机的时间越来越长，有的人因为玩儿手机不吃饭、不睡觉。这样做对眼睛、对身体都没有好处（hǎochù，benefit）。

读后判断 True or false

1. 人们可以用手机支付。（　）

2. 手机不能帮我们学习。（　）

3. 人们用手机的时间越来越长。 (　　)

4. 有的人有了手机就不喜欢吃饭。 (　　)

5. 长时间看手机对身体不好。 (　　)

二、口头表达 Oral expression

任务名称：你比画我猜。

Task: Act and guess.

任务要求：学生两人一组，老师事先准备好包含“把”字句的卡片。组员 1 按照卡片所说的内容做出相应的动作，组员 2 看同伴的动作，猜卡片上的句子。每组活动限时 3 分钟，猜出句子最多、最准确的小组获胜。

Requirements: Two students work in a group. The teacher should prepare cards, each with a 把-sentence on it in advance. Group member 1 makes corresponding actions according to the sentences on the cards. Group member 2 observes the actions of each one's peer and guesses the sentences on the cards. Time for each group is limited to 3 minutes. The group that guesses the most sentences most accurately within the time limit wins.

Reference words: 把

三、书面表达 Written expression

任务名称：手机使用小调查。

Task: Survey on the mobile phones.

任务要求：请同学们从手机品牌、购买原因、常用功能、每天使用时长等方面调查一下目前班上同学的手机持有及使用状况，然后完成下列表格。

Requirements: Please ask your classmates about the brands, purposes of purchasing, common functions and time length of using, etc. of their mobile phones to make clear the current owning and using situations of their mobiles, and then complete the following table.

Reference words: 贵　看书　学习　玩儿游戏　看电影　好看　便宜……

使用的手机品牌 Mobile phone brands	
买手机时考虑的因素 Factors to consider when buying mobile phones	
最常用的手机功能 The frequently-used mobile functions	
每天使用手机的时长 Time length of using mobile phone everyday	

补充词汇 Supplementary Words

duōgōngnéngcháng
多功能床
multifunctional sickbed

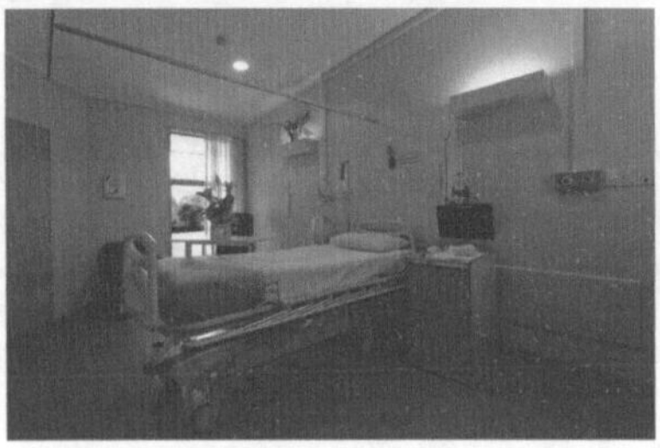

hūxījī
呼吸机
respirato

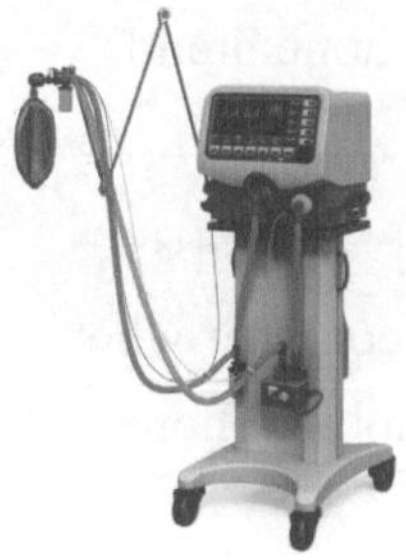

shūyèbèng
输液泵
infusion pump

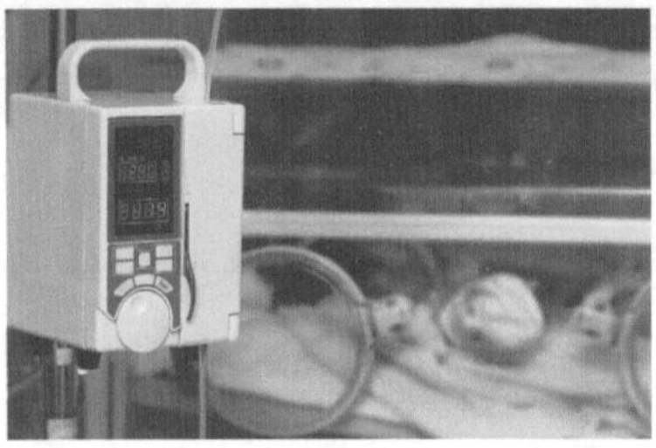

shǒudòng chúchànyí
手动除颤仪
manual defibrillator

第十四课 Lesson 14

Wǒ kàn bu qīngchu

我看不清楚

I can't see clearly

学习目标 Learning Objectives

1. Language functions: Students learn how to exhort others; students are able to invite others and accept others' invitation.
2. Language points: Potential complement; Aspectual particle "着" (2); Adverb "还是" (2); Adverb "更"; Adverb "才" (2); Interrogative pronouns expressing arbitrary meanings.
3. Medical knowledge: Students are expected to know how to have their eyesight checked.
4. Social culture: Students are expected to understand China's contemporary wedding custom.

热身活动 Warming-up

1. 哪些行为对视力有伤害？
What behaviors can harm the eyesight?

2. 在你们国家，参加婚礼一般送什么礼物？
In your country, what kind of gifts do you usually give at weddings?

课文（一）
Text（Ⅰ）

Wáng Chén zài yǎnkē zhěnshì.
（王　晨　在　眼科　诊室。）

dàifu:　Nǐ zěnme le?
大夫：你怎么了？

Wáng Chén:　Zuìjìn kàn dōngxi hěn móhu,　kàn bu qīngchu.
王晨：最近看东西很模糊，看不清楚。

dàifu:　Zhèyàng duō jiǔ le?
大夫：这样　多久了？

Wáng Chén:　Kuài liǎng gè xīngqī le.
王晨：快　两个星期了。

dàifu:　Shìlìbiǎo shàng de tú'àn nǐ néng kàndào dì jǐ háng?
大夫：视力表　上　的图案你　能　看到第几行？

Wáng Chén:　Dì-yī háng.
王晨：第一行。

dàifu:　Nǐ zuìjìn yòng yǎn duō ma?
大夫：你最近用　眼多　吗？

Wáng Chén:　Tǐng duō de,　wǒ chángcháng tǎngzhe wánr yóuxì.
王晨：挺　多的，我　常常　躺着　玩儿游戏。

dàifu:　Xiànzài hěn duō niánqīngrén hé nǐ yíyàng,　yīnwèi wánr shǒujī,
大夫：现在　很　多　年轻人　和你一样，因为玩儿手机，

shāngle yǎnjing.
伤了　眼睛。

Wáng Chén:　Wǒ de yǎnjing hái néng huīfù ma?
王晨：我的　眼睛还　能　恢复吗？

dàifu: Xiànzài hái huīfù de liǎo, rúguǒ nǐ háishi zhèyàng yòng yǎn,
大夫：现在 还恢复得了，如果你还是这样 用 眼，

shíjiān cháng le jiù huīfù bù liǎo le.
时间 长 了就恢复不了了。

Wáng Chén: Tài kěpà le! Wǒ mǎshàng bǎ shǒujī li de yóuxì dōu shān le,
王晨：太可怕了！我 马上 把手机里的游戏都 删 了，

yǐhòu bù wánr le.
以后不玩儿了。

(Wang Chen is seeing a doctor at the ophthalmic consulting room.)

Doctor: What's the matter with you?

Wang Chen: Recently I see things in a blur. I can't see clearly.

Doctor: How long have you been like this?

Wang Chen: Almost two weeks.

Doctor: Which row of the letters on the visual chart can you see at your best?

Wang Chen: The first row.

Doctor: Do you use your eyes much recently?

Wang Chen: Yes. I often play mobile games while lying in bed.

Doctor: Nowadays, there are many young people hurting their eyes because of playing games, just like you.

Wang Chen: Can my eyes recover?

Doctor: They can still recover for now. If you keep using eyes like this, they can't recover after a long time.

Wang Chen: It's so horrible. I'll delete the games in my phone immediately and not play mobile games any more.

生词 New words

1. 模糊	móhu	*adj.*	indistinct

2. 清楚	qīngchu	*adj.*	clear
3. 这样	zhèyàng	*pron.*	this way, such, like this
4. 视力表	shìlìbiǎo	*n.*	visual chart
视力	shìlì	*n.*	vision, eyesight
表	biǎo	*n.*	chart
5. 图案	tú'àn	*n.*	pattern, design
6. 行	háng	*m.*	used for sth. in a line
7. 躺	tǎng	*v.*	to lie
8. 年轻人	niánqīngrén	*n.*	young people
年轻	niánqīng	*adj.*	young
9. 了	liǎo	*v.*	to finish
10. 可怕	kěpà	*adj.*	horrible
11. 删	shān	*v.*	to delete

语言点 Language Points

一、可能补语　Potential complement

动词和结果补语或趋向补语之间，加上“得”或者“不”，就成了可能补语。可能补语表示动作能否实现某种结果或者达到某种状态。肯定形式是：动词 + 得 + 结果补语 / 趋向补语。否定形式是：动词 + 不 + 结果补语 / 趋向补语。正反疑问形式是“肯定式 + 否定式”。例如：

A potential complement is formed by adding “得” or “不” between the verb and the resultative complement or the directional complement. It indicates whether an action can achieve a certain result or a certain state. The affirmative form is: verb + 得 + resultative complement/directional complement. The negative form is: verb +不 + resultative complement/directional complement. The positive and negative question form is "positive form + negative form". For example:

1. 最近看东西很模糊，看不清楚。

2. 现在还恢复得了，如果你还是这样用眼，时间长了就恢复不了了。

3. 今天的作业太多了，你写得完写不完？

※ 练习：请用可能补语完成对话或句子 Please complete dialogues or sentences with potential complement

1. A：生理学太难了，你听得懂吗？

   B：________________________。

2. A：数学作业这么多，你写得完写不完？

   B：________________________。

3. 我们三个人点五个菜是不是太多了？ ______________。

4. 每天玩七八个小时手机，眼睛太累了，时间长了 ______________。

二、动态助词"着"（2） Aspectual particle "着" (2)

动态助词"着"可以用在两个动作之间，表示动作执行者进行第二个动作（主要动作）时的状态和方式，即表示伴随的动作。前面的动词带宾语时，"着"用在V和O之间。例如：

The aspectual particle "着" can be used between two verbs to indicate the state and manner of the actor when he or she performs the second action (the main action), that is, to indicate the accompanying action. If the first verb is followed by the object, "着" is used between V and O. For example:

1. 我常常躺着玩儿游戏。

2. 不要听着歌写作业。

3. 美丽和月亮在宿舍躺着看书。

※ 练习：请用动态助词“着”完成句子　Please complete sentences with the aspectual particle “着”

1. 别 ______________ 打电话。（开车）

2. 妈妈喜欢 ____________ 做饭。（看电视）

3. 马大为常常 ____________ 跑步。（听歌）

4. 美丽喜欢去咖啡馆，在那里她可以 ____________ 看书。（喝咖啡）

三、副词“还是”（2）　Adverb “还是” (2)

副词“还是”表示动作行为或者状态继续保持不变，同“还”。例如：

The adverb “还是” indicates that the action or state remains unchanged being the same as “还”. For example:

1. 现在还恢复得了，如果你还是这样用眼，时间长了就恢复不了了。

2. 医生告诉他不要一直玩儿手机，可是他还是这样做。

3. 病人已经吃药了，但是血压还是有点儿高。

※ 练习：请用副词“还是”完成对话　Please complete dialogues with the adverb “还是”

1. A：今天早上我吃药了，可是头 ______________________________。

   B：你去医院看看吧。

2. A：上午我去他办公室，他不在；刚才我去，___________________。

   B：你明天再去吧。

3. A：你复习了两个星期，现在觉得生理学不难了吧？

   B：不，_____________________________________。

4. A：马上要考试了，孩子不玩儿游戏了吧？

   B：虽然要考试了，___________________________。

综合练习 Comprehensive Exercises

一、根据拼音写汉字 Write Chinese characters according to Pinyin

1. móhu__________　　3. zhèyàng__________　　5. tǎng__________

2. háng__________　　4. qīngchu__________　　6. kěpà__________

二、辨字组词 Discriminate between Chinese characters and make words

1. 清________ / 请________　　2. 行________ / 听________　　3. 样________ / 校________　　4. 怕________ / 的________

三、替换练习 Substitution drills

1. 你的眼睛 现在 恢复 得了。

这些饭	我	吃
明天下午的比赛	我	参加
这些东西	我一个人	拿

2. 时间长了 就 恢复 不了了。

现在不去	买
迟到（chídào，be late）了	考
不吃药	好

3. 我马上把手机里的游戏都删了。

作业	写了
晚饭	做了
饭	吃了

四、选词填空 Use the following words to fill in the blanks

清楚　　这样　　行　　年轻人　　可怕

1. 你家门口有一个穿蓝衣服的_______。
2. 这个电影太_______了！我不想看了。
3. 我们都不知道他为什么_______做。
4. 每一_______的字数都不一样。
5. 我坐在最前面，也看不_______老师写的字。

五、用所给词语完成对话 Complete the dialogues with given words

1. 儿子：妈妈，这个字我不会写，您能教教我吗？

   妈妈：________________________________。（这样）

2. 同学：美丽，我不小心点了四个菜，我们一起吃吧。

   美丽：________________________________。（了 liǎo）

3. 朋友：手术做完后你就能走路了吗？

   病人：不行，________________________。（躺）

4. 老师：________________________________？（清楚）

   学生：能。

5. 家属：请问，这个手术一个小时能做完吗？

护士：______________________________。（不）

六、根据课文内容回答问题 Answer the following questions according to the text

1. 王晨怎么了？
2. 王晨的眼睛不舒服多长时间了？
3. 王晨最近用眼多吗？
4. 王晨的眼睛还能恢复吗？

七、根据课文内容填空 Fill in the blanks according to the text

王晨最近看东西很______，看不______，______快两个星期了。视力表上的图案，他只能看到______。最近他______挺多的，常常______玩儿游戏。大夫说现在眼睛还恢复______，时间长了就恢复______了。王晨要______游戏都删了，______不玩儿了。

课文（二）
Text（II）

Wáng Chén zài gěi Mǎ Dàwéi dǎ diànhuà.
（王 晨 在给马 大为 打 电话。）

Wáng Chén: Dàwéi, wǒ gēge wǔ yuè èrshí hào jǔxíng hūnlǐ, huānyíng nǐ lái cānjiā.
王晨：大为，我哥哥五月二十号举行婚礼，欢迎你来参加。

Mǎ Dàwéi: Gōngxǐ gōngxǐ! Kěshì zhēn bàoqiàn, nà tiān wǒ kěnéng qù bu liǎo.
马大为：恭喜 恭喜！可是 真 抱歉，那天 我 可能 去不了。

Wáng Chén: Wèi shénme?
王晨：为 什么？

Mǎ Dàwéi: Wǒ fùmǔ nà tiān lái, wǒ děi qù jīchǎng jiē tāmen.
马大为：我父母那天来，我得去机场接他们。

Wáng Chén: Fēijī jǐ diǎn dào?
王晨：飞机几点 到？

Mǎ Dàwéi: Zǎoshang bā diǎn.
马大为：早上 八点。

Wáng Chén: Nǐ kěyǐ dài tāmen yìqǐ lái, rén duō le gèng rènao.
王晨：你可以带他们一起来，人多了 更热闹。

Mǎ Dàwéi: Wǒ pà láibují.
马大为：我怕来不及。

Wáng Chén: Láidejí. Hūnlǐ shíyī diǎn cái kāishǐ.
王晨：来得及。婚礼十一点 才开始。

Mǎ Dàwéi: Nà tài hǎo le! Wǒ hái méi cānjiāguo Zhōngguórén de hūnlǐ ne. Wǒ yào zhǔnbèi shénme ne?
马大为：那太好了！我还 没 参加过 中国人 的婚礼呢。我 要 准备 什么 呢？

Wáng Chén: Shénme yě búyòng zhǔnbèi.

王晨：什么 也不用 准备。

(Wang Chen is calling up Ma Dawei.)

Wang Chen: Dawei, my brother is going to have the wedding on May 20th. Welcome to attend!

Ma Dawei: Congratulations! But, sorry, I maybe can't make it that day.

Wang Chen: Why?

Ma Dawei: My parents will come that day. I have to pick them up at the airport.

Wang Chen: When will the plane land?

Ma Dawei: Eight in the morning.

Wang Chen: You can bring them to the wedding. More people make more jollification.

Ma Dawei: I'm afraid that we will not make it on time.

Wang Chen: Don't worry. The wedding will begin at eleven.

Ma Dawei: That's great! I haven't attended a Chinese wedding yet. What should I prepare?

Wang Chen: Nothing to prepare.

生词 New words

1. 举行	jǔxíng	*v.*	to hold
2. 婚礼	hūnlǐ	*n.*	wedding
3. 欢迎	huānyíng	*v.*	to welcome
4. 恭喜	gōngxǐ	*v.*	to congratulate
5. 抱歉	bàoqiàn	*adj.*	sorry
6. 父母	fùmǔ	*n.*	parents
7. 机场	jīchǎng	*n.*	airport
8. 接	jiē	*v.*	to pick up

9. 更	gèng	*adv.*	even more
10. 热闹	rènao	*adj.*	bustling
11. 怕	pà	*v.*	to worry about, to be afraid of
12. 来不及	láibují	*v.*	to have no enough time (to do sth.)
13. 来得及	láidejí	*v.*	to be able to do sth. in time

语言点 Language Points

一、副词"更" Adverb "更"

副词"更"用于比较，常用在形容词前表示程度的加深。例如：

The adverb "更" is used for comparison and is often used in front of adjectives to express the deepening of the degree. For example:

1. 人多了更热闹。
2. 马大为的汉语说得不错，金龙说得更好。
3. 今天 32 度，明天更热。

※ 练习：请用副词"更"完成对话 Please complete dialogues with the adverb "更"

1. A：你觉得汉语难吗？

   B：有点儿难，但是 ________________。

2. A：这里春天很舒服，我很喜欢。

   B：秋天 ________________。

3. A：你觉得红的好看还是黄的好看？

B：____________________________。

4. A：这种葡萄好甜！

B：你吃过新疆葡萄吗？____________________________。

二、副词“才”（2） Adverb “才” (2)

副词“才”出现在表示时间的词语后，表示动作行为发生得晚或者用的时间长。与副词“就”相对。例如：

The adverb “才” appears after the words expressing time, indicating that the action take place late or last a long time. It is opposite to the adverb “就”. For example:

1. 婚礼十一点才开始。
2. 马大为八点十分才到教室。
3. 他今天花（huā，spend）了一个半小时才到学校。

※ 练习：请选择“就”或“才”填空 Please select “就” or “才” to fill in the blanks

1. 美丽晚上八点 _______ 睡觉了。
2. 金龙半个小时 _______ 写完了，马大为三个小时 _______ 写完。
3. 这是个大手术，五个小时 _______ 做完。
4. 我家离医院很近，走路十分钟 _______ 到了。

三、疑问代词表任指 Interrogative pronouns expressing arbitrary meanings

在汉语中，疑问代词“什么”“哪儿”“谁”“怎么”用在陈述句中，可以代指某一范围内所有的对象。“什么”指“任何东西”，“哪儿”指“任何地方”，“谁”指“任何人”，“怎么”指“任何方式”。后面经常有副词“都”或者“也”相呼应。例如：

In Chinese, the interrogative pronouns "什么", "哪儿", "谁" and "怎么" can refer to all the things within a certain range when being used in declarative sentences. "什么" refers to "anything", "哪儿" refers to "anywhere", "谁" refers to "anyone", and "怎么" refers to "any way". It is often followed by adverb "都" or "也". For example:

1. 什么也不用准备。

2. 我哪儿都没去过。

3. 李真谁都不认识。

※ 练习：组词成句　Group words into sentences

1. 也　不想　吃　什么　我

______________________________。

2. 马大为　去　哪儿　都　想

______________________________。

3. 我　看　怎么　不清楚　也

______________________________。

4. 玩儿手机　谁　喜欢　都

______________________________。

综合练习 Comprehensive Exercises

一、根据拼音写汉字 Write Chinese characters according to Pinyin

1. jǔxíng________　3. huānyíng________　5. rènao________

2. bàoqiàn________　4. fùmǔ________　6. jīchǎng________

二、辨字组词 Discriminate between Chinese characters and make words

1. 接________ 新________
2. 迎________ 近________
3. 更________ 便________
4. 闹________ 问________

三、替换练习 Substitution drills

1. 我怕<u>来不及</u>。

明天考不好
写不完作业
他今天来不了

2. <u>婚礼十一点</u>才<u>开始</u>。

我昨晚三点	睡觉
他十一点	吃早饭
我找了一天	找到我的手机

3. <u>什么</u>也<u>不用准备</u>。

哪儿	不想去
什么	不知道
谁	不认识

四、选词填空 Use the following words to fill in the blanks

热闹　接　更　怕　来得及

1. 哈尔滨的冰雪节人特别多，非常_______。
2. 他的病比以前_______严重了。
3. 现在还早，去机场_______。
4. 我们都能来医院照顾你，你别_______。
5. 你今天下午几点的飞机？我去机场_______你。

五、用所给词语完成对话 Complete the dialogues with given words

1. 妈妈：快来吃早饭。
   儿子：____________________。（来不及）
2. 医生：你的头疼好点儿了吗？
   病人：____________________。（更）
3. 王晨：你快点儿，我们上课要迟到（chídào，be late）了。
   朋友：____________________。（来得及）
4. 老师：你的作业都写完了吗？
   学生：____________________。（抱歉）
5. 医生：这是个小手术，你不用太担心。
   病人：____________________。（怕）

六、根据课文内容回答问题 Answer the following questions according to the text

1. 王晨的哥哥什么时候举行婚礼？
2. 为什么马大为说他可能去不了？

3. 那天马大为父母的飞机几点到？

4. 王晨让马大为做什么？

七、根据课文内容填空 Fill in the blanks according to the text

王晨的哥哥五月二十号________婚礼，王晨给马大为打电话请他来________。可是，马大为的父母那天要来，他可能去________，马大为觉得很________。马大为父母的飞机早上八点到，王晨________马大为带父母一起来，人多了________。婚礼十一点________开始，应该________。马大为很高兴，因为他还没________中国人的婚礼呢。

语言任务 Language Tasks

一、阅读理解 Reading comprehension

越来越多的人喜欢用手机，每天看手机的时间也越来越长。有的喜欢用手机玩儿游戏，有的喜欢用手机看电影，还有的喜欢用手机买东西，等等。很多年轻人因为长时间用手机伤了眼睛，看不清楚东西。医生说为了自己的眼睛，要少玩儿手机，少躺着玩儿游戏，减少（jiǎnshǎo，reduce）用眼，这样视力才有可能恢复。

读后判断 True or false

1. 有的人喜欢用手机看书。（　）
2. 人们用手机的时间越来越长了。（　）
3. 用手机不能买东西。（　）
4. 用手机不能看电影。（　）
5. 为了自己的眼睛，要少用电脑。（　）

二、口头表达 Oral expression

任务名称：去医院看眼睛。

Task: Go to see an ophthalmologist.

任务要求：1. 两个学生一组，一个是眼睛不舒服的病人，一个是医生。

2. 医生询问病人眼睛的情况，病人描述症状并回答医生的问题。

Requirements: 1. Two students work in a group. One acts as a patient feeling uncomfortable on his/her eyes, and the other as a doctor.

2. The doctor asks about the patient's eyes, and the patient describes the symptoms and answers the doctor's questions.

Reference words: 模糊　清楚　视力表　行　最近　躺着　玩儿游戏　可怕

三、书面表达 Written expression

任务名称：中西婚礼比较。

Task: Comparison between Chinese and western weddings.

任务要求：请同学们分别说一说中式婚礼和西式婚礼的不同，并完成下列表格。

Requirement: Please ask your classmates to describe the differences between Chinese wedding and western wedding, and then complete the following table.

中式婚礼 Chinese wedding	1.
	2.
	3.
西式婚礼 Western wedding	1.
	2.
	3.

结论 Conclusion	

Reference words: 举行 婚礼 参加 了 带 更 热闹 准备

补充词汇 Supplementary Words

yànguāng
验光
optometry

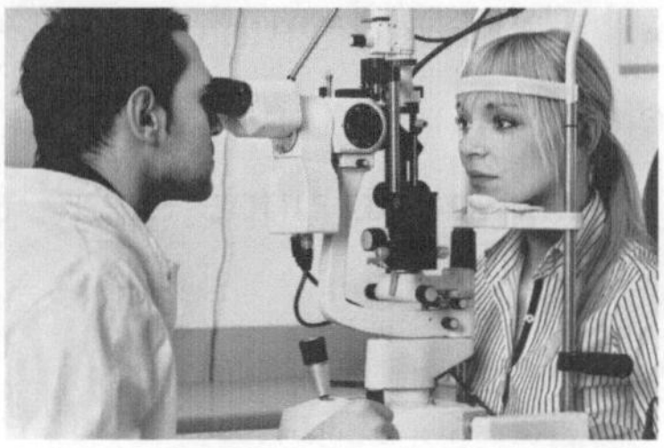

yǎnjìng
眼镜
glasses

mòjìng
墨镜
sunglasses

yǐnxíng yǎnjìng
隐形眼镜
contact lens

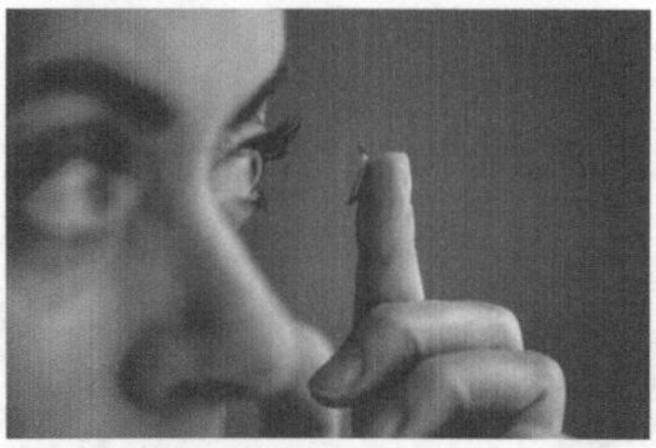

第十五课 Lesson 15

Bǎ miánqiú qǔ chūlai

把 棉球 取出来

Take the cotton ball out

学习目标 Learning Objectives

1. Language functions: Students can introduce the process of completing something; students are able to introduce how to accomplish something.
2. Language points: Fixed structure "先……再……然后……最后……"; Fixed structure "V + 起来"; Preposition "对"; Fixed structure "一……也 / 都 + 不 / 没 + V / VP"; 把-sentence (2).
3. Medical knowledge: Students are expected to understand the method of emergency hemostasis.
4. Social culture: The etiquette of inviting friends.

热身活动 Warming-up

1. 你流过鼻血吗？原因是什么？

Have you ever had nosebleeds? Why?

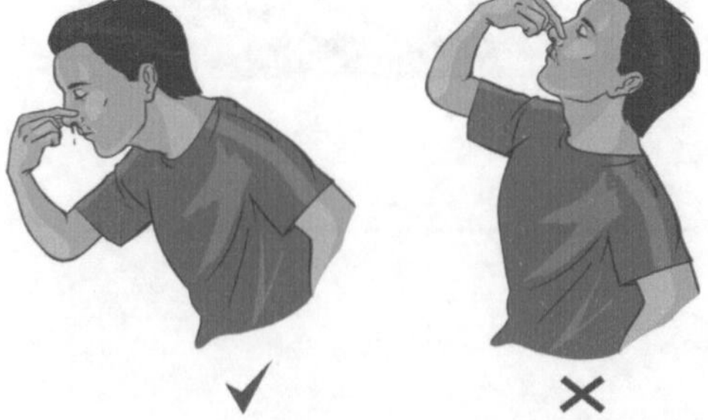

2. 你知道哪些止血的方法？

What methods do you know to stop bleeding?

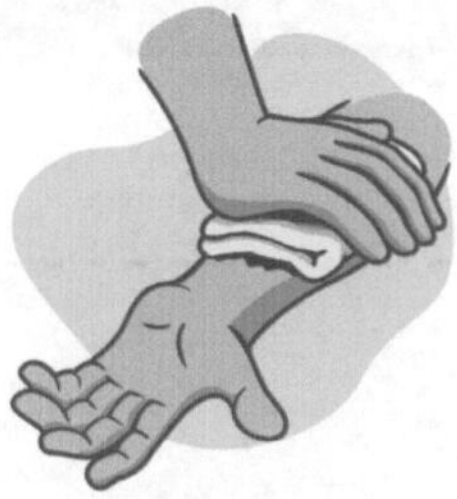

课文（一）
Text（Ⅰ）

Mǎ Dàwéi hé Jīn Lóng zài sùshè liáotiānr.
（马大为和金龙在宿舍聊天儿。）

Mǎ Dàwéi: Míngtiān xiàwǔ méiyǒu kè, wǒmen qǐng Wáng Chén, Lǐ Zhēn lái sùshè wánr ba.
马大为：明天下午没有课，我们请王晨、李真来宿舍玩儿吧。

Jīn Lóng: Hǎo! Kěshì, wǒmen fángjiān li tài luàn le. Wǒmen jīntiān děi hǎohāor shōushi shōushi.
金龙：好！可是，我们房间里太乱了。我们今天得好好儿收拾收拾。

Mǎ Dàwéi: Zěnme shōushi?
马大为：怎么收拾？

Jīn Lóng: Xiān bǎ chuáng zhěnglǐ hǎo, zài bǎ zhuōzi shàng de shū fàng zhěngqí, ránhòu bǎ dì sǎo yi sǎo, zuìhòu bǎ lājī rēngdiào.
金龙：先把床整理好，再把桌子上的书放整齐，然后把地扫一扫，最后把垃圾扔掉。

Mǎ Dàwéi: Nà wǒ néng xiān bǎ zìjǐ de shìqing zuòwán ma?
马大为：那我能先把自己的事情做完吗？

Jīn Lóng: Nǐ yǒu shénme shìr?
金龙：你有什么事儿？

Mǎ Dàwéi: Wǒ yào xiān bǎ bīngjīlíng chīwán, zài bǎ yóuxì dǎwán.
马大为：我要先把冰激凌吃完，再把游戏打完。

Jīn Lóng: Kàn qǐlai, nǐ duì dǎsǎo fángjiān méi xìngqù.
金龙：看起来，你对打扫房间没兴趣。

Mǎ Dàwéi: Duì, yìdiǎnr xìngqù dōu méiyǒu.
马大为：对，一点儿兴趣都没有。

(Ma Dawei and Jin Long are chatting in their dorm.)

Ma Dawei: We don't have class tomorrow afternoon. Let's invite Wang Chen and Li Zhen to our dorm.

Jin Long: OK. But our dorm is too messy. We need to tide it up thoroughly.

Ma Dawei: How to tide it up?

Jin Long: First, we need to clear up our beds. Then, we put the books on our desks in order. And then, we sweep the floor. And at last, we throw away the rubbish.

Ma Dawei: Well, can I finish my own businesses first?

Jin Long: What things?

Ma Dawei: First, I need to eat up the ice cream. Then, I need to finish the mobile game.

Jin Long: It seems that you are not interested in cleaning up the dorm.

Ma Dawei: No, not at all.

生词 New words

1. 乱	luàn	*adj.*	messy
2. 整理	zhěnglǐ	*v.*	to tidy up
3. 放	fàng	*v.*	to put, to place
4. 整齐	zhěngqí	*adj.*	tidy
5. 地	dì	*n.*	ground, floor
6. 扫	sǎo	*v.*	to sweep
7. 最后	zuìhòu	*n.*	last
8. 垃圾	lājī	*n.*	garbage, rubbish
9. 扔	rēng	*v.*	to throw
10. 掉	diào	*v.*	to drop
11. 自己	zìjǐ	*pron.*	oneself
12. 事情	shìqing	*n.*	event, thing
13. 打游戏	dǎ yóuxì	*VO*	to play games

打	dǎ	*v.*	to play
14. 看起来	kàn qǐlai		it seems
起来	qǐlai	*v.*	to sit up, to stand up
15. 对……有／没有兴趣	duì…yǒu/méiyǒu xìngqù		to have/have no interest in
对	duì	*prep.*	in, to
兴趣	xìngqù	*n.*	interest
16. 打扫	dǎsǎo	*v.*	to clean

语言点 Language Points

一、固定结构“先……再……然后……最后……”
Fixed structure“先……再……然后……最后……”

固定结构“先……再……然后……最后……”连接表承接关系的分句，表示动作行为发生的先后顺序。该结构用于完整地叙述事情发生的经过，我们也可以选择使用其中两至三项，简要叙述事情发生的过程。例如：

The fixed structure“先……再……然后……最后……”connects the clauses of continuing relationship, indicating the sequence of the actions. This structure is used to completely describe the course of the event. We can also selectively use two or three of them to briefly describe the course of the event. For example:

1. 先把床整理好，再把桌子上的书放整齐，然后把地扫一扫，最后把垃圾扔掉。

2. 我要先把冰激凌吃完，再把游戏打完。

3. 下课以后，马大为先回宿舍休息，再去体育馆锻炼，然后去学校附近的饭馆吃饭。

※ 练习：请用“先……再……然后……最后……”回答问题　Please use the structure “先……再……然后……最后……” to answer questions

1. A：下课以后，你做什么？

   B：____。

2. A：上个星期六，你做什么了？

   B：____。

3. A：快放寒假了，你有什么打算？

   B：____。

4. A：我想学好汉语，应该怎么做？

   B：____。

二、固定结构“V + 起来”　Fixed structure “V + 起来”

“V + 起来”做插入语或句子的前一部分，表示估计或者着眼于某一方面。例如：

“V + 起来” is used as a parenthesis or the first part of a sentence to indicate estimation or focusing on a certain aspect. For example:

1. 看起来，你对打扫房间没兴趣。
2. 生理学学起来很难。
3. 这件衣服穿起来很舒服。

※ 练习：选出“起来”在句子中的位置　Choose the position of “起来” in sentences

1. A 汉语歌 B 听 C 很好听 D。
2. 我 A 觉得 B 篮球 C 学 D 不太难。
3. 每天锻炼 A 身体 B 说 C 简单，D 做起来很难。
4. A 中国菜 B 吃 C 很好吃 D。

三、介词“对” Preposition “对”

介词“对”用来引出动作的对象，或者表示对待。例如：

The preposition “对” is used to introduce the object of the action, or to express treatment. For example:

1. 你对打扫房间没兴趣。
2. 马大为对运动很有兴趣。
3. 王医生对病人很好。

※ 练习：组词成句 Group words into sentences

1. 金龙 学习汉语 对 很有兴趣

____。

2. 病人 李护士 对 很好

____。

3. 王老师 特别好 学生 对

____。

4. 金龙 对 不太 打扫房间 有兴趣

____。

四、固定结构“一……也 / 都 + 不 / 没 + V / VP” Fixed structure “一……也 / 都 + 不 / 没 + V / VP”

“一……也 / 都 + 不 / 没 + V / VP”表示否定，有强调的语气。例如：

“一……也 / 都 +不 / 没 + V / VP” indicates negative, with an emphatic tone. For example:

1. （我对打扫房间）一点儿兴趣都没有。
2. 来中国的时候，我一个汉字也不认识。
3. 哥哥一点儿都不喜欢爬山。

※ 练习：组词成句　Group words into sentences

1. 一点儿　不想收拾　他　也

________________________________。

2. 一次医院　去过　也　没　我

________________________________。

3. 篮球比赛　赢过　一次　都　没　我们学院

________________________________。

4. 一杯水　喝　没　我　也　今天

________________________________。

综合练习 Comprehensive Exercises

一、根据拼音写汉字 Write Chinese characters according to Pinyin

1. dǎsǎo________　3. shìqing________　5. zhěnglǐ________

2. zuìhòu________　4. zhěngqí________　6. xìngqù________

二、辨字组词 Discriminate between Chinese characters and make words

1. 扫________ 当________

2. 地________ 他________

3. 理________ 里________

4. 情________ 请________

三、替换练习 Substitution drills

1. 先把床整理好，再把桌子上的书放整齐。

作业写完	房间收拾好
饭吃完	桌子收拾干净
书整理好	地扫一扫

2. 看起来，你对打扫房间没兴趣。

你的身体好多了
你很喜欢吃中国菜
他一点儿也不想去上课

3. 我们今天得好好儿收拾收拾。

打扫打扫
整理整理
休息休息

四、选词填空 Use the following words to fill in the blanks

整理　打扫　起来　兴趣　一点儿

1. 我对唱歌没有_______。

2. 你的身体看_______好多了。

3. 工作人员来________病房（bìngfáng，ward）了。

4. 桌子上的书太乱了，你快去________一下。

5. 那个病人说做手术的时候________也不疼。

五、用所给词语完成对话 Complete the dialogues with given words

1. 儿子：妈妈，我现在可以看电视吗？

   妈妈：________________________________。

   （先……再……然后……最后……）

2. 美丽：你经常在家做饭吗？

   同学：________________________________。（对……有兴趣）

3. 医生：________________________________。（起来）

   病人：我也觉得好多了。

4. 女儿：爸爸，你的头还疼吗？

   爸爸：________________________。（一点儿也不）

5. 美丽：________________________。（把）

   月亮：是这个红色的吗？给你。

六、根据课文内容回答问题 Answer the following questions according to the text

1. 金龙为什么要收拾房间？
2. 金龙想怎么收拾房间？
3. 马大为想先做什么？
4. 为什么马大为不想打扫房间？

七、根据课文内容填空 Fill in the blanks according to the text

明天下午没有课，马大为想请王晨、李真_______。金龙说房间里_______，今天得好好儿_______。先把床_______，再_______放整齐，然后_______扫一扫，最后把垃圾_______。马大为想先把自己的事情_______，他要先把冰激凌_______，再把游戏_______。他对打扫房间_______。

课文（二）
Text（II）

Yí wèi māma dàizhe háizi lái kàn jízhěn.
（一位 妈妈 带着 孩子来 看 急诊。）

māma: Yīshēng, háizi de bízi shuāipò le, yìzhí liú xiě.
妈妈：医生，孩子的鼻子摔破了，一直流血。

yīshēng: Nǐ bǎ háizi fàngdào yǐzi shàng, fúzhe tā de tóu. Wǒ kànkan. Bízi li de máoxì-xuèguǎn shuāipò le.
医生：你把孩子放到椅子上，扶着他的头。我 看看。鼻子里的 毛细血管 摔破了。

māma: Zěnme zhǐ xiě ne?
妈妈：怎么 止血 呢？

yīshēng: Bǎ xiāodú miánqiú sāijìn bízi li jiù xíng.
医生：把消毒 棉球 塞进鼻子里就行。

māma: Hái huì zài liú xiě ma?
妈妈：还会再流血吗？

yīshēng: Bú huì de, búyòng dānxīn.
医生：不会的，不用 担心。

māma: Shénme shíhou bǎ miánqiú qǔ chūlai?
妈妈：什么 时候把 棉球 取出来？

yīshēng: Míngtiān xiàwǔ.
医生：明天 下午。

māma: Zìjǐ zài jiā qǔ kěyǐ ma?
妈妈：自己在家取可以吗？

yīshēng: Bùxíng, nǐ háishi bǎ háizi dài guòlai, ràng yīshēng qǔ.
医生：不行，你还是把孩子带过来，让 医生 取。

māma: Hǎo de, xièxie yīshēng.
妈妈：好 的，谢谢 医生。

(A mother takes her kid for emergency treatment.)

Mother: Doctor, my kid's nose was broken and has been bleeding.

Doctor: Put your kid on the chair and hold his head. Let me see. The blood capillaries in his nasal cavity are broken.

Mother: How to stop bleeding?

Doctor: Put the sterilized cotton balls into his nostril.

Mother: Will his nose bleed again?

Doctor: No. Don't worry.

Mother: When shall we take out the cotton ball?

Doctor: Tomorrow afternoon.

Mother: Can we take the cotton ball out by ourselves at home?

Doctor: No. You should take your kid to the hospital and let the doctor take it out.

Mother: OK. Thank you, doctor.

生词 New words

1. 孩子	háizi	*n.*	child, kid
2. 鼻子	bízi	*n.*	nose
3. 破	pò	*v.*	to be broken
4. 流血	liú xiě	*VO*	to bleed
流	liú	*v.*	to flow
血	xiě/xuè	*n.*	blood
5. 扶	fú	*v.*	to hold, to support
6. 毛细血管	máoxì-xuèguǎn	*n.*	blood capillary
7. 止血	zhǐ xiě	*VO*	to stop bleeding
止	zhǐ	*v.*	to stop
8. 消毒	xiāodú	*v.*	to disinfect, to sterilize
9. 棉球	miánqiú	*n.*	cotton ball

10. 塞	sāi	*v.*	to fill in
11. 取	qǔ	*v.*	to take

语言点 Language Points

“把”字句（2） 把-sentence (2)

“把”字句动词后加趋向补语，表示宾语发生了位置上的移动。其基本结构是：

主语 + 把 + 宾语 + 动词 + 趋向补语

The verb of a 把-sentence with a directional complement after it indicates that the position of the object moves. Its basic structure is:

S + 把 + O + V + directional complement

1. 把消毒棉球塞进鼻子里就行。
2. 什么时候把棉球取出来？
3. 不行，你还是把孩子带过来，让医生取。

※ 练习：组词成句　Group words into sentences

1. 把　带　病人　过来　你　吧

______________________________。

2. 把　病历　送　过来　请你

______________________________。

3. 我把　白大褂　送过去　给马大为

______________________________。

4. 美丽　帮我　把　买回来了　咖啡

______________________________。

综合练习 Comprehensive Exercises

一、根据拼音写汉字 Write Chinese characters according to Pinyin

1. háizi________　　3. liú________　　5. fú________

2. qǔ________　　4. bízi________　　6. zhǐ________

二、辨字组词 Discriminate between Chinese characters and make words

1. 取________ / 最________　　2. 孩________ / 刻________　　3. 止________ / 上________　　4. 球________ / 玩________

三、替换练习 Substitution drills

1. 你把孩子放到椅子上。

手机	桌子上
书	书包里
衣服	床上

2. 你还是把孩子带过来，让医生取。

照片	他看看
手机	他修修
病人	医生检查检查

3. 你 <u>扶</u> 着 <u>他的头</u>。

拿	手机
带	钱
打	伞

四、选词填空 Use the following words to fill in the blanks

把　出来　过来　放　着

1. 你下午来医院_______药拿回去。
2. 不要把白大褂_______在桌子上。
3. 他生病了，最近一直在床上躺_______。
4. 上课了，快把书包里的书拿_______。
5. 我的手机在桌子上，你帮我拿_______吧。

五、用所给词语完成对话 Complete the dialogues with given words

1. 妈妈：都十二点了，你怎么还不睡？

   儿子：__________________________。（把）

2. 美丽：你看见我的汉语书了吗？

   同学：__________________________。（着）

3. 家属：护士，我们明天住院，要带什么东西？

   护士：______________________________________。（把）

4. 金龙：大为，你知道我的手机在哪儿吗？

   大为：在你的书包里，__________________________。（进去）

5. 大为：金龙，你的手机怎么了？

金龙：________________。（破）

六、根据课文内容回答问题 Answer the following questions according to the text

1. 孩子怎么了？
2. 医生说怎么止血？
3. 什么时候可以把棉球取出来？
4. 谁可以把棉球取出来？

七、根据课文内容填空 Fill in the blanks according to the text

孩子的________摔破了，一直________。医生让妈妈把________放到椅子上，________他的头。医生看了一下，说孩子鼻子里的毛细血管________，要把棉球________止血，明天下午再把棉球________，但不能自己在家取，要把孩子________，让医生取。

语言任务 Language Tasks

一、阅读理解 Reading comprehension

儿子摔伤鼻子以后，鼻子就经常流血。特别是冬天，早上起床的时候儿子常常会流鼻血。我用手捏（niē，pinch）着他的鼻子，一般捏两三分钟就能止血。除了流鼻血以外，儿子还常常感冒。带他去医院检查，医生说儿子得的是鼻炎（bíyán，rhinitis）。

读后判断 True or false

1. 儿子的鼻子以前摔伤过。 （ ）

2. 儿子的鼻子经常流血。 ( )

3. 鼻子流血后可以用手捏着止血。 ( )

4. 除了流鼻血，儿子身体没有别的问题。 ( )

5. 儿子的鼻炎已经好了。 ( )

二、口头表达 Oral expression

任务名称：如何收拾房间。

Task: How to tidy up the room.

任务要求：1. 两个学生一组，讨论打扫房间的具体安排。

2. 说出打扫的步骤和具体安排，并劝说同屋一起做。

Requirements: 1. Two students work in a group to discuss the specific arrangements for cleaning the room.

2. Tell the roommate the steps and specific arrangements for cleaning the room, and persuade him/her to do it together.

Reference words: 乱　先……再……然后……最后……　打扫　把　整理　整齐　收拾　垃圾　扔掉　起来　对……有兴趣

三、书面表达 Written expression

任务名称：怎样把房间打扫得又快又好?

Task: How to clean the room quickly and well?

任务要求：写出打扫房间的步骤。

Requirement: Write down the steps of cleaning the room.

1. 先	
2. 再	

3. 然后	
4. 最后	

Reference words: 乱　把　整理　收拾　打扫　垃圾　扔掉　整齐

补充词汇 Supplementary Words

miánbàng
棉棒
cotton swab

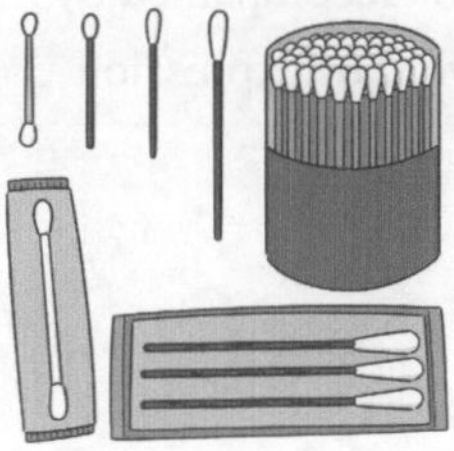

diǎnfú
碘伏
iodophor

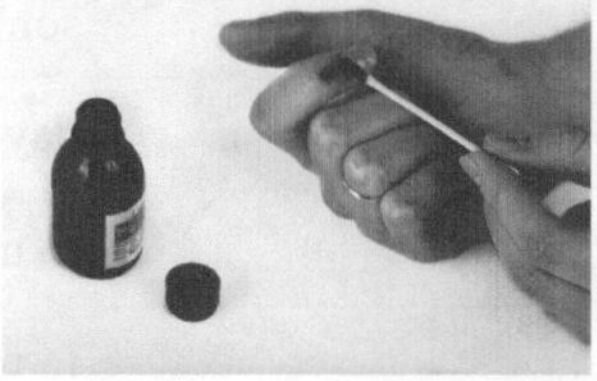

shābù
纱布
gauze

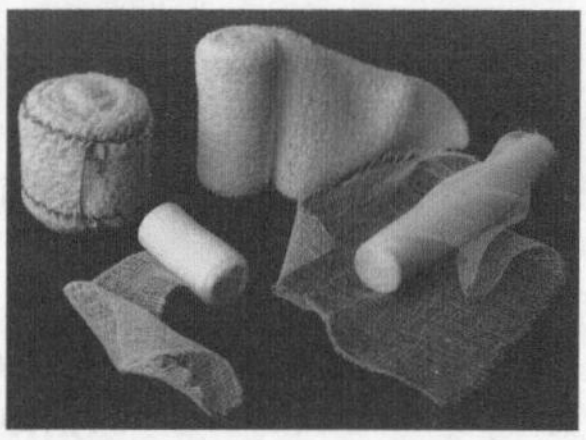

chuāngkětiē
创可贴
adhesive bandage

shǒushùdāo
手术刀
scalpel

nièzi
镊子
forceps

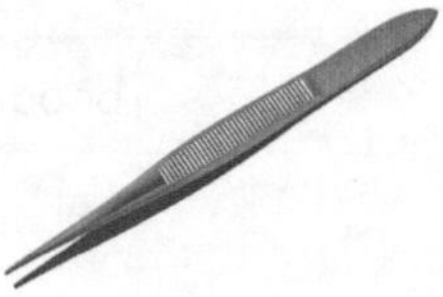

词汇总表
Glossary

A				
按	àn	*v.*	to press	13
按时	ànshí	*adv.*	on time	9
熬夜	áoyè	*v.*	to stay up	2
B				
把	bǎ	*prep.*	used to shift the object ahead of the verb, which must be reduplicated or accompanied by some other word or expression	13
白天	báitiān	*n.*	daytime	3
搬	bān	*v.*	to move	1
搬家	bānjiā	*v.*	to move house	1
帮	bāng	*v.*	to help	13
帮忙	bāngmáng	*v.*	to help	10
帮助	bāngzhù	*v.*	to help	8
棒	bàng	*adj.*	great	8
报名	bàomíng	*v.*	to sign up	6
抱歉	bàoqiàn	*adj.*	sorry	14
杯	bēi	*m.*	a cup of	4
北	běi	*n.*	north	8
北门	běimén	*n.*	north gate	8

鼻子	bízi	*n.*	nose	15
比	bǐ	*prep.*	than	5
比较	bǐjiào	*adv.*	pretty	12
比赛	bǐsài	*n./v.*	competition; to compete	6
标准	biāozhǔn	*adj.*	standard	11
表	biǎo	*n.*	chart	14
别	bié	*adv.*	don't	9
冰激凌	bīngjīlíng	*n.*	ice cream	7
病	bìng	*n./v.*	illness; to fall ill	2
病历	bìnglì	*n.*	clinical case, medical records	10
不但	búdàn	*conj.*	not only	8
不但……而且……	búdàn…érqiě…		not only...but also...	8
不到	bú dào	*VP*	less than	12
不过	búguò	*conj.*	but	7
不要	búyào	*adv.*	do not	2
不小心	bù xiǎoxīn	*AP*	careless, by accident	13
		C		
才	cái	*adv.*	just	11
参加	cānjiā	*v.*	to take part in	6
查房	cháfáng	*v.*	to make the rounds of the wards	13
差	chà	*adj.*	poor, bad	5
差不多	chàbuduō	*adj.*	similar	8
产科	chǎnkē	*n.*	obstetrics	4
长	cháng	*adj.*	long	1
肠息肉	chángxīròu	*n.*	intestinal polyps	12
尝	cháng	*v.*	to taste	12
常常	chángcháng	*adv.*	often, usually	1

唱	chàng	*v.*	to sing	1
唱歌	chànggē	*v.*	to sing (a song)	1
吵	chǎo	*adj.*	noisy	8
出来	chūlai	*v.*	to come out	12
出院	chūyuàn	*v.*	to discharge from hospital	9
除了	chúle	*prep.*	except, besides	1
除了……以外	chúle…yǐwài		except, besides	1
窗户	chuānghu	*n.*	window	13
春天	chūntiān	*n.*	spring	5
次	cì	*m.*	time	7
聪明	cōngming	*adj.*	smart	11
从	cóng	*prep.*	from	1
存	cún	*v.*	to save	10
		D		
打	dǎ	*v.*	to play	2
打	dǎ	*v.*	to play	15
打车	dǎchē	*v.*	to take a taxi	9
打吊针	dǎ diàozhēn	*VO*	to be put on a drip	11
打开	dǎkāi	*v.*	to open	13
打篮球	dǎ lánqiú	*VO*	to play basketball	2
打扰	dǎrǎo	*v.*	to interrupt, to bother	3
打扫	dǎsǎo	*v.*	to clean	15
打算	dǎsuàn	*v.*	to plan	7
打游戏	dǎ yóuxì	*VO*	to play games	15
打针	dǎzhēn	*v.*	to have an injection	12
大概	dàgài	*adv.*	probably	1
大家	dàjiā	*pron.*	everybody	7

大夫	dàifu	*n.*	doctor	9
带	dài	*v.*	to take	4
担心	dānxīn	*v.*	to worry	8
单	dān	*n.*	sheet, list	13
胆囊	dǎnnáng	*n.*	cholecyst	11
胆囊炎	dǎnnángyán	*n.*	cholecystitis	11
但是	dànshì	*conj.*	but	1
蛋糕	dàngāo	*n.*	cake	10
当	dāng	*v.*	to serve as, to be	4
当时	dāngshí	*n.*	at that time, then	10
刀口	dāokǒu	*n.*	cut	9
得	dé	*v.*	to get, to have	11
得	děi	*mod.v.*	need to	7
低	dī	*adj.*	low	1
低压	dīyā	*n.*	diastolic blood pressure	1
地	dì	*n.*	ground, floor	15
第	dì	*pref.*	before numerals to form ordinal numbers	7
第一	dì-yī	*num.*	first	7
店	diàn	*n.*	shop, store	8
吊针	diàozhēn	*n.*	infusion	11
掉	diào	*v.*	to drop	15
冬天	dōngtiān	*n.*	winter	5
懂	dǒng	*v.*	to understand	5
度	dù	*m.*	degree	5
锻炼	duànliàn	*v.*	to do exercises	6
对	duì	*prep.*	in, to	15
对了	duìle	*v.*	by the way	12

对……有/没有兴趣	duì…yǒu/méiyǒu xìngqù		to have/have no interest in	15
E				
儿科	érkē	*n.*	pediatrics	4
儿子	érzi	*n.*	son	9
而且	érqiě	*conj.*	but (also), and that	8
F				
发	fā	*v.*	to send	2
发微信	fā wēixìn	*VO*	to send a message on WeChat	2
房子	fángzi	*n.*	house	1
放	fàng	*v.*	to put, to place	15
放假	fàngjià	*v.*	to have a vacation	7
放松	fàngsōng	*v.*	to relax	7
放心	fàngxīn	*v.*	to be at ease, don't worry	2
飞机	fēijī	*n.*	aircraft, plane	12
分诊	fēnzhěn	*v.*	to make a triage	8
分诊台	fēnzhěntái	*n.*	redirect stand	8
风	fēng	*n.*	wind	5
扶	fú	*v.*	to hold, to support	15
父母	fùmǔ	*n.*	parents	14
附近	fùjìn	*n.*	nearby	8
复查	fùchá	*v.*	to recheck, to reexamine	9
复习	fùxí	*v.*	to review	2
腹	fù	*n.*	abdomen, stomach	9
腹痛	fùtòng	*n./adj.*	stomachache, abdominal pain	9
G				
干净	gānjìng	*adj.*	clean	13

感觉	gǎnjué	*v./n.*	to feel; feeling	9
感冒	gǎnmào	*v./n.*	to catch a cold; cold	4
刚	gāng	*adv.*	just	3
刚才	gāngcái	*n.*	just now	2
高	gāo	*adj.*	high	1
高压	gāoyā	*n.*	systolic blood pressure	1
告诉	gàosu	*v.*	to tell	6
歌	gē	*n.*	song	1
个子	gèzi	*n.*	height	10
给	gěi	*v.*	to give	4
跟	gēn	*prep.*	with, and	5
跟……一样（……）	gēn…yíyàng（…）		the same as, as...as	5
更	gèng	*adv.*	even more	14
恭喜	gōngxǐ	*v.*	to congratulate	14
挂号	guàhào	*v.*	to register	8
怪不得	guàibude	*adv.*	no wonder	11
关	guān	*v.*	to turn off, to close	13
过	guò	*v.*	to cross	3
过来	guòlai	*v.*	to come over	3
过去	guòqu	*v.*	after a verb to indicate a motion away from the speaker	10
过	guo	*part.*	an aspectual particle to indicate the action has occurred	8
		H		
还是	háishi	*adv.*	expressing a preference for an alternative	13
孩子	háizi	*n.*	child, kid	15
海边	hǎi biān		seaside	5

寒假	hánjià	*n.*	winter vacation	7
行	háng	*m.*	used for sth. in a line	14
好	hǎo	*adv.*	very	10
好好儿	hǎohāor	*adv.*	well	2
后天	hòutiān	*n.*	the day after tomorrow	2
呼叫铃	hūjiàolíng	*n.*	call bell	13
护士站	hùshizhàn	*n.*	nurse station	13
护照	hùzhào	*n.*	passport	8
话	huà	*n.*	words	5
欢迎	huānyíng	*v.*	to welcome	14
缓解	huǎnjiě	*v.*	to relieve	11
换	huàn	*v.*	to change	13
恢复	huīfù	*v.*	to recover	9
回	huí	*v.*	to reply, to answer	2
回	huí	*v.*	to return, to go back	4
回国	huí guó	*VO*	to return to one's country	7
回来	huílai	*v.*	to come back	4
会议	huìyì	*n.*	conference	10
会议室	huìyìshì	*n.*	conference room	10
婚礼	hūnlǐ	*n.*	wedding	14
J				
机场	jīchǎng	*n.*	airport	14
极	jí	*adv.*	extremely	7
急性	jíxìng	*adj.*	acute	11
季节	jìjié	*n.*	season	5
家	jiā	*m.*	used for households or businesses	1

家人	jiārén	*n.*	family member	3
检查	jiǎnchá	*v.*	to test, to check	12
交	jiāo	*v.*	to associate with, to make friends with	11
交朋友	jiāo péngyou	*VO*	to make friends with sb.	11
叫	jiào	*v.*	to ask, to order	1
教授	jiàoshòu	*n.*	professor	4
接	jiē	*v.*	to pick up	14
结果	jiéguǒ	*n.*	result	12
结婚	jiéhūn	*v.*	to marry, to get married	7
结束	jiéshù	*v.*	to finish, to be over	6
姐姐	jiějie	*n.*	elder sister	7
进	jìn	*v.*	to enter	3
进来	jìnlai	*v.*	to come in	3
进去	jìnqu	*v.*	to enter, to get in	3
经常	jīngcháng	*adv.*	often	8
景色	jǐngsè	*n.*	scenery	12
久	jiǔ	*adj.*	long	11
就	jiù	*adv.*	will	3
举行	jǔxíng	*v.*	to hold	14
剧烈	jùliè	*adj.*	violent, strenuous, fierce	9
觉得	juéde	*v.*	to think, to feel	5
K				
咖啡	kāfēi	*n.*	coffee	4
开	kāi	*v.*	to prescribe	12
开会	kāihuì	*v.*	to have a meeting	10
开机	kāijī	*v.*	to start up	13

开始	kāishǐ	*v.*	to start	11
开心	kāixīn	*adj.*	happy	7
看病	kànbìng	*v.*	to see a doctor	8
看见	kànjiàn	*v.*	to see	2
看起来	kàn qǐlai		it seems	15
康复	kāngfù	*v.*	to recover	11
考	kǎo	*v.*	to test, to examine	2
考试	kǎoshì	*v.*	to test, to exam	2
颗	kē	*m.*	usually used for sth. small and roundish	12
可	kě	*adv.*	(used for emphasis) just	6
可怕	kěpà	*adj.*	horrible	14
空儿	kòngr	*n.*	free time	6
口腔	kǒuqiāng	*n.*	oral cavity	6
口味	kǒuwèi	*n.*	taste	8
KTV	KTV	*n.*	Karaoke TV	1
快要	kuàiyào	*adv.*	soon, be going to	4
困	kùn	*adj.*	sleepy	2
		L		
垃圾	lājī	*n.*	garbage, rubbish	15
辣	là	*adj.*	spicy	8
来不及	láibují	*v.*	to have no enough time (to do sth.)	14
来得及	láidejí	*v.*	to be able to do sth. in time	14
篮球	lánqiú	*n.*	basketball	2
俩	liǎ	*num.-m.*	two, a pair	8
脸	liǎn	*n.*	face	10
脸色	liǎnsè	*n.*	complexion	2

凉	liáng	*adj.*	cool	9
量	liáng	*v.*	to measure	1
聊天儿	liáotiānr	*v.*	to chat	11
了	liǎo	*v.*	to finish	14
流	liú	*v.*	to flow	15
流血	liú xiě	*VO*	to bleed	15
路上	lùshang	*n.*	on the road	7
乱	luàn	*adj.*	messy	15
		M		
麻烦	máfan	*v./adj.*	to bother, excuse me; troublesome	13
马大哈	mǎdàhā	*n./adj.*	ma-da-ha (a slang used to call someone who is very careless); careless, forgetful	6
忙	máng	*v.*	to be busy with	10
毛细血管	máoxì-xuèguǎn	*n.*	blood capillary	15
美	měi	*adj.*	beautiful	12
门	mén	*m.*	branch of study	2
门口	ménkǒu	*n.*	gate	1
米	mǐ	*m.*	meter	1
棉球	miánqiú	*n.*	cotton ball	15
名	míng	*m.*	used for persons	4
明白	míngbai	*v./adj.*	to understand; clear, obvious	3
明年	míngnián	*n.*	next year	7
模糊	móhu	*adj.*	indistinct	14
		N		
拿	ná	*v.*	to bring, to take	10
那	nà	*conj.*	then	13

那里	nàlǐ	*pron.*	there	5
那儿	nàr	*pron.*	there	7
男孩儿	nánháir	*n.*	boy	10
难	nán	*adj.*	difficult	2
呢	ne	*part.*	used at the end of a statement to indicate an action or a situation is continuing	10
年轻	niánqīng	*adj.*	young	14
年轻人	niánqīngrén	*n.*	young people	14
女儿	nǚ'ér	*n.*	daughter	9
暖和	nuǎnhuo	*adj.*	warm	5
		O		
呕吐	ǒutù	*v.*	to vomit	9
		P		
怕	pà	*v.*	to worry about, to be afraid of	14
判断	pànduàn	*v.*	to judge	2
碰	pèng	*v.*	to hit, to touch, to bump	13
便宜	piányi	*adj.*	cheap	8
屏	píng	*n.*	screen	13
破	pò	*v.*	to be broken	15
葡萄	pútao	*n.*	grape	12
		Q		
起来	qǐlai	*v.*	to sit up, to stand up	15
前天	qiántiān	*n.*	the day before yesterday	9
切除	qiēchú	*v.*	to cut off	12
清楚	qīngchu	*adj.*	clear	14
情况	qíngkuàng	*n.*	matter, situation	12
请	qǐng	*v.*	to invite	1

请假	qǐngjià	*v.*	to ask for leave	11
秋天	qiūtiān	*n.*	autumn	5
取	qǔ	*v.*	to take	15
取号	qǔ hào	*VO*	to take a queue number	8
去年	qùnián	*n.*	last year	11
全	quán	*adv.*	all, whole	10
		R		
然后	ránhòu	*conj.*	then	8
让	ràng	*v.*	to let, to make (sb. do)	4
热闹	rènao	*adj.*	bustling	14
人员	rényuán	*n.*	staff	13
扔	rēng	*v.*	to throw	15
如果	rúguǒ	*conj.*	if	3
如果……就……	rúguǒ…jiù…		if...	3
		S		
塞	sāi	*v.*	to fill in	15
伞	sǎn	*n.*	umbrella	4
扫	sǎo	*v.*	to sweep	15
沙发	shāfā	*n.*	couch	10
删	shān	*v.*	to delete	14
伤	shāng	*v.*	to hurt	3
上	shàng	*n.*	last	4
上	shàng	*v.*	used after a verb to indicate the result of an action	13
上班	shàngbān	*v.*	to go to work	1
神经	shénjīng	*n.*	neuro	4
生病	shēngbìng	*v.*	to get sick	2
生理学	shēnglǐxué	*n.*	physiology	2

师傅	shīfu	*n.*	form of address for any stranger	13
食堂	shítáng	*n.*	canteen	8
事情	shìqing	*n.*	event, thing	15
事儿	shìr	*n.*	matter	2
视力	shìlì	*n.*	vision, eyesight	14
视力表	shìlìbiǎo	*n.*	visual chart	14
收拾	shōushi	*v.*	to tide up	13
手机屏	shǒujīpíng	*n.*	mobile screen	13
瘦	shòu	*adj.*	thin	10
舒服	shūfu	*adj.*	comfortable	1
输	shū	*v.*	to lose	6
暑假	shǔjià	*n.*	summer vacation	5
数学	shùxué	*n.*	mathematics	5
数学课	shùxuékè	*n.*	math class	5
摔	shuāi	*v.*	to fall	3
帅	shuài	*adj.*	handsome, amazing	10
水平	shuǐpíng	*n.*	level	9
顺利	shùnlì	*adj.*	smooth	7
说话	shuōhuà	*v.*	to speak, to talk	4
司机	sījī	*n.*	driver	11
送	sòng	*v.*	to give, to send	10
虽然	suīrán	*conj.*	although	1
虽然……但是……	suīrán…dànshì…		although…	1
随便	suíbiàn	*adj.*	random	13
所以	suǒyǐ	*conj.*	so, therefore	6
		T		
它	tā	*pron.*	it	13

躺	tǎng	*v.*	to lie	14
特别	tèbié	*adv./adj.*	especially; special	2
疼痛	téngtòng	*adj.*	painful	11
体育	tǐyù	*n.*	sports	6
体育馆	tǐyùguǎn	*n.*	gym	6
天气预报	tiānqì yùbào		weather forecast	7
甜	tián	*adj.*	sweet	12
填	tián	*v.*	to fill	2
填空	tiánkòng	*v.*	to fill in the blank	2
调	tiáo	*v.*	to change, to adjust	6
调课	tiáo kè	*VO*	to change the class time	6
调整	tiáozhěng	*v.*	to adjust	8
听力	tīnglì	*n.*	listening	5
听说	tīngshuō	*v.*	to hear	4
挺	tǐng	*adv.*	quite	3
痛	tòng	*adj.*	painful, sore	9
头	tóu	*n.*	head	1
头晕	tóuyūn	*v.*	to be dizzy	1
突然	tūrán	*adj.*	sudden	4
图案	tú'àn	*n.*	pattern, design	14
推荐	tuījiàn	*v.*	to recommend	8
退休	tuìxiū	*v.*	to retire	4
		W		
外科	wàikē	*n.*	surgery	4
完	wán	*v.*	to finish, to be over	2
晚饭	wǎnfàn	*n.*	dinner	10
网上	wǎng shang		online	12

往	wǎng	*prep.*	towards	1
忘	wàng	*v.*	to forget	6
微信	wēixìn	*n.*	WeChat	2
维修	wéixiū	*v.*	to maintain, to repair	13
维修单	wéixiūdān	*n.*	repair sheet	13
温度	wēndù	*n.*	temperature	5
问题	wèntí	*n.*	question, problem, matter	2
午饭	wǔfàn	*n.*	lunch	3
		X		
西	xī	*n.*	west	1
希望	xīwàng	*v.*	to hope, to wish	11
息肉	xīròu	*n.*	polyp	12
下雪	xià xuě	*VO*	to snow	7
夏天	xiàtiān	*n.*	summer	5
先	xiān	*adv.*	first, firstly	1
消毒	xiāodú	*v.*	to disinfect, to sterilize	15
消化	xiāohuà	*v.*	to digest	9
消炎	xiāoyán	*v.*	to diminish inflammation	12
消炎针	xiāoyánzhēn	*n.*	antiphlogistic injection	12
小孩儿	xiǎoháir	*n.*	kid	4
小时	xiǎoshí	*n.*	hour	12
小心	xiǎoxīn	*adj.*	careful	13
校长	xiàozhǎng	*n.*	principal	4
写病历	xiě bìnglì	*VO*	to write medical records	10
心电图	xīndiàntú	*n.*	electrocardiogram	1
心脏	xīnzàng	*n.*	heart	4
型号	xínghào	*n.*	type	13

兴趣	xìngqù	*n.*	interest	15
……性	…xìng	*suf.*	used to form mounds and adjectives	11
修	xiū	*v.*	to repair	13
需要	xūyào	*v.*	to need	8
学	xué	*v.*	to learn	2
雪	xuě	*n.*	snow	7
血	xuè/xiě	*n.*	blood	15
血压	xuèyā	*n.*	blood pressure	1
		Y		
牙	yá	*n.*	tooth	8
牙套	yátào	*n.*	tooth socket	8
严重	yánzhòng	*adj.*	serious	3
药	yào	*n.*	medicine	9
要是	yàoshi	*conj.*	if	9
要是……就……	yàoshi…jiù…		if, suppose	9
一……就……	yī…jiù…		as soon as	8
医学	yīxué	*n.*	medical science	5
医学课	yīxuékè	*n.*	medical course	5
一会儿	yíhuìr	*num.-m.*	a little while	13
一样	yíyàng	*adj.*	same	5
已经	yǐjīng	*adv.*	already	1
以前	yǐqián	*n.*	before	6
以外	yǐwài	*n.*	except, beyond	1
一边	yìbiān	*adv.*	at the same time	7
一边……一边……	yìbiān…yìbiān…		while	7
一直	yìzhí	*adv.*	straight, straight forward	1

因为	yīnwèi	*conj.*	because	2
应该	yīnggāi	*mod.v.*	should	12
赢	yíng	*v.*	to win	6
游泳	yóuyǒng	*v.*	to swim	7
有的	yǒude	*pron.*	some	3
有的……有的……	yǒude…yǒude…		some...some...	3
有名	yǒumíng	*adj.*	famous	4
有意思	yǒu yìsi	*VO*	interesting	4
又……又……	yòu…yòu…		both…and…	2
预报	yùbào	*n./v.*	forecast; to forecast	7
院长	yuànzhǎng	*n.*	director of a hospital	4
越来越	yuè lái yuè		more and more	4
越……越……	yuè…yuè…		the more...the more...	5
晕	yūn	*adj.*	dizzy, faint	1
		Z		
再	zài	*adv.*	again	6
在	zài	*adv.*	in the process of	10
咱们	zánmen	*pron.*	we, us	2
糟糕	zāogāo	*adj.*	bad	3
早日	zǎorì	*adv.*	soon	11
长	zhǎng	*v.*	to grow, to come into being	12
丈夫	zhàngfu	*n.*	husband	9
找	zhǎo	*v.*	to look for, to visit	6
照顾	zhàogù	*v.*	to take care of	3
照片	zhàopiàn	*n.*	picture, photo	10
这么	zhème	*pron.*	so, such	2
这样	zhèyàng	*pron.*	this way, such, like this	14

着	zhe	*part.*	aspectual particle added to a verb or an adjective to indicate a continued action or state, often with the particle "呢" at the end of the sentence	12
整理	zhěnglǐ	*v.*	to tidy up	15
整齐	zhěngqí	*adj.*	tidy	15
正	zhèng	*adv.*	right, just	10
正在	zhèngzài	*adv.*	right in the middle of (doing sth.), in the process of	10
止	zhǐ	*v.*	to stop	15
止血	zhǐ xiě	*VO*	to stop bleeding	15
终于	zhōngyú	*adv.*	finally	7
周六	zhōuliù	*n.*	Saturday	6
周末	zhōumò	*n.*	weekend	1
主任	zhǔrèn	*n.*	director	9
住院	zhùyuàn	*v.*	to be hospitalized	3
注意	zhùyì	*v.*	to pay attention to	9
自己	zìjǐ	*pron.*	oneself	15
走	zǒu	*v.*	to walk, to go	1
最后	zuìhòu	*n.*	last	15
最近	zuìjìn	*n.*	recently	1
醉	zuì	*v.*	to be drunk	10
左右	zuǒyòu	*n.*	around, about	10
做心电图	zuò xīndiàntú	*VO*	to take an ECG	1

专名 Proper nouns

B			
冰城	Bīngchéng	Ice City	7
冰雪节	Bīngxuě Jié	Ice and Snow Festival	7
H			
哈尔滨	Hā'ěrbīn	Harbin	7
汉字	Hànzì	Chinese character	5
J			
吉米	Jímǐ	name of a Russian student	2
L			
刘	Liú	a Chinese surname	9
刘文	Liú Wén	a Chinese name	10
S			
三亚	Sānyà	Sanya	7
X			
新疆	Xīnjiāng	a provincial administrative region in China	12
Z			
张	Zhāng	a Chinese surname	13